Also by Gerald Weeks

Treating Infidelity: Therapeutic Dilemmas and Effective Strategies, with Nancy Gambescia and Robert Jenkins

Erectile Dysfunction: Integrating Couple Therapy, Sex Therapy, and Medical Treatment, with Nancy Gambescia

Hypoactive Sexual Desire: Integrating Sex and Couple Therapy, with Nancy Gambescia

If Only I Had Known . . .

A Norton Professional Book

If Only I Had Known . . .

Avoiding Common Mistakes
in Couples Therapy

Gerald R. Weeks, Ph.D.
Mark Odell, Ph.D.
Susanne Methven, M.S.

W.W. Norton & Company
New York • London

Manufacturing by Haddon Craftsmen
Book design by Leeann Graham
Production Manager: Leeann Graham

Library of Congress Cataloging-in-Publication Data

Weeks, Gerald R., 1948- .
If only I had known–: avoiding common mistakes in couples
therapy / Gerald R. Weeks, Mark Odell, Susanne Methven.
p. cm.
"A Norton professional book."
Includes bibliographical references and index.
ISBN 0-393-70445-9 (pbk.)
1. Marital psychotherapy. I. Odell, Mark. II. Methven,
Susanne. III. Title.

RC488.5.W442 2005
616.89'1562–dc22   2005047798

W. W. Norton & Company, Inc., 500 Fifth Avenue,
New York, N. Y. 10110
www.wwnorton.com

W. W. Norton & Company Ltd., Castle House,
75/76 Wells St., London WIT 3QT

4 6 8 9 7 5 3

Contents

Acknowledgments

We are grateful to all of our colleagues and students who have been open and trusting enough over the years to admit their mistakes, therapeutic errors, and downright blunders. Learning from one's mistakes is truly invaluable to becoming a therapist. Hopefully this book will help you avoid some of the mistakes we have all made.

We would like to thank Deborah Malmud, Senior Editor at Norton, for her support in this project. Casey Ruble and Andrea Costella provided superb editorial assistance. We also appreciate the contribution of Jennifer Gilroy in reading early drafts and giving us feedback.

If Only I Had Known . . .

Mistakes?! What Mistakes?

In the field of psychotherapy a variety of media, including books, articles, workshops, presentations, seminars, and specialized training, has been produced to make therapists more effective at helping clients change. Many resources are "how-to" in nature, giving the reader numerous principles and examples to follow about what works in therapy. A naïve reader may assume that there is an element of "plug and play" involved in therapy, where the therapist's major concern is correctly identifying the problem he or she is facing with a given client, finding the recommended intervention or approach for that problem, and then implementing the solution in cookbook fashion. As Odell and Campbell (1998, p. 91) noted about the literature, "most case studies ... show that therapy *was success-ful*. ... If therapy were baseball, case studies would be press accounts of clutch hits, tremendous defensive plays, and shrewdly calculated managerial strategizing that made the win happen. The only problem is, we know a lot more about how to win baseball games than we do about helping people make long-lasting changes in their lives, despite there being no shortage of theory."

1

This book is of a different nature. It deals with how therapists can learn from common mistakes made in couple counseling. Much of the information presented here about mistakes was derived from the supervision of hundreds of beginning therapists, as well as many more seasoned ones. I (Gerald Weeks) attended over 500 case conferences in which seasoned therapists discussed cases that were going badly or in which they had made a mistake. I was the first to catalog some of the common mistakes made in couple therapy and was giving workshops on this topic as far back as the early 1990s (Weeks & Treat, 1992, 2001). In addition, we the authors have made professional presentations on this material. Feedback from these sessions has been positive, as attendees leave not only understanding that struggling with couple therapy is not unusual, but also feeling more knowledgeable about common errors and the practical steps they can take to avoid them. There is no way to catalog all the possible mistakes a couple therapist can make, but following is a brief typology of generic mistakes we have observed:

- Failing to acknowledge that mistakes exist
- Failing to use theory when intervening
- Failing to use a chosen theory or theories correctly
- Failing to discard a theory when it is not applicable
- Failing to act when action is clearly warranted
- Failing to restrain oneself from intervening when it is not time

This introduction discusses the definition of a mistake, why mistakes are hard to see, and what to do about them. An overview of the book follows.

What Is A Mistake?

To examine errors, of course, one first must be able to identify what they are. This is not as easy as it may seem. A discussion with ten seasoned therapists would probably provide at least 15 or more different views on what mistakes are, with a number of views in direct opposition to each other. One therapist may view something as a mistake whereas another would not. In addition, the clients' views of mistakes are the ones that matter most, and, although they may be different from the therapist's view, they are not often solicited. Thus, mistakes by their very nature are controversial.

Mistakes can be categorized as one of two types: philosophical/conceptual or applied. Philosophical/conceptual mistakes are usually made at the level of values and worldview, something most clients and therapists working together assume that they have in common. Unfortunately, this is not always an accurate assumption. Conceptual mistakes occur when therapists make assumptions about what is happening in a couple without having adequate information, or when their own point of view is not open to correction. Applied mistakes include intervening incorrectly by using theory poorly, too rigidly, or neglecting to use it at all. For example, in one case a wife presented with hypoactive sexual desire. She began treatment by talking about a television show she had seen that supported her belief that sex is much too important in our culture. She wanted to have an intellectual discussion of the problem. The therapist became engaged in a conversation with her about the TV show. The husband was clearly impatient and wanted to talk about the lack of sex. Some could argue that the therapist was appropriately joining with the wife whereas others could argue that the therapist was helping her avoid the problem or discounting the husband.

Philosophical Mistakes

In recent years, therapy has been seen more as a collaborative effort between the therapist and client than as a series of interactions or interventions done by the therapist to the client. Postmodern thinkers in particular probably would reject the use of the terms *mistakes* and *errors* because this language suggests that if there are "wrong ways," there must be "correct" or "right ways" to do therapy. It also hints at expertise and hierarchy, concepts that postmodernists do not endorse. However, pragmatically, they would probably agree that there are better ways to collaborate, and much of the narrative literature describes those preferred ways.

A major philosophical blind spot occurs, however, when therapy is seen primarily as a collaborative exercise occurring between people who are essentially peers, such that hierarchy is removed in principle and mistakes, therefore, cannot be made. This blind spot is the failure to see that the therapist and client do not have a shared understanding of the therapist's role. No matter how the therapist thinks about what he or she is doing with the client, the client will almost without exception view the therapist as (1) a credentialed, trained, and qualified expert, (2) a source of new information, perspective, and ideas, (3) a guide to the solution of problems that bring the client to therapy, and (4) not the focus of the conversation or a person to whom the client will offer reciprocal assistance with regard to the therapist's struggles and personal life. All of these characteristics of the therapist define the legally regulated, state-sanctioned, professional relationship that includes the acquisition of informed consent and the rendering of a fee for a service. Hierarchy is inherent in the enterprise, as is the therapist's responsibility to act in certain ways to help the client. Further, even when the therapist strives to include the client as a cocreator of a new, meaningful narrative and deliberately explains the problems of hierarchy to the client, the relationship's momentum derives from the therapist's position, not the client's. He or she can educate the client about how collaborative therapy is, but the client is never in a truly equal position, because the therapist still must do the socializing and educating about what therapy involves. The therapist can attempt to give up his or her "privileged" position, but it is the very volition to do so that exposes the inherent privilege in the first place; if it did not exist, it could not be surrendered even in principle. Conversely, the client has no privileged position to give up to start with—the very nature of being a client means that help is sought. If there really were no hierarchy, there would be no need to talk about it or try to remove it. And there would not be any fees.

Mistakes of Theory

Therapists can err at the theoretical level by misunderstanding a theory, misapplying it, or not using one at all. Marriage and family therapists historically have had a degree of admiration for theoretical mavericks or atheoretical, "fly by the seat of the pants" masters such as Carl Whitaker, who just *did* and theorized later. However, the days of relatively sparse theoretical approaches are long gone, and the field's maturity now requires a standard of care complete with theoretical justification and, often, manualized treatment protocols (Sexton, Weeks, & Robbins, 2003). Whitaker's interesting therapeutic practice of falling asleep in session, for example, would not be a good intervention choice today.

At all levels of experience, theoretical considerations are a concern. Novice clinicians understandably are uncomfortable moving quickly between theory and practical application, simply as a function of inexperience. It is not uncommon to find full-time practitioners who are unfamiliar with the cohesive language or use of theory. More seasoned clinicians, however, can no longer be uninformed about theory. We would argue that most therapists have multiple theoretical preferences and habits, but that they rarely think about them specifically or articulate them and therefore are less effective in putting them to use. The simple solution to this problem is for therapists to expend the effort to develop a more cogent, communicable theory of change. Once this meta-theory is in place, more specific applications of it, including the bits and pieces of established psychotherapeutic theories, follow quite naturally. This particular problem has occurred in sex therapy with some degree of frequency. For many years, sex therapy was largely behavioral and sex therapists did not focus on couple issues. The following excerpt shows how the therapist operating from this position could go in the wrong direction:

Therapist: Okay, we now know the problem is premature ejaculation. This is good news because it is an easy problem to remedy. I want to start you on some homework assignments that will help the problem, okay?

Wife: But all we ever do is fight. I don't want to be around him.

Therapist: You are here to help the sexual problem. You won't be fighting all the time. Give this a try when you are getting along.

The therapist is trying to use a concept in sex therapy known as "bypass." He is trying to bypass the couple's main issue and just deal with the sexual problem from a behavioral perspective.

Not having a foundational theoretical template is a big problem, but so is not having a solid command of the theories one chooses to use. Some theories, such as cognitive-behavioral and behavioral theories, solution-focused theory, and some of the experiential theories, are relatively straightforward and less likely to be misunderstood, though they may certainly be mishandled or misapplied. Structural theory, transgenerational and Bowenian theories, and strategic theories may be more likely to be misunderstood and correspondingly misapplied. We have noted on a number of occasions the misunderstanding and misuse of strategic therapy in particular, both as a function of the appeal of its "trickiness" and its appearance of being comparatively simple. Predictably, the results are not good. The solution to this problem is for therapists to maintain at least a working knowledge of the major therapy theories.

The following example demonstrates how misused theories fail to get the job done. In this case, a Bowenian therapist is working with a couple for whom sexual issues are their presenting problem. Although considering family of origin contributions is certainly a legitimate area of exploration, the therapist's misapplication of differentiation of self misses the mark.

Therapist: I'm wondering about how each of you experienced sexuality in your families of origin. (*to wife*) For instance, was it ever okay for your mother to initiate sex with your father?

Wife: I don't really know that much about their sex life. They were pretty private about stuff like that.

Therapist: How would it feel to you to ask her about that at some point?

Wife: I could ask her, I guess, but I don't know what she'd say. It's not the kind of thing we talk about much. She'd probably give me that raised-eyebrows look that says it's none of my business. Besides, I've always been quite comfortable approaching my husband when I'm interested in sex. With the kids, though, my energy's not as great as it was 15 years ago.

Husband: That's true. She's not really shy when it comes to sex, and we didn't have much trouble there for a long time, but the kids come first most of the time, and I don't mind that. But I do get frustrated that it's almost always me that starts things. I would like for her to start the ball rolling more frequently.

Therapist: (*to wife*) What would happen if you asked your mother about how she approached your father sexually? It may be that if she was uncomfortable with that, you also might be unconsciously anxious in the same way, because you learned about being a sexual woman from her.

The therapist's insistence on pushing the wife toward a "going home again" moment may prove counterproductive, especially if the therapist stays solidly on this track. Differentiated people know where family of origin boundaries lie because they are responsible in part for their creation, and they know which ones are worth pushing on and which ones aren't. The wife's level of differentiation may be quite adequate, and the couple's sexual issues may be rooted in practical and marital dynamics far more than in unresolved family of origin issues.

Therapists missing a theoretical base or who are not solid on theory typically lack a consistent sense of direction with cases and are unable to come up with therapeutic alternatives when they get stuck. They often characterize themselves as "eclectic" and prefer to be spontaneous in their work. In addition, they tend to get bogged down in similar issues and dynamics across many couples. Their response to the consistent lack of progress is usually to say that they do not like working with couples, that couples therapy is too hard, that one or both members of the couple have serious individual pathologies, usually requiring individual treatment, or that the couple's relationship was beyond salvaging. Supervision, at the least, is needed, if not additional coursework or targeted additional training.

Working from a theoretical orientation is usually more deliberate and stepwise. Therapists who want to develop a greater facility with theory can periodically check internally why they are doing what they are doing in a given situation. The self-reflection process should be more than stating that the intervention is based on intuition or hunches, although this may be part of the explanation. Therapists should ask themselves why a given intervention or approach is recommended or at least defensible from a theoretical point of view. Achieving theoretical competence can be readily done in supervision with someone or, in some cases, in self-supervision. Therapists need to be able to think and talk conceptually, so using theoretical language is a good way to gain better theoretical grounding. Obviously, there is a great deal of overlap between theories, with the same construct being called different things according to different theories. Our concern is that therapists have some rationale based in theory to support their actions with clients, not necessarily a precise theoretical understanding.

Theoretical rigidity is the last theoretically focused problem leading to therapist errors. Theory is a lens intended to help the therapist observe, explain, and intervene with certain constructs that show up behaviorally. All theories are lenses that do a more or less adequate job. The greatest mistake therapists can make is not changing themselves or what they are doing to provide a context in which clients can change. The intersystem approach developed by Weeks and colleagues (DeMaria, Weeks, & Hof, 1999; Weeks & Hof, 1994, 1995) allows therapists maximum flexibility to be themselves and fit therapy to the client. Therapists who only use one approach or one kind of intervention on all clients are forcing clients into a theoretical lens that may not necessarily fit very well. As a result, therapy is not likely to be optimal. At its worst, this kind of serious restriction on therapeutic possibilities could constitute malpractice.

Most therapists are generalists and are not overly attached to any particular theory. Those who are wedded to a particular theory generally will not hold onto it if it is clearly missing the mark. A good postulate here is: Fire your theory before you fire your client or your client fires you. If theoretical rigidity is apparent in a therapist, the immediate question is why. In some cases therapists lack training and exposure to a range of approaches. More commonly, therapists choose an approach or theory that best fits the couple's problem and their own personalities. This may not be a problem if the therapist is sufficiently open and flexible, but it can be a great problem if he or she is not. Rigid commitment to a particular approach even when other approaches are available and understood by the therapist usually means the therapist is experiencing problems such as global countertransference, burnout, or some personally relevant source of overwhelming difficulty that is hindering adaptability. In extreme cases, the therapist him- or herself may have some deeper pathology.

Mistakes of Timing

Another therapist error that shows up in couple treatment and elsewhere has to do with the timing of interventions. Obviously, an ill-timed intervention may be worse than no intervention at all, and therapists must become good judges of when action is appropriate. Sometimes therapists must assess the risk of intervention and let a seemingly good opportunity pass. Conversely, especially effective therapists can create contexts in therapy where the timing is both more apparent and more predictable, and thus their interventions tend to have a greater impact.

Understanding or controlling timing is much more difficult in practice than it might sound. There is no way of radically reducing errors of timing by following any kind of cookbook or step-by-step process. Indeed, even manualized treatment protocols inevitably have to include an awareness of the vagaries of therapeutically opportune moments and the inexactness of creating and acting on them.

Nevertheless, timing errors come in two reciprocal forms: missing available opportunities and taking opportunities that are not available (or "forcing" an intervention). In the former situation, a therapist may have established a good working alliance with both members of the couple and made progress in addressing their clinical concerns. However, there may be a core issue or pattern or problem that has yet to be effectively tackled by the therapist. The therapist avoids the issue, either consciously or unconsciously, and may effectively train clients to avoid the underlying issue as well.

Clients will often gently encourage therapists to deal with issues or will even explicitly invite the therapist to explore the issue. One response is to tell clients that the topic will be returned to at a later time or that something else needs to be worked on first. However, if clients repeatedly bring up the topic and it does not get addressed, therapists may be avoiding it. They may be concentrating on the crisis of the week rather than sticking with patterns or more important themes (see Chapter 7). This may be due to therapists' being uncomfortable with the emotional intensity of the topic, feeling out of control in session, or fearing failure.

A useful example can be seen in a couple that came for therapy with a brand new clinician. The therapist was exceedingly nervous at the beginning, both because of his lack of experience and because he was being supervised by a live team behind the mirror. The clients were quite comfortable with that arrangement as it was standard practice at that clinic, and they easily settled into describing why they were seeking treatment. The clients were fairly pleasant with each other and there was relatively little emotional intensity; they had come to counseling to get something done in their relationship. The therapist had great difficulty tracking their talk and after about half the session had passed, the couple asked the therapist where they should focus counseling. The clients were essentially inviting the therapist to give direction to the therapy. Despite the fact that he was receiving direction from the team, he was not ready to take charge of the session. Unfortunately but predictably, the couple did not return for a second session.

Forcing interventions usually is just as ineffective and sometimes is worse than inaction. Therapists may put in a great deal of effort but intervene inappropriately for the same reason they may not intervene: fear of failure. The therapist seizes what might be a small window of opportunity for fear that another one is not going to come. Our experience is that trusting the process of therapy to bring opportunities to intervene is usually a good strategy; what is important usually presents itself in a number of ways and at a number of times. Patience is a virtue worth developing. With couples, there is often a greater sense of implied pressure on the therapist to act, but the therapist can respond by allowing time and a broader perspective to give greater insight into the clients' situation before making a move (see Chapter 6).

One very gifted supervisee found herself particularly frustrated with several of her couple clients simultaneously. She had received about four couple cases in a short amount of time and was in the early phase of treatment with each of them. With each case, she ended sessions feeling increasingly exasperated, especially as she believed she had been successful at joining with them and felt like she had a good sense of what was going on. She wanted to confront the clients about their motivation, but was wisely hesitant about doing so. Through supervision, it became clear that, although she had indeed successfully started therapy and did have a good theoretical conceptualization of the clients' issues, she was vastly overestimating how quickly they would be able to embrace change. Her impatience, as well as her struggle to restrain herself from "getting them moving," as she called it, were hampering her ability to work effectively. Once she freed herself from her desire to perform therapeutic miracles, the entire therapy process slowed down and gained depth.

Therapists who consistently err by jumping at opportunities to intervene may be less aware that their own processes contribute to negative outcomes and may attribute negative outcomes to the clients. Therapists may be overconfident and force interventions if they do not do a very good job of listening and make decisions about "what's really going on" more quickly than is advisable. When this is the case, errors are much more likely to show up, as the therapist is not working with the actual people in the office but rather with the people he or she has constructed in his or her mind.

Therapists who specialize in particular problems or populations sometimes do not appreciate how quickly they make assumptions about clients based on minimal information. For example, a therapist who works with a large group of incest survivors may be prone to see symptoms of incest where none exist. One well-established clinician who worked with a very challenging population almost exclusively admitted, half in jest, that she would not know what to do with an "ordinary" client. Making assumptions about clients may be effective and time-efficient for therapists working with specialized populations, but generalist couples therapists must proceed with some caution. Fortunately, most therapists realize after missing something with a client that they indeed missed something, and they slow down to find where they lost track.

In practice, then, mistakes by the therapist are real, both in behavior and in consequences. Even if one rigidly adheres to a systemic point of view that therapists' actions are determined by the systemic rules governing the therapist and clients' interactions, what the therapist does or does not do will significantly affect what happens in treatment. The therapist is responsible for his or her actions. Therefore, avoiding mistakes is a worthwhile goal.

Why Mistakes Are Hard to Recognize

Mistakes are difficult to recognize for many reasons. Factors include those relating to clients themselves and to the therapist, both of which affect the process of therapy itself. Further, there are interactional variables at play, such that the fit between a given couple or one or the other member of a couple and the therapist is not good. In these cases, mistakes can be generated from the gestalt of the client-therapist system.

Client Factors

Therapists generally agree that the practice of couple therapy is more difficult than either individual or family therapy. When a mistake is made in individual therapy, it is not unusual for the client to correct the therapist and proceed. In family therapy, the parents perceive that they are involved for the sake of the child, at least initially, so they may be more patient, as well as less clear, about how family therapy is actually done and, thus, the family may be less confident about the nature of mistakes in family therapy. In other words, individuals and families are more forgiving of mistakes. The couple therapist, on the other hand, is faced with two peers who may not see problems in the same way, who may think that the other partner is more to blame, and who may want the therapist to "fix" the other person. Thus, the therapist must initially walk a tightrope between validating each person's perspective and reframing the problem in such a way that both partners have a role. In addition, couples often have a great sense of distress, including the possibility of ending their relationship, and this can lead to a greater sense of pressure on themselves and the therapist attempting to help them. Clients may reduce their tension from conflict by attempting to triangulate the therapist. Or they may demonstrate various behaviors, like attempting to win arguments at all costs, staying focused on problems in the past, or not wanting to deal with underlying issues, all of which lead to difficulties in therapy. Couples, therefore, are quick to see mistakes, such as the therapist's siding with the other partner or being ineffective in some way, for example in the pace of therapy.

Clients may also be ambivalent about their relationship and yet not aware of it. They may be overt about wanting to participate in therapy to make things better but unwittingly committed to certain thoughts or behavior patterns that ultimately work against the relationship's success. They may not see their own contradictions, and they may refuse to see them even when the well-meaning therapist points them out. Any clinician who has done couple therapy where one or both partners has an active but unacknowledged addiction has faced this dynamic. When the addiction issue is raised, the couple therapy may crash. So, is raising the subject of addiction a mistake? Probably not, but then again, it may be a mistake, at least for the purposes of couple therapy. Confusing, isn't it?

Mistakes are usually not easy to see. At the level of individual cases, mistakes more often become visible when, for example, clients suddenly reduce their emotional disclosure in therapy, become less willing to take risks in session or out, begin to resist the direction therapy is going, or become outright combative. When they drop out or miss sessions, or cancel and do not reschedule, the therapist should think about whether mistakes may have been made. Couples tend to be more combative with each other than with the therapist, but sometimes both will take on the therapist. In some cases this may be due to a mistake on the therapist's part; other times the therapist may not have erred at all but rather pushed hard on entrenched system rules that the clients are afraid to change. Indeed, sometimes a therapist's mistake proves to be a good thing, at least temporarily, for the clients. When both partners agree that their therapist is not helping, they at least have that in common. There are plausible client-related reasons for the behaviors noted previously, including that therapy is working and clients are afraid of change and what it will bring, or other reasons that have little or nothing to do with the therapist.

Therapist Factors

It is tempting, even at times ego-protecting, to explain behavior, and especially therapy failure, as the sole responsibility of the client. However, examining therapist responsibility can be a valuable discipline and lead to better client retention. At a more macro level, a good rule of thumb is to identify the kinds of cases that you typically find difficult or particularly challenging and then to look specifically at reasons.

One key indicator of the potential to make mistakes is when the therapist's own reactivity or emotional intensity is sparked. In these countertransferential situations, the therapist is likely to err. A range of emotional experiences can trigger errors. For example, therapists who find themselves bored, angry, or hoping for a cancellation or a no-show may be working with clients with whom they have already erred or are likely to err. Relief at not dealing with these clients can mask an accumulation of errors and failure to examine reasons for clients' not pursuing therapy. Conversely, therapists should be wary when they feel strongly attracted to or protective of clients, want to rescue them, or make inordinately personal disclosures. In these situations the likelihood of making a serious error is greatly increased, and again, the therapist must reflect on why these feelings and behaviors are present. Supervision or collegial conversation should be sought diligently.

Some therapists may have difficulty broaching the subject of mistakes due to feelings of shame. The experience of shame is about the self, which is the focus of evaluation. Feelings of shame can derive from negative evaluations of one's performance as a therapist. Shame can be a powerful force in slowing or preventing improvement, and unless it is confronted and dealt with, progress can be slow. Supervisors can help therapists recognize and process their own feelings of shame. The supervisor might suspect therapist shame if supervisees do not respond to comments, change topics, or consistently rationalize client behavior as avoidance rather than addressing their own role in the therapy process.

As previously mentioned, lack of theoretical knowledge or inappropriate application of theory can lead to errors like not being able to figure out the next therapeutic steps. Lack of awareness, for example, of cultural issues may lead to blind spots and mismatching of worldviews between the therapist and the couple. Lack of self-awareness may result in countertransference, especially if family of origin issues affect the therapist's ability to confront clients or deal with conflict. Low differentiation may mean that the therapist is drawn into the problematic behavior sequences between the couple. Lack of skill, for example with communications training, can mean that couples will not increase the depth of their communication. Over time, with good supervision and training, a therapist learns to trust the process of therapy. With experience, the therapist can, for example, avoid jumping to conclusions about what the problem is and make a sufficient assessment. He or she will also get better at both controlling the structure of sessions to avoid replaying dynamics the couple experiences at home and at concentrating not only on the content of what is said but also on the process (*how* things are said).

What to Do About Errors

Mistakes range in seriousness from recoverable to fatal to the therapy process or even to the clients or therapist. This does highlight the importance of assessment, discussed in a later chapter, as the therapist wants to evaluate the potential benefit of therapy. Usually mistakes are recoverable if they are recognized soon enough and are not too serious. However, especially in cases where there is violence, addiction, or severe psychopathology, it is important to assess the potential benefit of couples counseling.

A critical first step is admitting that mistakes can be made. The next step is to recognize, as much as possible, when they occur. Then the task is learning to avoid the mistakes that you are particularly susceptible to and developing workable alternatives to them. If you suspect you have made an error, you usually should ask the clients about it. The mere act of asking can help you recover the mistake if indeed one has been made. In fact, for many couples, such conversations are very powerful agents of change that offer new possibilities through the modeling of good problem-solving skills and, therefore, new positive experiences of conflict. Greater trust, greater effort, and deeper therapeutic intimacy often result, from which even more effective therapy is generated. For example, a therapist might start a session as follows:

Therapist: I was thinking about our last session and I think that I got too caught up in focusing on the problem of your disagreements about your children. When I thought about it, it seemed to be just one symptom of your general level of disagreement.

Wife: The discussion about the kids was good, but I don't think it gets to the real problem.

Husband: (*to therapist*) You're right—we never seem to agree about anything!

Therapist: I'm sorry I didn't pick that up. Maybe we should start with that problem first.

Some couples, however, will not necessarily tell the therapist about a mistake that he or she has made, even if asked, and may simply discontinue treatment. In this case, good supervision can help the therapist see any patterns that might be interfering with his or her effectiveness.

Overview of the Book

This book addresses a number of common mistakes made in couple therapy. Both seasoned and beginning therapists will benefit from this book. Seasoned therapists will become more aware of the subtler and personally based causes of mistakes. Beginning therapists will learn not only about these kinds of mistakes, but also about those that are based on a lack of knowledge and the wisdom that comes through clinical experience. Throughout the text, we provide guidelines designed to help readers avoid making mistakes. We do not want readers to view these ideas as flawless, ironclad rules, principles, or truths. Most of all, we want clinicians to remember two things about the guidelines: First, the first few sessions of couple therapy are the most difficult. The therapist is trying to establish a relationship with both partners and help them both see their part in the problem. A mistake during this initial phase of treatment can permanently disrupt the course of treatment or cause the couple to terminate prematurely. Thus, the guidelines are most important during the first few sessions. Second, after the engagement phase, the therapist may intentionally decide to violate one of these guidelines for strategic reasons. The therapist should be aware that this strategy can disrupt treatment unless careful attention is given to process; even then, there is a genuine risk that it will not bring about the desired result. The therapist may or may not explain that he or she is going to depart from what is normally done and gain the couple's permission to proceed.

In general, chapters begin by identifying the failures and defining the problem, then present case studies that are composites of real clients, and finally offer suggestions for how to avoid these common problems. In Chapter 1 the need to maintain balance and control over the structure and process of couple counseling is discussed. Couples are a challenging clinical population. Therapists must "win the battle for structure" (Whitaker & Keith, 1981) so that they can provide an environment in which each partner can behave appropriately. This gives therapy the best chance to succeed.

In Chapter 2 we discuss one element of structure: confidentiality. We show why confidentiality is more complex for couples and share several models for handling confidentiality well.

Chapter 3 covers the systemic concept of therapist neutrality. Couples usually will not continue in therapy if one partner perceives that the therapist has sided with the other partner.

In Chapter 4 we discuss the importance of getting a full list of client problems. Therapists must pay attention to the temporal aspects of how clients define the problem they bring to counseling. Especially if there are many hurts in the past, it is important to monitor the clients' storytelling.

In Chapter 5 we continue to focus on how to listen for a full range of problems. Some problems may not be revealed directly. Therapists must listen with a "third ear" for issues such as abuse, affairs, addictions, and severe pathology.

Chapter 6 addresses reasons to complete assessments before intervening. Couples may not raise certain issues until the therapeutic relationship is established. Assessment and intervention inform each other, but a key outcome of this phase of treatment is to create a relational definition of the problem.

The importance of attending to process is the subject of Chapter 7. Clients are often unaware that the ways in which they communicate with each other and whether their behaviors are congruent with what is said powerfully influence each other.

Conflict is described as a normal part of the couple relationship in Chapter 8. Couples may be covert, overt, or a combination of both about conflict. The intensity of conflict, either high or low, needs to be managed in session, or the clients may perceive that the session is no different from what happens at home.

In Chapter 9 the continuum of how couples perceive situations is laid out. Couples who agree or have minor differences are relatively easy to work with. Most theoretical models fail to address these couples, focusing instead on couples who agree on practically nothing.

Chapter 10 compares and contrasts the most important couple technique, reframing, with the traditional interpretation technique. In couple counseling, reframing is most appropriate as it is a systems technique. Examples of bilateral and systemic reframes are given.

In Chapter 11 therapists are encouraged to handle commitment carefully. It is important that the therapist not underestimate or undervalue the importance of commitment to the relationship.

Spirituality in couple counseling is addressed in Chapter 12. Individuals' sense of spirituality can be an important resource or a barrier in couple counseling. It also can have major implications for the couple's relationship, for good or ill.

We hope that by pointing out common mistakes we can help therapists become more aware of potential pitfalls and learn how to avoid them or quickly recover from them. Of course, this book also serves as a reminder that in spite of our best intentions, mistakes can and will be made. Hopefully the guidelines presented here will help you make fewer mistakes or, if you are a supervisor, will assist you in helping your students and supervisees prevent mistakes. However, we will never reach a point where errors, mistakes, blunders, and countertransference reactions do not occur. Being a productive therapist rather than a perfect therapist is in the best interest of the couple. Isomorphically, the partners also learn from this attitude that they do not have to be perfect for each other but rather productive in promoting happiness and harmony in the relationship. Mistakes will be made. Admit them, learn from them, and establish a process with the couple that allows everyone to recover from the mistake and move forward.

CHAPTER ONE
The "Battle for Structure"

Family therapy pioneer Carl Whitaker maintained that the therapist must win what he called the "battle for structure" (Whitaker & Keith, 1981). Winning this battle means taking control of the process and content of therapy. This does not mean that the therapist unilaterally sets the agenda but rather that he or she takes the lead with the couple in setting an agenda, implementing treatment, and working thematically or staying focused on the issue unless there is good reason to depart from the agenda.

Becoming adept at winning the battle for structure with couples is a skill many therapists never master, and, after too many frustrating failures, some end up avoiding couple therapy altogether. We cannot overstate how different couple therapy is from individual therapy and, to a lesser degree, from family therapy. For therapy to have the best chance to succeed the therapist must be in charge of how it proceeds, including setting and enforcing rules and determining who attends and how the participants will conduct themselves in session.

Therapists may lose the battle for structure if they:

- Fail to decide who the client is—individual or couple
- Fail to recognize that structuring the therapeutic relationship starts from the first client contact
- Fail to establish and enforce ground rules for couples
- Unintentionally unbalance therapy
- Search for the objective "truth" with regard to the couple's story
- Fail to address their own issues about authority and confronting clients

The specifics of winning the battle for structure vary from client to client, but the therapist must win it in each case. If the therapist loses the battle for structure, the couple will replay the same dynamics in session that they enact at home. Many couples will notice this quite quickly, and some will comment on it. Others will give the therapist the benefit of the doubt, attributing his or her relative inaction to the legitimate need to gather data on their behavior. When the clients express distress that their therapy experience is no different than their regular everyday experience, the therapist has failed to make structural or process changes that will support relational change.

Failing to win the battle for structure can also lead to unbalanced therapy. When therapy becomes unbalanced, one partner essentially blames the other for their problem. Part of winning the battle for structure is balancing the system by helping each partner to see their contribution to the problem. Balancing the system gives partners a systemic or holistic way of viewing the problem.

Winning the battle for structure positions the therapist to effect change with motivated, cooperative clients who are working with a shared sense of goals. The implicit message to the couple is that the therapist is sufficiently competent to handle their situation, and, if they are willing to entrust themselves to him or her, a good outcome is likely. Winning the couple's trust sometimes can take longer or be more difficult than one might think, but it is also something that can be explicitly discussed, even as part of winning the battle for structure. From time to time in our clinical work, we have had conversations that gently confront clients with what they believe our agenda as a therapist is. If they explicate something inaccurate that marginalizes the other partner (e.g., "I want you to make Joe realize that he has to start listening to me") we secure a better sense of trust by reassuring them that we want them to have a relationship that they both find valuable. Both partners must "win," or both "lose."

Why Couples Present a Challenge to Structure

Couples are the most difficult of all client systems to control. With individual clients, the therapist is usually able to make fairly straightforward alliances, even though there may be challenges dealing with the client's old patterns and pathology. The vast majority of individual clients are able to work within a therapeutic relationship in which the therapist empathizes with, is supportive of, and confronts the client directly as needed. Family counseling can consist of a variety of member constellations, but the usual focus is parents coming to treatment to help their children. Parents overtly put aside their dyadic differences to cooperate and learn the necessary skills and practices to change their family. If they cannot do this, the therapist addresses their lack of consensus in parenting, consistent with a structural approach to family treatment. Such family work often moves to couple therapy.

By contrast, couples form stable and sometimes dysfunctional systems, with each partner often consciously or unconsciously blaming the other for his or her or their problems. The couple often presents as if they both have sought treatment to change, and, in fact, they may be genuinely committed to doing so. However, even if they aren't aware of it, partners may have an underlying agenda to get the therapist to take sides and change the other person. Generally, members of couples find it easier to see their partner's contributions to their difficulties than they do their own. Therefore, the therapist sometimes walks a very fine line between having a solid alliance with each individual and, for therapeutic reasons, maintaining the option of taking one partner's side from time to time. Maintaining balance can be very difficult, especially in the face of one partner's hyper-emotionality or even emotional volatility by both partners. The couple may form a complementary behavior pattern, with one partner being emotional and the other rational. The therapist may unintentionally unbalance the couple system because of countertransference reactions.

The following dialogue shows the therapist struggling to gain control with a hyperemotional couple:

Wife: (*crying*) I have tried for years but he never listens to me about anything. He secludes himself and won't let me in.

Husband: (*angry*) For the record, that's just not true. I listen to you, but when you boss me around, and that's just about all the time, I tune you out and need my space.

Therapist: How can I help each of you get what you need?

Husband: (*angry*) Make her stop crying and bossing me around.

Wife: (*tearful*) He is always angry with me.

Therapist: (*to husband*) Can you talk to your wife without being angry?

The therapist in this case is caught in the couple's emotionality and probably is aware of it to a degree. Therapists dealing with hyperemotionality often feel desperate to somehow reduce the emotional lability in order to get something done. Rather than set some ground rules, set an agenda, or explore the basis for the hyperemotionality, all of which would be legitimate ways of deescalating the uncontrolled intensity, the therapist chooses to focus on the feelings at hand. Simply going back and forth with the feelings mirrors what the couple does at home and does little to move the therapy forward.

In order to promote therapeutic success, a therapist may need to spell out what is and is not acceptable behavior in therapy. The clients can choose whether or not to comply with these guidelines. If clients are unwilling, therapy will end and the therapist will not waste time and energy trying to help clients who are more interested in being right and in control than in making relational progress.

Who Is the Client? Determining Whether to Conduct Individual or Couple Sessions

The battle for structure begins as early as the first phone call. A person may call to request individual therapy for a couple problem or may request couple therapy but state that he or she wants to meet with the therapist first for an individual session. Assuming the therapist has the opportunity to actually speak with the caller rather than simply taking an appointment someone else has set up, the therapist must do some probing to see whether individual or couple counseling is best. It is not always easy to discern whether a caller's description warrants one or the other.

Couple counseling is the best course of action when the problem presented is obviously couple-related. This gives the therapist an opportunity to establish a relationship with the couple, obtain an overview of the problems from both partners' perspectives, discuss the ground rules, and help the couple decide on the best way to proceed, all the while observing and possibly intervening in the ongoing relational dynamics that govern their relationship. Seeing the clients as a couple for the first few sessions allows all these tasks to be accomplished more thoroughly than would be possible with individual sessions. It also strengthens the bond between the therapist and the couple. The therapist can begin developing a treatment plan in collaboration with the couple and reframe the problems relationally.

This makes subsequent interventions easier because they are based on an already-established relational foundation.

Occasionally, however, couple therapy may not be possible for pragmatic reasons, even when the couple's relationship is the identified target of therapy. These reasons include one partner's wanting to "check out" the therapist, one partner's unwillingness to participate in treatment, or some other problem such as scheduling for one of the partners. The therapist cannot automatically infer some kind of pathology from these kinds of circumstances. On the other hand, the therapist should be aware that the initiating partner might come alone to establish a therapeutic advantage for him- or herself. In other words, an individual initial session could be benign or could be malevolently motivated. Sometimes it is somewhere between these extremes. The therapist must be aware of each of these possibilities and look for evidence of any underlying problematic agenda. If one is discerned, it must be addressed concretely by asking explicit questions or commenting directly on whatever perceptions the therapist has.

Establishing Ground Rules for Therapy

The therapist can establish whatever ground rules he or she deems necessary and applicable for a couple's benefit, especially after seeing how the couple relates with each other and the therapist. These rules will help to structure counseling and promote systemic changes. Some common ground rules include:

- Both partners must show up for each session, or the appointment is considered broken. This rule supports the systemic nature of couple counseling and is best implemented after discussion and agreement between the therapist and couple. Exceptions should be made only with explicit forethought. In other words, one partner showing up alone unexpectedly is not acceptable.
- Partners must give the therapist 24 hours notice of an appointment cancellation and not cancel because of a fight or

one partner's reluctance to attend. The therapist may need to address cancellations of appointments early in treatment. Cancellations may be an indicator that the therapist needs to do some additional relationship building with one of the partners or make sure that problems are being defined relationally. This is also the time to watch out for power games into which the therapist is being triangulated.

- The partners must initially describe the problem to the therapist and then learn to speak to each other with the therapist as a facilitator.
- Partners must learn to speak for themselves using "I" language.
- Partners must show respect for each other and avoid patterns of communication that are destructive. The therapist will point out when these patterns appear. The partners must be willing to move in this direction, even though they may not arrive at the destination instantaneously. The therapist may have to be very directive at times to shut these patterns down. The partners need to be prepared for the possibility of the therapist's directive intensity. This definitely is *not* Carl Rogers!
- Each partner must be willing to accept his or her responsibility in the problems' creation, occurrence, or maintenance. Some clients genuinely need a good deal of help in perceiving this, so it may take some time for them to get here. The willingness to learn to see what is unseen is part of the commitment the client must make to treatment.
- The partners must assume responsibility for carrying out homework assignments. This includes a willingness to inform the therapist about the limitations of their capabilities. The couple also must help the therapist be realistic with them about homework. Therapists sometimes underappreciate the significance of what clients are asked to do in terms of homework and then erroneously assume the clients are unmotivated when they do not fully comply.

- The couple must agree to a rule of confidentiality should there be individual sessions at some point. The therapist and the couple will determine the particular rule of confidentiality. The mechanics of the process are described in Chapter 2.
- The therapist or the partners may request an individual session after the first few sessions or earlier if the therapist and other partner agree.
- The partners must agree to remain committed to the process long enough to give therapy a sufficient chance to be effective. The therapist must adequately explain how therapy works and how long it may take for them to achieve their goals. A couple's decisions about whether to stay together and work out their problems or leave therapy or the relationship must not be made prematurely. Rules regarding decisions about whether to proceed in therapy or stay in the relationship may need to be made explicit.

Many couples comply fairly well with the rules, even when they aren't made as explicit as the foregoing suggests. But there will be clients for whom the rules themselves present a problem, and they will break them. The therapist *must* address this issue purposefully. For some clients, breaking the rules is unintentional but habitual; the intensity of the emotions they feel in conflict overwhelms their rationality and they jettison the rule on respect, for example. The therapist cannot let this breach go unchallenged, and repeated interruptions by the therapist may be required to short-circuit the pattern. Clients can easily turn their frustration on the therapist under these conditions and the therapist must be prepared to receive the brunt of the clients' upset and use it as a moment of introducing change. This can be very powerful. It allows for a different kind of interaction under emotional conditions for the client, and it reinforces the therapist's neutrality and power in helping the clients change.

For some clients, however, the breaking of rules is not as benign. These clients will choose, sometimes quite overtly, to test the therapist's mettle and quickly find an excuse to break one or more of the ground rules. They're interested in seeing how much power the therapist is willing to use, and whether the therapist is "tough enough" to handle them. This dynamic may indicate individual pathology on the part of the client, or it may indicate genuine ambivalence on the client's part about their relationship. In either case, the challenge presented is huge. The following case example shows how one challenge played out.

Husband: (*to therapist, angrily*) I don't agree with how my wife handled my daughter's comments. She should have been more mature and been the bigger person, and I'm not going to discuss it. (*He stands up and moves toward the door as if to exit.*)

Wife: (*to therapist*) See? He won't even give me the chance to talk about it with him! He gets mad and always walks out whenever it comes up!

Therapist: Bob, I need for you to sit down and work through this. If we're going to make changes, as we all agreed early on, we can't revert back to what doesn't work. You can take some time right now to gather yourself together, but we can't just run from it. Please sit down.

Husband: (*moving back to his chair, but still standing*) I'm not willing to let her just drag me over the coals again about how wrong my daughter was and how wrong I was for not standing up for her. She just wants to put me under her thumb! I don't agree with that!

Therapist: I understand. (*pause*) Do you really believe your wife wants to break you?

Husband: Sometimes she does!

Wife: I don't—

Therapist: (*interrupting the wife*) Hold on. (*longer pause, to husband*) I wonder if there may be any other possibilities.

The therapist was able to break the pattern of the husband's withdrawal and reengage him in the problem-solving process by challenging both his habit of leaving and his wife's habit of pushing him to engage her directly when he was emotionally flooded. The ground rules had to be maintained for change to occur. The fact that the therapist did not directly confront the husband's emotion but rather asked him a cognitively focused question allowed him to "save face" while maintaining a sense of safety.

Another case example demonstrates the importance of enforcing rules. In this case a couple was working with a trainee. During a particularly emotionally intense session, one partner had suddenly walked out of the therapy room. The therapist had been so surprised when she left that she did not know how to respond. She finished the session with the remaining partner, who said that in their prior counseling the woman had frequently walked out and that was usually the beginning of the end of therapy. The trainee then consulted her supervisor. The supervisor said that, assuming both clients returned for the next session (and calling and speaking with both of them about that would be a good idea), that issue must be addressed very quickly. In the next session, both partners showed up, and the therapist reiterated the importance of not leaving midsession. Thirty minutes later, the woman got up and left again in the midst of an intense conversation, and again the therapist did not stop her.

In consultation with the supervisor, it was decided that, assuming the clients were repeating an established pattern, the therapist would inform the clients that if either of them left midsession, the session would immediately end and the question of whether the therapist would continue with them at all would be raised. In the next session, the clients were informed of this, and the session proceeded with both partners staying for the whole time. In the next session, however, the woman got up and headed for the door, and the therapist told her that if she left, she might be refused further services. The woman hesitated, then said she didn't care, and walked out. The therapist ended the session and told the man that the woman would need to call her if she wanted to discuss continuing.

Some days later the woman called and asked to schedule another session, and the therapist said she would not be available for a few weeks as other clients were filling her caseload. She told the woman to call again in a week or so, which she did. The therapist asked if she had walked out on any conflicts with her partner since their last therapy session, and she said she had. The therapist told her she would not continue their counseling until the woman had not walked out on a conflict at least three times in a row. The clients did not return to therapy.

In this case, the therapist's credibility and leverage had been seriously eroded by the clients' being able to impose their pattern on the therapy itself by breaking the rules. The therapist was able to recover and even creatively addressed the dynamic outside of the therapy room, but therapy itself was unsuccessful. Had she allowed the pattern to continue in treatment, it is likely that the clients would have terminated anyway without change.

Avoiding Unbalanced Therapy

Although unbalancing therapy is warranted in some circumstances, when it occurs inadvertently or without the therapist being aware of it, it is problematic. For example, in strategic therapy the therapist may sometimes purposely unbalance the therapy by suggesting to a husband to continue to start quarrels with his wife, the rationale being that without quarrels a real relationship can not exist. However, this unbalanced intervention focuses on the husband without addressing the wife's role in the disputes. When this kind of unbalancing occurs, therapy tends to deteriorate. The goal of the couple therapist is to maintain strategic neutrality with the couple so that both partners perceive him or her as fair. Strategic neutrality means that neither partner is able to ascertain when the therapist will intervene next and who will be in the "hot seat." It also means that the therapist is on the side of the couple relationship. The therapist demonstrates neutrality by confronting each partner on his or her part in creating dysfunctional patterns, by pushing each of them to initiate changes, and by helping them respond well to changes the partner makes. Chapter 3 provides an in-depth discussion of ways of maintaining therapist neutrality.

Certain circumstances can jeopardize balanced therapy. We will discuss the following: when individual sessions are needed; when issues of medication or diagnosis arise; when clients become hyperemotional, overly rational, or volatile; and when therapists search for an objective "truth" with regard to the couple's story.

Individual Sessions

Earlier in this chapter we suggested that it is generally best to see the couple together. Some therapists follow this rule without exception because they believe not doing so will inevitably unbalance the therapy. There are times, however, when the therapist may wish to see one or both partners individually for one or several sessions. This should be done with a clear rationale in mind (for example to purposely unbalance therapy), even if the therapist chooses not to share the rationale with the couple. Other times the couple may request individual sessions. Splitting the couple should not be done just because it is requested or because the therapist has been trained that it should be done. For example, one clinic had a policy of seeing the couple first, then each partner in turn, and then the couple. This system was problematic and led to a high dropout rate, difficulty with issues of confidentiality because they were not clarified in the first session, and a disruption in the formation of the therapeutic alliance between the therapist and the couple.

Again, splitting the couple should be done with a clear justification. The rationale must make clinical and theoretical sense to the therapist who chooses it, even if it does not pass muster with another therapist. Possible justifications include: one partner needing some individual therapy, one partner needing to share information that might be more hurtful to the other partner than he or she can handle at the time, one partner needing to bond more with the therapist, or one partner needing to share a secret that is preventing progress and that the therapist suspects is being hidden. Whatever the justification is, the therapist should consider the possible important implications for the couple and the couple therapy.

Prior to splitting the couple, several issues need to be handled. First, make sure the rules of confidentiality are clear to all parties. (For a more in-depth discussion of confidentiality, see Chapter 2.) Second, do the therapist and the partners all agree that it is acceptable to have individual sessions if the rules of confidentiality, now explicated, do not suit them? In other words, the motivation for an individual session by one of the partners may stem from a desire to share secrets that the therapist will maintain, not holding the partner accountable for the impact the secret has on therapy progress. But if the rule of confidentiality is clarified to preclude the therapist from sharing secrets, that motivation erodes. Individual sessions are contraindicated if either partner or the therapist feels that they will unbalance the therapy. Third, decide who will be seen, how, for how long, and about what. Generally speaking, it is useful to offer both partners the opportunity to be seen individually. They can rotate individual sessions, split a session, or double the number of sessions weekly. Even if one partner does not want to be seen, that person knows the therapist gave him or her the opportunity and he or she might wish to be seen later. The number of individual sessions should usually be limited to about three or four, unless a concrete rationale can be offered for more. Seeing one partner or both individually for more than a few sessions may represent a shift to individual therapy with a strong individual attachment forming with the therapist. When couple sessions resume and the therapist shifts back to an overtly systemic perspective, the partners may feel betrayed if the therapist does not take sides. The therapist may have never lost the systemic perspective, but it may be difficult for the partners to see that the therapist has maintained neutrality. In order to avoid this problem, it is best to limit individual sessions and to make it clear that each person is to talk only about him- or herself and how he or she contributes to the couple problem. Allowing individual clients to vent about their partners and pathologize each other sets up a pattern in which clients expect the therapist to endorse their view. This is sometimes a very difficult tendency to countermand.

Fourth, consider the nature of the couple's pathology. Some couples are just too risky to be seen individually by the couple therapist and should be referred to another therapist for individual work. Referrals may be best for clients who rigidly externalize their problems, have borderline personality disorders, or generally have a poor sense of boundaries. These types of couples tend to blur the boundaries between the couple work and the individual work. Therapists who see such couples individually may find that the clients cannot be managed in the individual sessions and often tell their partners that the therapist is beginning to subscribe to their point of view. The partner then gets upset and may drop out or believe the therapist no longer has a systemic view. The therapist may be able to maintain a systemic view in spite of this behavior, but the partner's perception has now changed. In problematic situations, the therapist can always say at the outset that he or she will try individual sessions, but if at any time it is not working for all three parties, any one of them may terminate the individual sessions and make a referral. The therapist will quickly get a sense of whether the partners are able to abide by the rules established for seeing the therapist individually.

The following case example illustrates some of the principles discussed about splitting couples for individual sessions. Brian and Amanda had been married for 9 years. They were both in their fifties and each had been previously married once. Brian had a couple of grown children from his first marriage. The couple had been in individual and marital therapy several times prior to seeing the therapist. They were beginning this therapy to work on the wife's lack of sexual desire. After a number of sessions with a lack of progress, the wife reported that she thought she had been sexually abused as a child. A prior therapist had dismissed this idea. She felt she needed to work on this issue without her husband. Initially, the male therapist suggested going to a female therapist for the potentially extensive individual therapy. The wife wanted to continue with the male therapist because she liked and trusted him and felt he knew what he was doing. The therapist suggested a treatment protocol that included individual sessions for the potential sexual abuse and periodic couple sessions where the wife could update her husband on progress. During treatment, if anyone felt the individual sessions were unbalancing the couple therapy, they would have to stop. Both partners agreed. This couple had good boundaries and an understanding of therapy. In fact, the wife was a therapist. Her individual therapy lasted about a year. She slowly began to remember incidents from her childhood and work through them. During the monthly couples sessions, her husband heard about her progress, maintained his relationship with the therapist, and worked on managing his relationship with his wife until she was through the emotional turmoil of recalling the sexual traumas.

Once the individual therapy was completed the couple therapy resumed at a regular pace. The husband was delighted with the progress his wife had made and how the situation had been handled. With the sexual abuse resolved, it was possible to make headway on the lack of sexual desire. Weeks and Gambescia (2002) noted that sexual abuse is not the only factor that leads to lack of sexual desire. The therapy shifted back to an explicitly systemic perspective with an examination of how the couple's dynamics were being manifested by the wife's lack of sexual desire.

In considering the foregoing case, it could be argued that working through the wife's experiences of sexual abuse with her husband in regular attendance would have been just as effective, perhaps more so. It would have offered them both the opportunity to manage a very vulnerable issue in an intimacy-building way that could have enhanced their connectedness, all with the guidance of the therapist working from a relational perspective. On the other hand, it could have been a bad decision if the husband was unable or unwilling to be sufficiently empathic or supportive of the wife, or if she was simply unable or unwilling to become increasingly vulnerable in his presence. The point is that there is risk in either choice. Splitting the couple in this case was effective, both for addressing the wife's individual concerns regarding her abuse history and for the couple's sexual difficulties.

Splitting couples must be done with great attention to process. Therapists who fail to follow some of these basic guidelines will find that they have lost their ability to be an effective therapist for the couple. Therapeutic neutrality will be compromised either because the therapist begins to side more with one partner than the other or because one or both partners perceive that the therapist has sided with the other partner and agrees that the problem is in that partner.

Medications and Diagnoses

Another issue that has received little attention in the literature is what to do when one or both of the partners need medication. Historically, systems thinkers have been biased against medication because of the old idea that it is part of the medical model of individual therapy, and they often do not receive much training in the use of medications. When both partners need medication and a referral is made, the therapy is not unbalanced as easily. However, when it is clear that one partner needs medication, therapy may become unbalanced. Suppose, for example, one partner is clinically depressed. Neglecting to treat the depression will impede the progress of restoring the marriage, but making a referral to a psychiatrist could send a message that the person in need of psychiatric help is causing the problem.

The same dynamic may come into play when the question of diagnosis is raised. As Odell and Campbell (1998) discussed, diagnostic labels can be used as weapons between partners intent on locating the problem in the other person. The therapist must consider carefully the effect that offering a diagnosis may have on the couple's relationship. There are ways to minimize the impact of medication or diagnosis with the couple, and often a well-crafted reframe is helpful and derails the possibility of unbalancing the system.

The process of reframing is discussed in greater detail in Chapter 10, so only a brief introduction is offered here. A successful reframe gives a new context to the way a problem is defined or attributed to a particular person so that a perceptual adjustment that changes the meaning of a problem occurs. Typically, the reframe offers a more benevolent explanation and moves the locus of responsibility, or blame, for a problem from one person to the couple as a twosome. A systemic reframe highlights the interlocking interactional contributions that both partners make to the problem, whereas a bilateral reframe does not emphasize the interlocking component but rather addresses each person benevolently but more or less separately. Both types of reframe are illustrated in the following case example.

Pat and Peter sought couples counseling. Over a period of time, Pat had become increasingly depressed, and Peter had distanced himself from the relationship. The therapist felt that Pat might be helped by medication for the depression but did not want to imply that the state of the marriage was her fault.

Systemic reframe. This marriage has been in serious trouble for many years, but you both want it to be better. You have struggled on your own and have not succeeded and have grown more and more demoralized. Each of you has developed a way of being in the relationship that allows it to continue. You should be congratulated for the sacrifices you have made for the sake of the marriage. Pat, you have been depressed and taken medication. Peter, you have been distant. You have both found ways to avoid confronting deeper issues in your relationship in order to protect it.

Bilateral reframe. Pat has tried for years to improve this struggling marriage. She has now become depressed and needs some medication to help her continue to fight for the marriage. Peter has also struggled for years in this failing marriage. He has not become depressed and does not need medication, but he has withdrawn from the marriage in order to reduce conflict. He did this to protect the marriage, but it seems that it only made the problem persist longer because both partners were not able to talk about how to make things better.

These two examples illustrate the ways a therapist can diffuse the responsibility onto both partners. The therapist does not want to create the perception that one partner is "sicker" than the other. The basic assumption that each partner is about equally healthy or unhealthy is valid in virtually all cases unless there is a bona fide psychosis operative in one of the partners. For example, one partner may develop a biologically based depression, an anxiety, or another similar disorder. Such types of illnesses may be unrelated to the marriage but significantly affect it just as any other illness would. In these cases, the therapy can be directed toward educating the couple and examining how the illness has changed their dynamic. A biologically based illness may create an overlay of couple dysfunction that needs attention; for example, the partner of someone who is depressed may become too much of a caretaker and exacerbate the depression. A balanced perspective is still needed in conceptualizing how the couple copes with the illness. A therapist with some familiarity with medical family therapy or psychoeducational approaches to treatment may be needed at this point as a referral or as a supplemental source of help.

Hyperemotionality, Rationality, and Volatility

Part of the therapist's responsibility is to monitor the emotional balance within the session, as well as to keep the couple emotionally engaged. Problems with balance can come as a result of hyperemotionality, rationality, or volatility between the partners. The therapist needs to keep a balance between rationality or thought and emotion in the sessions. There may be times when the sessions need to be emotionally intensified and other times when emotions need to be calmed.

Hyperemotionality. The most common way that a session can become emotionally unbalanced is when one partner becomes hyperemotional. This partner may express strong and persistent feelings such as anger, hurt, resentment, or depression. These feelings may be used to express the partner's belief that he or she has been victimized, abused, mistreated, unloved, uncared for, and so on by the other partner. This partner is trying to sway the therapist to side with him or her because he or she is the one who has been hurt the most, suffered the most, or has the greater degree of righteous indignation. And it may be true! Nevertheless, the therapist must be careful not to let these strong feelings unbalance the therapy too much or for too long.

Therapists do care about how clients feel and are often especially responsive and empathic when clients express suffering. People build good intimate relationships through the expression of pain and vulnerability. But the expression of hyperemotionality typically serves to build a connection with the therapist, often at the partner's expense. Although therapists need to empathically support the person expressing pain, spending an inordinate amount of time allowing for the ventilation of those feelings and helping the client to feel heard or validated can quickly lead to problems. It is also easy to fall into the trap of assuming that the one who appears to be suffering the most does not own any of the problem or owns just a small part of the problem. Some partners are simply more expressive, some are pathologically expressive (such as borderlines), and some have learned, sometimes unconsciously, that they can control relationships through emotional expression.

Rationality. On the other hand, some partners unbalance the session by being unemotional and rational. They are emotionally disengaged. These clients are trying to implicitly communicate that they are the calm and rational ones and therefore have a clearer perception of the situation, are more competent, and perhaps are easier to work with and live with. They will try to convince the therapist of their position using a logical, unemotional approach, often complete with an almost transcriptionlike recall of specific events that support their view. The therapist who has negative countertransference to emotional expression and positive countertransference to rationality and calmness may unbalance the therapy in favor of this partner.

Volatility. Emotion can also unbalance therapy in sessions with volatile couples. These couples engage with each other rapidly and with vigor, and their emotional escalation occurs so quickly that productive treatment becomes extremely difficult. It is akin to a dogfight, and the therapist who tries to intervene runs the risk of being ignored or, worse, bitten. Letting the couple take off into their war unimpeded in front of the therapist is not a good idea either, especially after the therapist has enough experience with them to know that their tendency is to escalate automatically. If setting minimal ground rules is not effective in keeping their intensity in check, the therapist may ultimately have little alternative other than to fire them as a couple, as therapeutic change is difficult if the intensity cannot be controlled. This is a last resort, however, and in our experience it does not occur very frequently.

Treatment options for hyperemotionality. We have found that two simple techniques work well to reduce emotional intensity:

(1) first validating feelings and then asking cognitively oriented questions, and (2) separating clients in session.

With the first technique, the therapist not only validates the feelings and their causes as perceived by the client but also helps the other partner to do the same, which, not surprisingly, can be difficult. Partners may be overly expressive because they have found it to be an effective way to get the other partner's attention or to increase their influence in the relationship. Even with significant validation, redirecting clients off their emotionally laden rant often takes quite an effort. In addition, the partner who is not on the rant may have real difficulty not escalating in response, let alone taking a validating stance. To do this validating well, it is almost always necessary to structure, as a task, the expression of feelings rather than try to cope with a spontaneous enactment that results in an emotional meltdown. Obviously, in-the-moment expressions tend to be harder to control, so we suggest that the therapist approach this task much as an enactment, even perhaps letting the clients know the task ahead of time or in a prior session.

Once the feelings have been validated, the therapist can begin to ask more cognitively oriented questions. Feelings and cognitions reciprocally oppose each other. The more questions therapists ask about thoughts or feelings, the more they amplify the cognitive aspect of the problem and the more they diminish the emotional aspect. For example, suppose a woman is crying and angry with her husband over forgetting their anniversary. The therapist would validate these feelings first by just focusing on the feelings that are overtly felt and then on those that might be deeper, such as hurt and rejection. The therapist could then ask a number of cognitively oriented questions such as:

- Has he ever forgotten your anniversary before?
- What does your anniversary mean to you?
- What do you think your anniversary means to your husband?

- What do you think it means that he forgot your anniversary?
- What did anniversaries mean to your parents?
- What did you learn about the meaning of anniversaries in your family?
- What are you saying to yourself about the fact that he forgot?
- Are the things you are saying to yourself rational? Do you really believe each of these thoughts or are some of them exaggerations?

The emotional partner will have to think in order to answer these questions. The more she thinks about these questions the less emotional she may become. The therapist continues the process until the partner is able to balance her feelings with her cognitive interpretation or meaning of the situation.

It is important to note, however, that something that may appear innocuous to the therapist may be much bigger to the couple, and for good reason. The foregoing questions may be quite useful at deescalating many couples, but the therapist must appreciate the very real possibility that answering some cognitively-oriented questions may produce legitimate escalation. For instance, suppose for a moment that the woman considering the questions concludes that the husband has forgotten the last several anniversaries, which leads her to suspect that their marriage is not a high priority to him. In response to the cognitive questions, she may conclude that, in fact, there is a pretty good body of evidence supporting just such a conclusion, and that line of thought may actually fuel her emotionality. Obviously, the therapist pursuing such a line of questioning needs to be reasonably confident that the answers to the questions will not be surprises that take the therapy in the wrong direction. If the therapist believes that the husband does not really value his marriage and that the wife's perceptions are essentially accurate, attempting to deescalate her using these cognitive strategies may not be well received.

The second simple technique to derail overexpression is to separate the couple in session. It is sometimes a wise idea to inform the couple that they are not ready to deal with this level of intensity therapeutically yet, but its expression is an indicator of just how important the issue is. In order to address the issue, the therapist can explicitly state that the person expressing the emotion needs to be validated, but also that the partner does not necessarily need to be present for that to happen and, in fact, may be harmed by hearing the emotion at this point. The therapist is offering protection to both partners from their own destructiveness. This approach must be explicitly framed as a temporary measure and not overused, but there are times when the only way to avoid a total blowout is to stop the couple midattack and assert the need to split the session.

It is crucial that the therapist use this technique as intentionally as possible so that the partners do not perceive it as the therapist's implicit surrender to their overwhelming negativity. If they conclude this, they may think the therapist is out of his or her league, discontinue therapy, or think that their relationship is hopeless. Couples often leave an emotionally intense discussion as a means of escape. In session, storming out can be used to hold therapy hostage to one partner's own degree of comfort with how things are going, as noted earlier. The separation technique can be used to model for couples how to use separation in an effective way. If someone does walk out, the therapist must address that partner and stress the importance of facing conflicts in a safe way, including temporary time-outs and the possibility of splitting the sessions for a while.

Treatment options for dealing with rationality. On the other end of the emotional expression spectrum are sessions with little or no action. These sessions are sometimes emotionally dead or lacking appropriate emotional intensity. One of the most obvious reasons a session may be dead is that the therapist has set the wrong agenda for the couple. In other cases, couples may have their therapy session later in the day and not feel as energetic as they would be earlier. Some will even comment that they are both drained and had thought about canceling. The clients look tired and the therapist may not want to press them to do the work that is needed out of "kindness." Such generosity is actually counterproductive and may have more to do with the therapist's lack of energy or discomfort with emotional intensity than with the couple's apparent fatigue.

Sparking some emotional intensity usually is relatively easy, even with tired couples. When confronted with clients who seem to have low energy, the therapist can start the session slowly by showing some concern about them and perhaps asking what has them so tired out. After a few minutes, the therapist can ask what they want to talk about during the session. Either of the clients, or the therapist, may toss out some ideas, and, in almost every case, one idea or another sparks emotion. When the therapist finds the topic that is salient to the couple's present situation, the couple suddenly becomes engaged and the session becomes emotionally energized. It is an amazing transformation to observe, but it requires some patience on the part of the therapist to let the couple discover what is emotionally charged for them. Even when they are tired, couples who come to the session still are fighting for a better relationship. They are invested. Finding the right theme is all it takes to enliven the session.

Several other strategies can be used to amplify the emotion in sessions. One of these strategies is to ask feeling-oriented questions. Suppose that in the earlier example about the anniversary the wife had expressed a thought about her husband forgetting the day but clearly was holding back how she felt. Maybe she teared up when she spoke about it and then quickly moved to another topic. The therapist might say, "I think there is more to him forgetting your anniversary than you are saying. I noticed you tearing up a little and you then switched topics." The following questions illustrate what could be asked:

- How do you feel about him forgetting?
- Are there deeper feelings about him forgetting?
- How do you feel when he forgets other important events in your marriage?
- What feelings would you like him to understand and acknowledge?
- What feelings do you find hard to express to him?

The repetition and probing into her feelings will probably bring more feelings to the surface. The therapist stays on the feeling theme, exploring the present feelings and why some feelings may be difficult to express.

Another way to facilitate emotions in a session is to try to supply the missing feeling or use visual images and analogies. The partner prone to speak intellectually about a problem may not respond or know how to respond to the kinds of questions listed above. They are unaware of their feelings. The therapist may try to supply the missing feelings by saying things such as "I get the feeling that something is missing. You must be feeling something about..." or, "If I were in your place and my sister had died two weeks ago, I think I would be feeling grief and loss. I realize these are painful feelings to experience."

The partners can also be asked to talk about what a particular feeling is like. They may be instructed to paint a picture for the therapist or to talk about what the feeling is like in terms of an analogy. Examples of these kinds of statement include:

- I feel like I'm in a dark cave and can't get out.
- I am being pulled in two directions.
- I want to run away.
- I see red.
- My anger is so strong that I imagine people spontaneously igniting.

- He is just like my father/mother/sister/etc.
- I want to become invisible.
- I become a witch.

The image or analogy gives the therapist information about the kind and intensity of the feeling. Further questioning and probing should help to make the feeling more explicit and the client more self-aware. Again, it is important for the therapist to stay thematically focused on the issue and the feeling rather than be diverted by the client who may not want to discuss a feeling that is forbidden, painful, or will create strife in the relationship.

Some couples, however, are reluctant to get into feelings because it is just not their way, and they have built a relationship around not being emotionally expressive with each other or, for that matter, anyone else. The therapist might ask the partners whether they are emotional with anyone else. If the partners are emotionally expressive in another relationship, their lack of expression with their partner is, in some way, functional for them. For persons who are unexpressive with everyone, it may be necessary to evaluate them in terms of their family of origin experience, including a trauma history. In any event, emotion-avoiding couples may be able to suppress emotions in circumstances most others would find naturally inviting or even inevitable. Therapists working with emotion-avoiding couples may need to be more provocative than they are accustomed to when working with ordinary couples. There are many ways to do this, such as asking "What if you had emotions?," suggesting hypothetical tragedies (see Odell, 2003, for one example), or using other approaches commonly utilized in emotionally focused therapy work (e.g., see Johnson, 2003).

The Endless Search for Truth

Some therapists forget their role as therapists and become detectives trying to discover the truth in some situation, especially when one partner's account of an event in the relationship diverges widely from the other's. A naïve therapist might assume that further questioning will reveal the "objective" truth about the event. Although inconsistencies or suspicious-sounding pieces in the couple's narratives should not be casually dismissed, searching for the truth does not often produce therapeutic results. The therapist who becomes convinced that one partner is credible and sides with that person will end up with unbalanced therapy that is therapeutically detrimental. Such a therapist is in effect abandoning the basic assumption that each partner has some part of the problem, that the problem definition is a matter of perception, and that reality is socially constructed between partners in a couple. Usually, the therapist can assume the "truth" is somewhere between the individuals' stories. In addition, as we point out in Chapter 10, the truth is often less important than finding a reality or frame for the situation that facilitates change.

There are occasions, however, when searching for truth is quite important. When clients have a stories that are very concrete on one or both sides and are mutually exclusive ("You were gone the entire month of June, 1997"; "No, I was not. I've never been gone more than 4 or 5 days our whole marriage."), or when one partner's version is extremely convincing, the therapist may need to consider the possibility that one client is revealing the truth and the other is presenting a distortion. Such a pattern is common with some couples, particularly when violence, infidelity, or substance abuse is involved. Genuine psychosis on the part of one or both partners is also possible. For couples where there is violence, infidelity, substance abuse, or a psychotic dynamic, the therapist must maintain control in ways that may be uncomfortable compared to "garden variety" couples. Often these couples are, at best, ambivalent about the issues coming to light or are genuinely unaware of them. One member of the couple may be afraid to tell the truth but want to, and the other may implicitly, or even explicitly, threaten the other person about the consequences should the truth come out. The therapist must always listen with a "third ear" for such underlying subtleties in the couple's dynamics. There are plenty of resources available for therapists who need to assess for violence, infidelity, substance abuse, and psychosis. Briefly, the therapist must take steps to ensure clients' safety, and if there is a threat, the therapist must be prepared to separate the couple and take whatever steps are necessary to safeguard all parties' welfare. Sometimes this precludes any couple work at all. We encourage even the most systemically oriented couple therapists to be prepared to jettison couple work when the circumstances warrant it.

Therapist Issues That May Influence the Battle for Structure

One thing to remember, and remember again: Ultimately, a couple's success or failure does not rest on the therapist's shoulders alone. In the final analysis, the responsibility for their relationship is theirs. Therapists can increase or decrease the likelihood of their clients' being willing to take that responsibility, and they should do whatever they can to find a way to work with their clients, but, in the end, the couple must choose to build their relationship or destroy it. Beginning therapists are especially prone to taking on more responsibility with difficult clients than they should. Couples are a particularly strong draw for many therapists who may have been the "peacemaker" between adults in their families of origin. It is a trap to avoid.

Beginning therapists or therapists with issues around authority-type figures should also be cautious when working with certain types of couples. We can think of several instances where a wife called for an appointment and talked about how her high-powered executive or professional husband was accustomed to being in charge both at work and at home, was sometimes even abusive, and had intimidated or manipulated previous therapists. These women were seeking a therapist who would not be intimidated by the husbands' power, fame, wealth, or the like. In other cases husbands have sought help with a domineering, unreasonable wife who was similarly unaccustomed to accepting input from people, professionals included. Winning the battle for structure with these kinds of couples is much more challenging than with some others. Therapists may need to seek supervision on these types of cases, or even refer the couple to a therapist with more experience and a greater degree of confidence. The therapist treating these types of cases must be able to see each person in the room as a vulnerable and needy human being like everyone else. Therapists will not serve their clients' best interests if they idealize an individual, are jealous, or are afraid to be themselves and to confront the couple as needed.

Maintaining control over structure and process cannot be emphasized enough. It is essential to secure control at the beginning of therapy or the couple will enact the same patterns that brought them to treatment. This issue is central throughout the whole course of treatment. As the therapy unfolds and the therapist moves from one issue to another, a constant monitoring of balance is required. The therapist can do a self-check from time to time to make sure the therapy is balanced in all the ways mentioned in this chapter. If the therapy has become unbalanced the therapist can reflect on what has happened or seek supervision. Catching an unbalanced situation early allows the therapist to correct the imbalance and move forward. The couple may need to be informed that the therapist has missed something that led to the unbalance and be allowed to talk about their perceptions. Otherwise, one of the partners may develop a mistrust of the therapist's ability to maintain control, be fair, or work effectively.

CHAPTER TWO

Confidentiality Traps

The discussion of confidentiality is one of the most important elements of informed consent. Informed consent is the formal, legal agreement that structures the relationship between the therapist and the clients. Each party can contribute to potential problems: the therapist by implementing a confidentiality agreement that is too simple and does not anticipate the complexities of couple work; the clients by not being open about their agendas for therapy. Mismatched communication about confidentiality can lead to legal or ethical problems. A good understanding of the nature of confidentiality forms a critical base for building trust in the therapeutic relationship. Common therapist mistakes with confidentiality include:

- Not being clear about the rules of confidentiality
- Not setting the rules of confidentiality from the outset
- Failing to enforce the rules of confidentiality
- Not anticipating problems with confidentiality given the presenting problem
- Not being flexible in setting the rules and gaining client consent to rules

Why Confidentiality Is More Complex With Couples

The importance of confidentiality when doing therapy with individuals is clearly stipulated in the various mental health professions' codes of ethics. However, with couple work, the matter becomes much more complex. One obvious reason for this is that it is not uncommon to see one or both of the partners individually for one or more sessions before couple therapy starts, during couple treatment, or in sequence after it. Seeing partners individually is common enough that it warrants special attention. The advisability of splitting partners was discussed in Chapter 1.

As noted earlier, it is common for clients to call desiring couple therapy but ask to come individually to the first session. Mark was typical of this situation. He called to request couple therapy but said he needed to come alone to the first session. The therapist did not inquire as to why he wanted to come alone and failed to establish any rule of confidentiality at the beginning of the first session. Mark quickly revealed that he had gone to a high school reunion and met an old girlfriend. His old girlfriend was single and doing well in her career. They had started seeing each other and before long were having an affair. Mark had been married 4 years and had a 1-year-old child. He felt obligated to stay married because of his child but said his passion was directed entirely toward his affair partner. He reported liking his wife and loving her deeply as a friend. He missed the time and passion they had before the birth of their child.

In a case such as this one, the therapist is stuck with the default position that Mark's individual confidence must be maintained. Mark assumed this would be the case and the therapist did not state otherwise. At this point, the therapist was in trouble. Presumably, the therapist knew that Mark's secret had huge implications for his marriage and the couple counseling they would be starting, but he chose to not discuss it out of fear of losing the client or the hope that somehow everything would come out without the therapist's prodding. If the therapist didn't know this, he was not qualified to do couple therapy.

Once couple therapy began, it involved a mix of some individual therapy for Mark and couple therapy. Over the initial course of therapy, Mark continued the affair. The therapist was in a position of having to pretend not to know the secret or to refer them. The therapist chose to do both individual therapy and couple therapy knowing that he, too, was deceiving Mark's wife and bound to a rule of confidentiality with Mark out of default. Had the wife found out about the therapist's knowing this secret she would have felt betrayed by him, at the very least. At worst, she would have had legitimate grounds to consider suing him for malpractice. Once she was under his care, he had an equal obligation to safeguard her well-being, and he clearly could not do this without violating Mark's confidentiality. In this case, it would have been safer to refer the couple to another therapist for couple counseling.

In some cases therapists may obtain information from sources beyond face-to-face, in-session contact: They may receive a phone call, fax, or email from a partner, see the partner in a context outside the therapy room (for instance, at a restaurant having a romantic dinner with someone other than the spouse), or receive information from an outside source. For example, a therapist may learn that a client he or she is seeing in couple therapy is having an affair with another one of his or her other clients. This is not a situation regularly addressed in graduate school! Additional complexities include the ambiguity in the codes of ethics, lack of training, and lack of literature in this area, all of which leave the therapist in a state of confusion and anxiety about what to do. Adding to the discomfort is the possibility of legal action taken against the clinician as a result of perceived or real harm stemming from mishandled confidentiality. All therapists know that it is important to act ethically, but many therapists simply do not know what to do in these types of circumstances, and there is little consensus on where to turn for guidance.

The codes of ethics of the American Psychological Association (2002), the American Counseling Association (1995), and the American Association of Marriage and Family Therapy (2001) do a less than adequate job of guiding the clinician in a number of situations regarding confidentiality with couples. The codes tend to deal in absolutes and provide simplistic principles without accounting for countervailing principles that therapists are also beholden to, or the complexity that therapists routinely face in their work. This may be an inherent limitation in codifying ethics, but it nevertheless means that therapists dealing with ethical issues may not receive definitive help when consulting the codes. They may wonder whether they have violated their particular code of ethics, whether they will be or should be reported, or whether they are vulnerable to legal action.

The codes of ethics of all the major professional organizations mentioned above state that the client, defined as an individual, may waive his or her right to privacy. The American Counseling Association's (ACA) assumption is that without such a formal, written waiver, information about one family member cannot be disclosed to another family member (see ACA Code of Ethics, B.2). The American Association of Marriage and Family Therapy (AAMFT) states that information can only be given to another family member with prior written permission (see AAMFT Code of Ethics, 2.2). It is also important to note that in the AAMFT Code of Ethics the therapist should continue treatment only so long as it is "reasonably" clear that the clients benefit from the relationship (see AAMFT Code of Ethics, 1.5). The importance of this principle will become clear later in the chapter.

Problematic Ethical Issues

Most couple therapy begins with both partners present. Obviously, beginning treatment with the couple as a couple not only gives the therapist an overview of the problems from both partners' perspectives and insight into the couple's interaction patterns and the like, but also allows the therapist to discuss the issue of confidentiality with both of them at the same time. However, this is not always the way therapy starts. As a result, ethical problems pertaining to information obtained from an individual prior to the start of couple therapy, decisions about who the client is, and the sequencing of treatment may arise.

When the therapist starts therapy by seeing just one partner, information that might prevent progress in couple's treatment if it is held in confidence may be revealed. Couple therapy is generally contraindicated in cases where there is an active affair, an addiction of any kind, instrumental spouse abuse, or severe psychopathology in either partner. This is not to say that couple therapy cannot be of great value in these circumstances; indeed, the literature has a wealth of evidence for the utility of couple therapy as a component in treating addictions, depression, severe mental illness, and so on (Sprenkle, 2002). However, the chances of the couple's making therapeutic progress as a couple are highly unlikely while an affair goes on, an addiction rages, or the like. In these instances, couple therapy may become focused on helping partners look at issues for each individual within the relationship and on identifying concerns about the viability of the relationship.

For example, if the partner who comes first states that he or she is having an active affair but would like to see if the marriage can be saved, the therapist already has a potential ethical dilemma. The therapist must decide who the client is and what the client's goal is. If the client comes alone and admits an affair or addiction but states that he or she wants to investigate saving the marriage, the therapist's client is the person in the room, not the relationship, regardless of the client's wishes and the therapist's intentions. Therapists must be aware of their own therapeutic agendas if they conceptualize the individual in an affair as one half of a couple who has not yet presented for treatment. However, the therapist can share information to help the client recognize that, in the therapist's view, maintaining the affair while working on the marriage is almost certainly oxymoronic, unless the possibility of an "open" relationship exists but has not been explored. The therapist may need to help the client decide what his or her goal really is. If the client really wants to work on the marriage and does not want to see if an open relationship is an option, he or she will need to discontinue the affair. If this is agreed upon, and the partner is invited, the therapist must to discuss with the initial partner the confidentiality issues that already exist.

Sometimes a partner will insist on an individual session first or state that the partner does not want to come to therapy. The therapist has little choice but to start the process and hope that nothing is revealed that will be a contraindication to doing couple therapy. If the client does reveal something, such as an active addiction, the therapist has two alternatives: He or she can suggest that the individual stop the behavior before starting couple therapy, or he or she can refuse to offer couple therapy by explaining that probably no progress will be made in the couple's relationship until the behavior ends. The therapist could also explain that if couple therapy is undertaken it would be with limited goals for the couple and that individual sessions would be needed for the partner whose problem will prevent progress. In so doing the therapist avoids an ethical and probably moral dilemma and has advised the individual client not to seek couple therapy elsewhere. The same is true for the couples facing affairs, abuse, or severe psychopathology. Therapists must use their best judgment in deciding whether couple therapy will "reasonably" benefit the couple. If contraindications to couple therapy exist, the clients are best advised to seek individual therapy first and, perhaps, couples therapy later.

Models for Confidentiality and Implementation Issues

Karpel (1980) is the only clinician we are familiar with in the field of family therapy who has tried to address the complex ethical and moral responsibilities of doing family and couple therapy. This fact is astounding given the amount of attention the literature devotes to issues of supervision and revisions in ethical standards. At the heart of it, there are three ethical positions that the clinician can take, with small variations on each, described below.

Therapists choose their ethical position based on their comfort levels and the particular couple. The therapist's comfort level can be comprised of various factors, including personal values and how they have been implemented in their clinical experience and the complexity of the situation. Many therapists prefer to choose the simple position of maintaining everything in confidence. For instance, in order to keep confidentiality simple, some therapists avoid all the multiple relationships they possibly can, whereas others are willing to consider multiple relationships on a case-by-case basis, seeking to minimize risk a much as possible. That is, seeing fewer members of a system individually decreases the chance of the therapist being told secrets. Attributes of the couple may also influence the choice of position. Couples who are open and tell the clinician readily that they do not have any secrets may predispose the therapist to choose one ethical position over the other. It is important to talk with the couple about what rule of confidentiality is to be used. If the couple is seen for the first meeting the clinician can discuss this issue near the end of the meeting. The therapist may describe the ethical positions or may choose the one he or she likes or thinks is most appropriate for the couple. The therapist may have prewritten contracts for each partner to sign or write it by hand in the session, including anything particular the couple wants.

The three ethical positions regarding confidentiality are as follows: keeping all individually revealed information confidential unless there is a waiver, sharing all information, and having accountability with discretion. Each position has advantages and disadvantages, and none is a guarantee against potential legal action.

Keep All Information Confidential Unless There Is a Waiver

The first position the therapist might take is consistent with the wording of the codes of ethics mentioned earlier. The therapist states that he or she will keep any information received from a partner individually confidential unless a signed written waiver gives the therapist permission to divulge the information. This position has several advantages. Partners may be more likely to reveal information to the therapist if they know their partner will not be told what they reveal. In effect, this position gives people permission to share any secret they like knowing it will not be transmitted to the partner. Therapists may like this position because it allows them access to the greatest amount the information possible. They may also take comfort in the knowledge that they are not responsible for sharing any secret information.

Under this condition, the therapist essentially has two individual clients that just happen to be in a relationship together and are in treatment at the same time in the same place. Taken to its logical conclusion, the partners should have separate case files, and each couple session would be documented individually in each file, as well as in a couple file that would be "owned" by both partners. The documentation in the individual files would emphasize each individual's pathologies and treatment, whereas the couple file would contain the couple issues. In point of fact, such an approach is done in some form in some agencies that do not treat couples as couples and by some clinicians untrained in couple therapy. It also affords the clinician the ability to diagnose each individual and even to bill third-party payers for couple sessions (although typically a couple session is not billed as two individual sessions). Obviously, taking the individualist position to an extreme is unworkable, and determining just how far to take it can be difficult.

This option also has some major disadvantages clinically. Suppose one of the partners reveals an active affair, addiction, or something else that would "reasonably" prevent a successful outcome in the couple's therapy and does not want this information revealed to the partner. The therapist is now in a bind. He or she must go back to couple therapy pretending not to know the secret, which obviously can result in extreme discomfort. Additionally, the therapist is now in a position of colluding with the client in concealing information and deceiving the partner. The therapist is also aware that a successful outcome to the couple therapy is unlikely but must proceed as if this secret does not exist. It may be difficult to terminate the couple therapy. The therapist may not be comfortable finding an excuse to terminate, especially if the secret is revealed after some period of time working with the couple. Finally, even after signing an agreement of confidentiality, the partner who finds out about the secret may be angry with the therapist for knowing the secret and for not taking action to let him or her know that the therapy was a charade. Therapists also must keep in mind that they are equally therapeutically responsible for *both* members of the couple.

Knowing secret information from one partner may even preclude the therapist from asking about it in the couple session. If the therapist does ask about it, the client may be believe that the question was based on confidential information and thus consider it a violation. For example, in the course of couple treatment, it is not uncommon for the therapist to ask about an affair, especially if there are indicators that one may be occurring but has not been revealed. In the case discussed earlier, the therapist knew about an affair. However, even if there are suspicious indicators in the couple session, the therapist cannot ask about it without risking the possibility that the cheating partner will legitimately accuse the therapist of violating his or her confidentiality, even if the therapist asks while pretending not to know. In other cases, the partner being cheated on may ask the therapist bluntly about whether partner is having an affair. There are significant implications for any response given by the therapist. An affirmative answer or even a "could be" answer may violate confidentiality. An answer of no is a lie and thus harms the asking client by implying that his or her perceptions are incorrect. A no-comment answer will, at the very least, damage trust and the therapeutic relationship while raising suspicions about what is not being said. Additionally, if couple dynamics can be partially explained by the presence of an affair and the therapist avoids discussing it, he or she is not doing good therapy, and standard of care concerns arise.

Share All Secrets

On the opposite end of the confidentiality spectrum is what could be called the "three-way rule." The therapist states that he or she will not keep any secrets and will share all information received. Any information among the three parties is considered public or nonconfidential. Essentially, the partners are asked to waive confidentially at the outset of therapy. This rule has the advantage of stressing openness and honesty to the couple. The therapist does not have to worry about being caught in the binds described earlier. He or she is free to share any information gained through any means whatsoever as long as it pertains to the couple. For example, if one partner sends the therapist an email about the fact that she has evidence of an affair, because of the position adopted by the couple this information would be revealed in the next session.

However, there is a potential drawback to this position. If a client knows that whatever is revealed to the therapist will be revealed to the partner he or she may be less likely to share secrets. For example, a client having an affair may deceive both the therapist and the partner. The therapist continues therapy but may be baffled, along with the partner, by the lack of progress. As a general rule, when therapy should be helping the couple to change but the couple is not making progress, one of the possible explanations is that there is a secret. If and when the secret does become known, the uninformed partner may be furious about the waste of time and the therapist may look foolish because he or she did not discern that there was a secret or what the secret might have been. Of course, many therapists will argue that a main cause of struggle in relationships is, in fact, secretivity and mistrust—something that emotionally focused therapy, for example, cites as lethal for intimacy (Johnson, 1996). Therefore, expecting therapy to produce significant positive change when secrets are not revealed is a serious mistake.

That said, the therapist operating with the three-way rule can explicitly address the possibility of secrets and inform the clients that secrets in marriage are usually detrimental to progress. The hope is that with growing trust in both the partners—and with the help of the therapist and the therapeutic process—there may be a greater willingness to take the risk of sharing secrets, even ones potentially devastating to the relationship. A useful analogy is getting out of debt. One cannot pay off all one's debtors until one knows the full extent of what is owed, painful as that may be.

Accountability With Discretion

The third option is what Karpel (1980) called "accountability with discretion." This position is a compromise between the previous two positions, but is closer to the three-way rule. Accountability with discretion involves informing the partners that the therapist will maintain information in confidence unless he or she believes it will be detrimental to the progress of the couple therapy. If the therapist believes any information obtained through any means will impede or be detrimental to couple therapy's producing change, the therapist will ask the person with the secret to share it with the partner in a conjoint session. If the partner refuses to share the information, the therapist will not share the specific information, but will say that he or she is aware of information from [name of the partner] obtained [in an individual session, phone call, email, etc.] that makes it impossible to do couple therapy. The advantage of this rule is that the therapist will not be caught in a bind and will have a way out if he or she is asked to keep a secret. The rule gives the therapist room to maneuver. Interestingly, common sense would suggest that it would promote secret keeping on the part of the partners. In some cases it does, but in other cases the partner wants to reveal the secret but does not know how to do it or does not feel safe. These clients find it more comfortable to tell the therapist first, knowing that the secret must then be revealed. The task of the therapist is to help the individual get ready to share the secret. We usually give the partner about three sessions to share the secret and to begin working on the individual problem. If the problem is an affair, the person must agree to stop it within 3 weeks and to continue to see the therapist both individually and as part of the couple to deal with the issue. If the problem is an addiction or some other issue, the partner must seek help from an addictions specialist (unless the therapist is trained in addictions work) and begin all the work required by the addictions specialist. The following transcript illustrates how to implement this strategy.

Therapist: I would like to talk to the two of you about confidentiality. Let me tell you how I like to handle this matter and get your reactions. I maintain all information that you tell me through whatever means in confidence. However, if you tell me something in an individual session, or through some other means, that I think will impede the progress of your couple therapy, I will ask you to take responsibility for it. This might mean individual sessions for one or both of you and a limited time period during which certain problems are stopped. You may or may not wish to tell me secrets and I will tell you whether I think it is important for your partner to know. If I think your partner should know, then I will suggest you tell them and coach you about how to do it. If there is an ongoing secret behavior I will help you to stop it in a given period before asking you to tell your partner. I will never reveal the nature of the secret, but if it interferes with your stated goal of doing couple therapy I may terminate therapy by saying that you have not fulfilled this agreement. Are you clear about this rule?

Husband and wife: Clear, clear.

Therapist: Any questions?

Wife: I guess you are saying that if my husband is doing something I should know about and will make this therapy a sham, you will ask him to tell me or you'll tell me that you can't work with us.

Therapist: Yes.

Wife: You have a hard job. I guess I would rather know something than nothing.

Husband: I'm here to save my marriage. I'll do whatever it takes.

Therapist: Are you both okay with this rule?

Couple: Yes.

Therapist: Let me put this in writing and get you to sign that you understand that this is the rule of confidentiality we will use.

This position has many complexities. A partner may reveal a secret but then not want it shared. The therapist has already informed the client about the consequences of this action. The therapist will make an announcement to the couple that he or she can no longer work with them because of information revealed by one of the partners in an individual session. Remember that the therapist is not obligated to reveal the specific information or secret. However, such a declaration raises a red flag for the uninformed partner. One of two consequences result: the uninformed partner is jolted out of his or her denial and suddenly knows what the secret is, or the uninformed partner demands to know what the other is hiding.

In our experience, there are three frequent outcomes with the accountability with discretion position. The first is that partners are looking for a "safe" way to reveal the secret. This position provides them with that sense of safety. Although the ultimate outcome can never be predicted, they know the secret will be handled in the context of couple therapy. The second is that they are ambivalent about revealing the secret and know that when the therapist attempts to end treatment the game will be at an end. They know the partner will press them for the information and they will then reveal it. The third outcome is that, when confronted with the secret, the partner will deny it, resulting in termination of couple counseling and perhaps the relationship. The partner with the secret is really looking for a way out of the marriage without having to say what he or she is doing. Typically, the other partner continues with the therapist to understand what has happened or to deal with his or her own denial of suspicious behavior or knowledge of a secret or an affair. The goal of therapy may shift to helping that partner exit the relationship because the other partner refuses to be honest or to assisting each partner separately to deal with their dishonesty and denial, respectively. Of course, therapists in this situation face the same bind as those who adopt the first position: they cannot reveal the secret to the partner continuing treatment even after couple therapy has ended. However, at this point the partner is usually able to discern the secret or break through his or her denial. In some cases, the partner continuing treatment may overcome his or her denial and admit that there was an affair, even though he or she has no concrete evidence. The therapist should continue to maintain the secret but may confirm that unless the other partner can dispel the accusation of an affair, their relationship will not change.

Two questions commonly arise about this strategy—the first regarding therapist level of comfort and the second regarding the implied position of power. Therapists may feel uncomfortable keeping the secret for a limited period of time or about confronting the couple and telling them that couple therapy must be terminated. This is to be expected, but keep in mind that the secret-keeping is time-limited and that confrontation is ethically required if the therapy is to "reasonably" produce change. Many beginning therapists are also concerned that keeping the secret even for only a brief time may lead the other spouse to feel betrayed. In our experience, this has never happened. The sense of betrayal is directed toward the partner. Some "uninformed" partners have even sympathized with the therapist for the dilemma their partner created for the therapist and they appreciate knowing the therapist did not participate in a therapeutic relationship based on deception.

The issue of the therapist's position of power is a more serious yet less frequently considered drawback. When the couple and therapist agree to proceed under this confidentiality position, the therapist is put in an extraordinarily powerful and responsible position. He or she decides what can be kept secret and what is "too important" to be kept secret. The therapist's vision of how a couple relationship should operate becomes the standard by which the clients' relationship is evaluated. Fortunately, this is usually not a problem. But consider this: What if the therapist himself is having an affair and does not believe it is necessary to reveal it in his own marriage? Does he view an affair by one of the partners similarly? Additionally, does the therapist have sufficient knowledge of the clients to be able to determine what is consequential for that couple? Imagine the harm done by a therapist who judges something inconsequential to the clients as crucial, or vice versa.

In most cases we prefer the third ethical option. Therapists who choose this option must be very clear about the details of the rule of confidentiality and have everything in writing. But even written documentation raises a hornet's nest of possible problems, all of which may have legal ramifications, as discussed in the following section.

Documentation Concerns

The case record is both a critical support and a source of potential vulnerability for the therapist. Done right, however, the documentation of a case can actually serve as the model by which to handle ethical dilemmas. We reiterate, however, that nothing clinicians do will ever fully insulate them against legal complaints or legal action.

As we have mentioned, treating individuals is fairly straightforward with regard to confidentiality, whereas couples work can take us quickly into murkiness. This is true for documentation as well. In a private practice setting, the clinician has the most freedom to generate case files according to both personal preference and professional requirements. It is comparatively simple under such circumstances to transfer one's ethical position to one's case files. If the therapist chooses to use either of the latter two confidentiality rules, the case file should reflect that the couple is the client. Therefore, we stress that the therapist's initial informed consent reflects his or her default ethical position. Progress notes should focus mostly on couple dynamics, and both partners "own" the case file's contents. As most professional issues courses mention, nothing from that file can be released to a third party without both partners' consent, common exceptions to confidentiality notwithstanding. Taking this position from the outset will greatly reduce the possibility of running into a problem with secrets in any individual sessions that may occur during the course of couple therapy.

Individual sessions that take place during couple work should be documented as individual sessions, but this information should not be identified as confidential within the couple treatment. Individuals working in agencies may wish to consult agency policy and obtain legal advice before implementing this strategy. Furthermore, the therapist must be prepared to keep a time-limited secret and confront the couple with the possible termination of therapy if the person with the secret does not comply with treatment. Maintaining this information in confidence produces cognitive dissonance for the therapist and will be uncomfortable. The therapist must carefully document all the sessions and be very attentive to the process of implementing this strategy. Lax implementation of the strategy can produce problems for the therapist. Finally, therapists must ultimately decide on which of the three ethical positions to take depending upon their comfort level and the couple's preference.

Under the best of circumstances, confidentiality concerns and the concomitant specter of legal repercussions can bring the therapist a good deal of stress and anxiety, as the following case example shows.

A couple who were in heavy conflict and on the verge of divorce presented for therapy. The therapist started by using the accountability with discretion confidentiality position. The couple agreed to this confidentiality rule and marital therapy commenced.

Over the course of the next few months, it became apparent that the husband had some significant individual psychopathology, consistent with antisocial personality disorder or a schizoid type, and the wife was codependent, a product of an alcoholic home with a history of abuse. The husband sent emails detailing the "truth" about the wife to the therapist, and these emails were then discussed in couple sessions, in accordance with the confidentiality rule that had been established. Then, one night, the wife called the therapist's pager in an emergency, stating in her message that the husband had abruptly left the home in a fit of rage and was driving around town with a gun. She was afraid he was suicidal. The therapist called the wife and told her to call the police and then asked if she knew where he might be. She said she did not have any idea and that the husband would not answer his phone. Minutes later, the husband called the therapist's pager and left a message claiming that he was not suicidal but that the *wife* was suicidal. The husband did not answer his phone when the therapist called, and when he called the wife back, she assured him that she was not suicidal. The husband eventually returned home and the incident was not discussed between the couple.

The husband sent the therapist an email the next day in which he said he had been suicidal but would not admit it to the wife. He then stated that he would deny it if the therapist raised it in couple therapy in the session scheduled for the next day, and that he intended to pursue legal action against the therapist if the therapist revealed the disclosure to the wife. Essentially, he was revoking his consent to release information and reinstating his individual confidentiality privilege. He stated that his attorney had informed him that his individual confidentiality would be legally protected, despite what he had agreed to in the beginning of therapy. Parenthetically, a strong argument could be made that the husband's revocation of consent did not occur until after the information he wanted confidential was revealed. Unfortunately, the paucity of case law on this issue was of little comfort to the therapist, who did not know what to make of this threat, legally or elsewise, and who did not want to become a nationally known figure on account of it. The therapist decided at that point to terminate couple therapy and make a referral. Unfortunately, the wife did not know any of this, and she needed to be informed. The husband said in his email that they would be coming for their scheduled session. The therapist was in a bind, no matter which way he went.

The therapist elected to tell the couple he would see them separately for most of this visit, and he met with the husband first. He confronted the husband about the bind the husband was placing him in, and told him that he would be unwilling to work with them under those conditions and that the husband's actions were detrimental to the goals of couple therapy. The husband stated he was glad to stop therapy, but he reiterated his threat about legal action should the therapist reveal anything to the wife. The therapist agreed to not tell the wife the specifics of their conversation, but stated that he would be honest with her about the impossibility of continuing to work with a couple that he himself could not trust. The wife knew that the husband had told the therapist that she was suicidal, and she had concluded correctly that the husband had been suicidal, so she was aware of some of what was going on. When the therapist met with the wife, he told her that he was unwilling to work with them as a couple because he couldn't be sure he could safeguard both of their individual well-being due to the contradictory information. The wife was upset but accepted the explanation. Then the therapist met with the couple and reiterated that he would need to refer them given what had happened. The entire episode was thoroughly documented in the couple file.

Several months later, the wife called the therapist and requested individual counseling, and the therapist accepted her with the reminder that what had occurred in their couple counseling was open up until the point that her husband revoked his consent. She was given a new file and counseling began.

The point of this example is that couple therapy brings with it a complexity that codes of ethics and case law do not adequately address. Approaching the issues carefully and wisely will do much to reduce some of the difficulties, but nothing will completely eliminate them, clinically or ethically.

CHAPTER THREE

Alliances and Coalitions

With a few exceptions, maintaining a position of neutrality, especially in the first few sessions, is one of the cardinal rules of couple therapy. Neutrality supports a systemic approach to couple counseling by viewing the couple as an interlocking system. Neutrality is not indifference or noninvolvement. Rather, the therapist is interested in each person's unique perception of the problem, even if he or she does not accept the client's definition of the problem. One partner's view is not seen as more correct than the other's. Neutrality is lost when the therapist unintentionally forms an alliance or coalition with one member of the couple at the expense of the other partner. (An alliance is a temporary affiliation wherein the therapist takes one person's side for a short period of time. A coalition is a stable and ongoing affiliation with one member of the couple.) Neutrality is also lost when the therapist places the blame or responsibility for couple problems solely on one partner. Alliances and coalitions may form when the therapist:

- Fails to understand the importance of neutrality to a systemic focus in counseling couples

- Fails to recognize how neutrality is lost
- Fails to recognize when exceptions to neutrality are appropriate
- Fails to implement neutrality well

The Importance of Neutrality

Neutrality is a fundamental assumption of systemic couple therapy, and clients generally require it, even when they don't expect it, welcome it, or help the therapist maintain it. When therapists maintain neutrality, they see the couple as an interlocking system in which each partner contributes in some way to the couple problem. In fact, the general belief is that the partners contribute about equally to the couple problem. In other words, the partners are of roughly equal health or pathology. Homogamy theories of mate selection have shown significant support for this idea, especially when partners select each other and are honest with each other. Of course, homogamy would not apply as well in cultures with arranged marriages, but most couple therapy is done with couples who have chosen each other.

The assumption that the couple is an interlocking system should be abandoned only with certain client couples and only after careful consideration. For instance, if one partner has been dishonest about his or her behavior (even unwittingly), the couple may not be operating as an interlocking system. The following case example illustrates this point.

A woman married a man who did not see himself as a sex addict and was unaware of the degree to which his behavior and thoughts were inappropriate. He concealed his behavior from her even though he continued to be a sex addict. When the woman discovered his addiction, she asked for therapy to correct the problem. In this case, the wife was the healthier partner and wanted her husband to be healthy. If, however, she had continued the relationship without confronting his behavior after she discovered it, we could view the couple as interlocking and assume that she was gaining something from his addiction or at least avoiding something negative. For instance, perhaps she feared intimacy and his addiction allowed her to avoid intimacy. Some therapists argue that at an unconscious level there are no secrets in a relationship (Charny & Parnass, 1995), but maintaining such a belief with clients is not usually helpful for therapy.

Similarly, when psychopathology occurs after a relationship is established, the therapist should not immediately assume that the couple is an interlocking system. Some mental disorders have a late onset or are situationally generated. One partner may develop some form of psychopathology, such as depression, after the partners have been a couple for a while. The disorder may be largely unrelated to the relationship. To say the healthy partner played a role in the development of the disorder or enabled it might be inaccurate. On the other hand, therapists must fully explore and rule out the fact that the marriage is not a significant contributor to the psychopathology. There is growing evidence that depression, for example, is often related to marital distress or discord (Beach, 2003, Howard & Weeks, 1995). Depression appears to be especially common when couples feel a sense of hopelessness about the resolution of long-standing problems and when a partner feels stuck in the relationship.

Maintaining neutrality is especially important when one considers the expectations of clients. When a partner enters treatment with the other partner, he or she wants to be treated with respect. How he or she wants the partner to be treated, however, is another matter. In the best case, each person also wants the partner to be treated well and expects the therapist to be fair and unbiased (another way to phrase neutrality), but frequently one or both parties want the therapist to take sides. Partners may even verbally acknowledge that part of the problem is theirs while secretly or overtly believing that the other partner is more, mostly, or totally to blame. Thus, each partner will try to convince the therapist that his or her position is the right, true, correct, accurate, or real view of the relationship.

The therapist may receive mixed messages that each partner wants to change and sees his or her own responsibility for the problem but still expects the therapist to fix the other partner. If this attitude underlies the couple's approach to therapy they will be exquisitely sensitive to the therapist's taking sides even though they may try to pull the therapist toward their position.

How Therapists Lose Neutrality

If every couple therapist understands the importance of being therapeutically neutral, how do they get inducted into the system in such a way that partners perceive side-taking, alliances, or coalitions? Therapists can lose neutrality for a variety of reasons; following is a discussion of some of the most common ones.

Factors Outside the Therapist's Control

In many cases, the therapist may be unaware of or unable to initially control the client's perceptions for the following reasons: the couple or partner may believe that they cannot be helped; that the therapist will take one partner's side because they are the emotional, injured, or "sick" partner; or that one partner is more articulate or persuasive. The therapist can gradually change these perceptions, but unless these perceptions receive immediate attention and the therapist probes, he or she may not know how the couple perceives the therapy, thereby risking a loss of neutrality. For example, it is quite common when treating a couple in which one partner is a therapist that the non-therapist partner believes he or she will be perceived with less credibility and as the one with the greater (or only) pathology.

Diagnostic Errors

Most couple therapists rarely use the *Diagnostic and Statistical Manual of Mental Disorders* (DSM-IV) (American Psychiatric Association, 1994) due to its emphasis on individual pathology. From early in the history of couple and family therapy, therapists focused on systems and believed that using the DSM diagnostic scheme had the effect of pathologizing one partner at the expense of the other. Theoretical and practical concerns have affected this stance. From a theoretical point of view, one must recognize that individuals exist within systems. Weeks (1994, and Weeks & Gambescia 2000, 2002) argued that couples consist of individuals. Thus, the DSM-IV could be applied to individuals, especially as many therapists who do couple therapy are trained as psychologists or individually oriented counselors and are well-versed in the diagnostic and statistical classification system. Each individual may or may not have his or her own pathology. The assumption is that couples form interlocking patterns of behavior such that each is likely to have his or her own pathology and reciprocal diagnosis. However, this is not always true, as one partner may be comparatively free of pathology.

Therapists must be well trained in diagnosis in order to avoid missing pathology in one or both parties. Therapists can make diagnostic errors for several reasons: by failing to maintain a systemic focus, by lack of training, or by personal identification with certain personality traits. The therapist can fail to maintain a systemic assumption by viewing one partner as healthier or contributing less to the problem than the other. Many higher-functioning couple members do not have Axis I disorders. However, both partners may have personality disorders. One common combination of personality types seen in couple therapy is the obsessive-compulsive husband and the histrionic wife. The obsessive-compulsive husband may come to the session on time, well dressed, well organized, and present his view of problems with clarity and rationality. His wife may appear late, be sloppily dressed, be disorganized, and present her view of the problems with confusion and hyperemotionality. Our culture places greater value on timeliness, organization, and rationality. Thus, the therapist may miss the fact that the husband has either the traits of or the personality for obsessive-compulsive personality disorder and begin to wonder how this man lives with a woman who is so emotionally intense and labile. The problem would not occur if the therapist recognized that both partners have a personality disorder. A systemic perspective of the personality match would suggest that one is overemotional and the other is underemotional. Thus, they complement each other. Each one has what the other is missing. The same idea could apply to any number of personality-disordered couples. Many training programs do not focus on Axis II diagnosis. So much material is available on Axis I diagnosis and these disorders are so vital in the mental health system and in obtaining reimbursement that Axis II training gets shortchanged. The therapist who has not been adequately trained will simply miss the personality disorders, but will be able to describe the fact that one partner has more problems than the other. Axis II disorders are also much more difficult to see than Axis I disorders, especially in higher-functioning clients. In fact, extensive training and experience are required if therapists are to be adept in assessing the presence of some Axis II disorders.

Therapists may identify with a partner with a particular personality disorder because they believe that one way of being is better than the other. In order to be successful in graduate school, a high level of organization and rational thinking is usually needed. Therapists may identify with the person who is most like them. Conversely, therapists may underidentify with the person least like themselves because they have personally rejected that constellation of traits in themselves, perhaps due to countertransference issues. The danger is that the person who is least like the therapist is more likely to be seen as the unhealthy partner.

Countertransference

One of the taboo topics in therapy is that therapists simply like some clients more than others. Clients may have traits that are more similar to certain therapists, have admirable characteristics, or be more compatible than other clients. Whatever the reasons for the countertransferential dynamic, it can pose a serious problem when dealing with a couple. We may not like each partner equally. Irrespective of the pathology present, our own personal history may predispose us to over- or underidentify with one of the partners. The gender of the clients is one issue. Some therapists are more comfortable relating to clients of the same gender whereas others relate better to the opposite gender. Therapists with unresolved family-of-origin issues around one parent may find this hinders them from relating to the client of the same gender as that parent. Therapist gender bias may affect the therapists ability to diagnose a client, see the couple's dynamics, or confront a client of a particular gender. The therapist who, for example, could never confront his or her father may have trouble confronting a male partner of a couple.

Cultural Issues

Clients whose culture differs from that of the therapist may pose another problem. Therapists may have little understanding of the clients' culture and, more importantly, be unaware of how that lack of understanding limits their ability to work well with the couple. A therapist who is of a different ethnicity, class, religion, or sexual orientation, among other demographic descriptors, than his or her client may find it more difficult to maintain neutrality. This problem can be exacerbated when the couple's difficulties are related to cultural issues. For example, immigrant partners from a developing nation with highly patriarchal norms may find themselves at odds over how to conduct their relationship in a new culture less friendly to such patriarchy. The couple may experience a crisis when the wife, for instance, becomes unwilling to accept formerly normative but now distasteful treatment from him. In such a case, the couple presenting for therapy at the wife's initiative would probably show the degree to which the husband has lost his power and privilege. In addition to supporting the wife's greater assertiveness, the therapist working with the couple would need to be especially sensitive to the husband's sense of power-lessness and possible bewilderment about why things changed. It would be easy to imagine the therapist missing the need for neutrality in such a case and simply failing to understand the husband's patriarchal past. Of course, if the therapist has the same value system as the male partner in the relationship, neu-trality is lost in the other direction and the wife's changes may be stifled.

Therapist Bias and Values

Therapists sometimes let their biases enter therapy when they should not. This is especially true when the therapist makes a judgment about the behavior or attitudes of one of the partners. For example, there has been some discussion in the literature about the "feminization of love" and the "masculin-ization of power" (e.g., see Starbuck, 2002). The former refers to the prioritization of stereotypically feminine ways of expressing love and the latter refers to the prioritization of stereotypically masculine ways of manifesting influence and using resources. A therapist working with a Hispanic couple, for example, who takes a position advocating the importance of the husband saying more affectionate and loving things to his wife (which she may like and he may not understand) is moving away from neutrality with regard to the clients' cultural background. It may be entirely justifiable to push the clients in such a direc-tion, but the therapist must acknowledge that his or her own cultural bias influences his or her course of action with the couple. In addition, the therapist must not allow the husband to be the sole target of change unless both partners agree that such a focus is welcome. Similarly, therapists who favor more traditional views must be aware of how their biases may get in the way of therapy with clients who desire a highly egalitarian marriage, and they must work to avoid letting this bias shape the therapy.

Value judgments based on the therapist's own history and psychology, religion, morals, and so on may bias the therapist toward an individualistic view of the problem and lead the therapist to make serious therapeutic mistakes. In one case, a couple came to therapy on the verge of divorce. The wife reported that she had seen a female therapist about her marital dissatisfaction. During the first and only session, this therapist had told her she should have an affair in order to find out whether another man could make her happy. The client knew this was inappropriate advice, had no wish to have an affair, and wanted to save the marriage. The therapist in question had terminated a long-standing marriage with an alcoholic husband by having an affair. She was imposing her own way of solving an unhappy marriage onto this client.

Although this may seem an obvious mistake, many other mistakes are not as easily discerned. When it comes to values, a degree of congruence between the client and the therapist is helpful. This is why it is invaluable to have an understanding of the implicit or explicit moral framework that organizes the couple's approach to their relationship. That alone, however, is not sufficient, because the therapist's own moral framework strongly influences (and *should* influence) how he or she approaches clinical work. If a therapist has a strong ethic about emotional or sexual exclusivity in a couple relationship, he or she may have a hard time dealing with a couple's idiosyncratic definition of exclusivity. Partners may, for example, define exclusivity as permitting sexual intimacy with persons outside the relationship as long as there is honesty between the partners and no emotional involvement with the other person. Sometimes, the requirement of sexual exclusivity can be broken only with partners of the same gender. The couple may reject the therapist's conception of exclusivity. Therapists can maintain their position of what might work best, they can choose to relinquish it in favor of the clients' views, or they can choose to refer. Whether or not the therapist and client can work together is less important than the *reason* they can or cannot.

Exceptions to Neutrality

In some situations the therapist should *not* be neutral. In cases involving infidelity or violence, maintaining a position of strict neutrality may be harmful. Although it may be appropriate for each partner to look at his or her part in the dynamics that lead to the act, the act itself must be condemned as wrong, unacceptable, or immoral. In short, although it is still important to consider how both partners contribute to the problem, the seriousness of these situations may preclude placing priority on therapist neutrality, especially during the early stage of treatment. Ideally, the therapist needs to ensure that the affair has stopped. In situations involving verbal or physical abuse, the abuse must stop and a plan for the emotional and physical safety of the partner must be established. Assuming these conditions are met and the couple wants therapy, the therapist can then explore with the couple how they reached the stage where an affair took place or where verbal/physical abuse occurred.

Enhancing Neutrality

From the first interaction, the therapist must communicate that he or she is on the side of the relationship. The relationship is the client and the target of change, although each partner will probably be required to change as well. Although this aim is easy to assert, in practice it is exceptionally difficult. Therapists must be aware of the most common mistakes that decrease neutrality: talking to one partner without talking to the other, being too attentive to one partner, using language that suggests the therapist only sees one side of the problem, agreeing with one partner against the other, and forgetting the basic assumption that the couple is an interlocking system. The following two examples show how easily mistakes can be made.

After a therapist greeted a new referral at the door to the clinic, he commented that he had the same type of car the couple had and really liked it. Once all participants were seated in his office, the wife said she could see how the therapy was going to go because the boys were already talking about their toys. The therapist's friendly chat infuriated the wife and led her to feel she would be starting therapy one-down. In another case, the therapist greeted a couple, who had been seen for several sessions, in the waiting room. The therapist commented on the wife's colorful blouse. The husband reacted by saying he felt his wife was going to get more attention because the therapist had already started with a comment to his wife. Some couples are so sensitive to the issue of neutrality that they will become upset over whose hand is shaken first if that is part of the therapist's greeting.

First meetings with couples are filled with land mines as far as neutrality goes. The best policy is to interact as little as possible with the couple until everyone is in the therapy room and then to say something to them as a couple. If the couple wants a little chat before getting started it is important to keep it balanced. It cannot be overemphasized that the couple must be appropriately socialized into couple work. They must understand that if they wish to see a change in their relationship, they will have to eventually be willing to reprioritize their being in a better relationship over their being right. For some couples, this is too much to ask, and therapy with them is usually doomed. For those who are willing to consider giving up their right to be right, work can proceed, and time will tell if they are successful in maintaining a gracious attitude.

It is usually wise to ask the couple a general question about what has brought them to therapy and what they wish to change. Give each partner equal time to speak so neither feels ignored and be careful to only make reflective statements. This, of course, assumes that the couple will be able to cooperate with each other in telling the therapist about what is going on.

Unfortunately, many couples are unable to do that, interrupting and arguing with each other about "facts." It may be necessary to become quite directive and assertive in structuring the session so that each partner's side can be told. It may also be necessary for the therapist to monitor, sometimes quite closely, how the couple describes the problem. This is one of the more exhausting aspects of couple work for all participants. After the therapist has gotten a reasonably uninterrupted description from one partner (assuming that was possible), it is generally wise to turn to the other partner and ask for his or her description of the problem. The therapist might say, "I understand how your partner sees the problem, tell me how you see it." The therapist must give equal attention to both partners. Internally, the partners are probably trying to guess whom the therapist thinks is right; this is fine—they *should* be constantly guessing about the therapist's position until they have learned that the therapist is going to remain neutral.

Maintaining neutrality is hard, especially in situations where there is great emotion for one or both partners. The therapist must validate each client's feelings, yet doing so sometimes costs the therapist his or her neutrality, even if only temporarily. It is crucial that both partners see that the therapist can align with both of them without necessarily taking sides permanently. If one or the other member of the couple cannot allow this, therapy will probably fail. The following dialogue shows how to validate perceptions without taking sides:

Wife: My husband does his own thing on the weekends, like playing golf, and I'm always stuck with the chores.

Husband: I need some down time, you're home all week.

Therapist: Let me see if I understand each of you. We will be talking about this a lot more, but I want to make sure I know where we are starting. (*to wife*) You appear to be saying your husband doesn't help out enough with the chores, especially on the weekends.

Wife: (*nodding*) Yes.

Therapist: (*to husband*) You are saying you need some time to unwind on the weekend.

Husband: (*nodding*) Yes.

Therapist: It seems that you are talking about chores, like who does what and when, and about how you have worked out your priorities so that each of you gets some time for yourself.

Couple: (*to therapist*) I think you said it well.

Therapist: Okay. That's one problem to discuss. I am also wondering whether you think you have enough time together so we can talk about the priorities of self, marriage, children, and work?

The therapist may receive feedback from a client that one of them feels the therapy is unbalanced or one-sided. Unfortunately, this feedback is usually nonverbal (Odell, Dielman, & Butler, in press) and frequently manifests in one of the couple members not wanting to continue in therapy. In the event that feedback, whether accurate or not, becomes known, it must become an immediate source of concern. Processing the therapeutic relationship with the couple will give the therapist an idea of whether he or she is actually taking sides or not. If the side-taking is just a perception on the part of one of the partners, the therapist should see if it can be altered. If the couple drops out after a couple of sessions the therapist should also examine whether lack of neutrality might be the cause of the early termination. In other cases, the therapy will become stuck because one partner is present but not participating. This situation can occur if the therapist has unconsciously decided to do primarily individual therapy with one member of the couple.

In addition to clearly defined pathology, some presentations of couple problems lead the therapist to focus more on one partner than the other. When one partner presents with blatant dysfunction it is easy to begin focusing on that person to the exclusion of the other. This partner begins to think that he or she is in the hot seat and that the therapist thinks he or she is the primary source of the problem. For example, one of the most common problems presented in couple therapy is conflict. One partner might be overtly angry, express the anger directly and frequently, and appear to be the instigator of the conflicts. The other partner might be defined as the victim of this conflict. What the therapist may fail to recognize is the passive-aggressive behavior of the other partner. In other words, the overt aggression on the part of one partner is mirrored by the covert aggression on the part of the other partner. The passive-aggressive partner might verbally agree to whatever the other partner wants but then not do it. The other partner becomes overtly angry and the passive-aggressive partner may withdraw or make excuses. Over time the pattern is likely to worsen. By the time the couple appears for therapy, the behavior of the overtly angry partner is much more obvious than that of the passive-aggressive partner. Maintaining a systemic focus can help therapists to look for what is not immediately apparent, which will increase their ability to maintain an appropriate degree of neutrality.

Sometimes one partner of a couple beginning therapy will clearly be suffering from an Axis I disorder. In these cases, the therapist may start to overemphasize the overt pathology in one partner, forgetting the systemic focus of therapy. The therapist may view the problem as existing within just one partner and assume that if that problem is treated the marital problems will disappear. As we mentioned earlier, depression is a good example. Depression is often viewed as a primarily biochemical, individual (rather than couple) problem. The therapist may further assume that the depression is the cause, rather than the effect, of the marital problems. As noted earlier, new research reveals that depression is, in fact, often the result of a distressing couple relationship.

Another example of how our training and research sometimes get in the way is in the treatment of insomnia. In one case, a wife mentioned insomnia in couple therapy. Because the research literature on insomnia has traditionally discussed only individual etiology or dynamics, the therapist immediately assumed that the problem was unrelated to the couple. The wife had been treated for her insomnia by several individual therapists and in different specialized sleep programs, but each treatment had failed. The new therapist initially tried some of the traditional individual techniques to treat her insomnia, but these too failed. The therapist then realized that the insomnia might serve some function in the woman's life or marriage, so he asked her how her life would be different if she did not suffer from insomnia. She reported that she hated her job and would probably quit, and that she would probably become enraged with her partner and leave him. She said that with her insomnia she did not have enough energy to make any changes. There was no doubt that her insomnia was the symptom she used to remain stuck in the relationship and in her present job. A series of strategic interventions directed toward the couple about her insomnia had the immediate effect of eliminating the problem. For example, the wife was told that it would be too risky to give up her insomnia until her partner had better control over his anger. She would need to continue to sacrifice her sleep in order to protect the relationship. Upon hearing this intervention, the husband said he did not want her to make this sacrifice.

A special problem also exists when the therapist must make a psychiatric referral. For many couples, such a referral is the same as saying that one partner is "sicker" than the other or that the problem resides just in one partner. The therapist may make a referral for treatment of depression or anxiety. The disorder may be an individual issue or a result of marital dysfunction. In either case, the therapist needs to make the referral and tie the problem to the relationship or discuss other problems that are clearly systemic in nature. For example, one partner may be depressed and the couple may be experiencing conflict. The depression may exacerbate the conflict, but the conflict may stem from underlying fears of intimacy in the couple. The fighting serves to maintain distance between them. The therapist can put the couple on the same level by stating that they each need to work on issues even though one needs the benefit of medication.

Clearly, maintaining a systemic focus can help the therapist to avoid forming unintentional alliances or coalitions and thus maintain neutrality. Violating the fundamental assumption that the couple is an interlocking system must only be done based on theoretically or clinically driven reasons. Maintaining a systemic focus, even when the couple actively resists this view, is a challenging task, but essential to a good outcome for the couple.

CHAPTER FOUR

Overemphasizing the Past or Present

Couples beginning therapy usually have at least one, if not several problems that eventually emerge. Generally speaking, the therapist begins by getting a list of problems, the current presentation of the problem, and then some historical background. One of the debates in psychotherapy and couples therapy has been how much historical information to obtain and when to obtain it. Some therapists do not care to collect much historical information at all; they simply want to know about the current problem. We feel that it is a mistake not to collect all relevant information, including history. The therapist must be flexible enough to move back and forth between the current problem and the history of the problem, which may be rooted in the couple's respective families. For example, a wife might say that her husband is always screaming and putting her down, while he denies it. After listening to a description of the current problem and asking them to enact it in the session, it appears the wife is overly sensitive to confrontation and conflict. At this point, obtaining some history would be useful. The therapist might learn that in her family there was never any conflict whereas his family was much more direct and conflict was viewed as healthy and constructive. Her family history may have predisposed her to believe that anything resembling conflict was unacceptable for a marriage and would lead to its dissolution.

The therapist has to be adept at weaving together both the present and the past at the right moments in order to clarify the problem. Exclusive emphasis on one or the other does not render a complete picture. Poor timing in obtaining information can lead one partner to feel blame. For example, using the example above, if the therapist were to spend too much time focusing on the wife's background she would probably feel that the problem lay only with her, while the husband may be equally culpable in the way in which he raises their marital problems. The goal is to obtain all the information without contributing to some of the problems described in Chapter 3, especially side-taking.

From the first session, clients will talk about their perspectives on what problems brought them to seek help. Couple therapy usually begins with the therapist inquiring about the couple's present problems, what brings them to therapy at this particular time or what kinds of problems they are having. Couples are expected to talk about their present problems and are usually willing to open up about their problems as they are experiencing them now. The therapist wants to find out what each person's perspective of the problem is, including information about the problem itself (what is happening now, when did it start, what kind of future each partner projects if the problem is not solved), environmental influences (various stressors and supports), and strengths and resources the clients may have, including elements they miss in their relationship. Thus, the "who," "what," "where," "when," and "how" of the problems are explored in early sessions.

The goal of the initial assessment is to gain a clear picture of the problem. This includes an understanding of the couple's current perception of the problem, how it evolved over time, and some of the historical roots of the problem. Partners may fail to appreciate both the past and present perspective. They may only want to talk about the here-and-now and avoid talking about the past in the belief, for example, that the past is irrelevant. Other couples might want to focus on the past and may sometimes use it as an excuse for not being able to act differently. They tend to tell a lot of stories about the problem and their theory about why they have the problem, without ever helping the therapist to understand the current dynamics of the problem. Some of the common errors therapists encounter in this balancing act are:

- Failing to focus on the present in order to obtain a clear, historically-rooted behavioral definition of the problem.
- Failing to focus on the past in order to gain some understanding of the present meaning of the problem.
- Failing to tactfully weave the two temporal perspectives together so that one partner doesn't begin to feel that the problem is exclusively his or hers.

The Therapist's Theoretical Orientation

Most couple therapists begin treatment by focusing on present problems. Given many clients' intensity about their problem(s), this makes perfect sense. Depending on the theoretical orientation of the therapist, therapy may never go beyond present patterns and sequences into the past at all. However, most therapy with couples includes some historic components, if for no other reason than that the couple brings it into the conversation. Still, most couple therapists address elements of the clients' past in their treatment, working from the present backward. The origin of the problem and its history over time might be explored, as might the relationship's general history. The exception to this way of working would occur with Bowenian, intergenerational, and psychodynamically/systemically oriented therapists, who place more value on addressing the past as the curative agent. They will move to talking about the past much more quickly and spend more time discussing past issues. That therapists with a solution-focused orientation would focus couples' attention on what they want to change and where exceptions to the problems are occurring.

Balancing the Past and Present

We are not suggesting the past is unimportant. Problems have histories that need to be understood and worked through. The first task is to understand how past problems and behaviors have become recurring patterns of behavior in the present. The second task is to help the individuals work through the issues in both the present and the past.

For example, Marie and Ralph came to therapy because they were unhappy with the distance in their relationship. They were committed to their relationship because of their religion and their vow to lifelong marriage. They used overworking and talking superficially as a way to maintain their distance, all within a greater sense of committed safety. To address the couple's goal of closeness, the therapist chose to work on their present pattern of communication and overworking first. It soon became clear that their present way of relating was based on patterns developed in childhood. They were both reared in families that they characterized as cold and rejecting. They both grew up feeling emotionally abandoned and unloved. During the initial phase of treatment the therapist made references to the past and how the clients were bringing their past into the present. Although Marie and Ralph had a covenant never to abandon each other, they were wary of getting too close. They feared that if they were truly known by each other, they would be rejected and abandoned the pain of which would be too great to bear. The progression of therapy allowed the therapist to spend more time helping the couple work through the early family of origin issues. This involved helping them understand that both sets of parents were overwhelmed with large families and trying to survive financially. Emotionally, it meant incorporating these early feelings in a framework that helped them experience the feelings less intensely.

A few sessions were held with Marie's parents and the couple so they could discuss how they felt and the situation in which they were reared. The parents admitted that they felt they had failed their children by having to work so much and talked about the challenges they faced when the father had lost a well-paying job and was not able to secure another job that paid as well. The parents had kept the father's change of jobs a secret from the children, thinking that if the children knew, it would make them feel anxious and insecure. These events had caused the family to drift apart, thinking that trying to become closer was impossible. But after these therapy sessions, all who attended felt a new sense of closeness. In this example, the therapist used both the present and the past therapeutically.

Staying appropriately focused becomes particularly difficult when clients want to dwell on the past, especially if their hurts have occurred there. The therapist usually wants to begin in the present and then move back and forth between the present and past in order to help the couple relate current problems with patterns of behavior learned early in life, in prior relationships, or even with each other. The simplest way to start the therapy productively is to explain how therapy works to the couple. Instructing the couple about what the therapist needs to know in order to be helpful will guide the couple in how to present information. Obviously, the therapist should clarify that dwelling on the past by telling one story after another is not going to help the therapist help the couple. The case of Jack and Audrey illustrates how a couple can remain stuck in the past if the therapist does not move them from this stuck position.

Therapist: Audrey, you are obviously very hurt by the way Jack treated you when he was drinking.

Audrey: He was mean, cruel, and vicious. I don't know why I
stayed.
Therapist: Jack has come a long ways in the past few months
from what you have both told me.
Audrey: He put me through years of torment. It is impossible
for anyone to understand.
Jack: I told you how sorry I am. I am going to stay sober and
build a future.
Audrey: You never said you were sorry for years—all you were
was selfish.
Therapist: You have to get all the old feelings of hurt out.
Jack: That's all she ever does.
Audrey: He doesn't care about how I felt!
Jack: I've taken responsibility for my actions.
Therapist: Audrey, what do you need for him to say?
Audrey: I lived with the devil for 8 years.

In this example, the therapist urged Audrey to talk about her
past feelings of hurt, anger, rage, and so on. In so doing, the
therapist only encouraged her to do more of what she did at
home. Audrey was controlling the session by staying stuck
in the past and the therapist was enabling it. The therapist
would have been wise to pursue one of the many options
at his disposal, such as validating Audrey's feelings and then
talking to her about why she stayed, exploring with her what
she was getting out of remaining the victim, asking about
whether she might have been replaying family history (her father was an alcoholic), about how things are different today,
or about what was preventing her from moving beyond the
past.

The therapist can lose control of this process by allowing one
partner or the couple to take over and tell stories about the
past. Each partner may have a detailed reconstruction of the
past, which is often disputed by the other partner. The partners may go into every detail possible about a single event.

The purpose of such stories is to demonstrate that the partner was wrong, bad, villainous, or the like. Apparently, they believe that by going into such detail they will prove the "truth" of their perception and thus bring about some kind of justice or restitution—or, at the very least, justify their own role in the couple's problems.

While establishing the therapeutic alliance, the therapist may feel the need to be polite and hear the stories but may, nonetheless, be bored or confused by all the details. In addition, it may be quite difficult to derail the storyteller's agenda. The point is not to get a large and seemingly endless array of stories, but to understand the patterns that the stories convey. When one partner starts to tell a long story about an event, such as a fight or a visit to in-laws, the other spouse has usually heard the story before and either ignores the speaker or animatedly attempts to debate this or that point. In fact, the couple may have done this on several occasions and may now be "trained" in how to tell the stories—who says what, what point is debated, the lesson from the story, and so on. The amount of time the therapist spends listening to the story can convey a lack of neutrality or balance. The storyteller's partner may have one or several reactions: concern that he or she will have more to refute the longer the therapist listens, withdrawal due to the perception that the therapist has been convinced of the other partner's point of view, or frustration that his or her story is not being heard.

The partner with the need to tell stories in such detail may do so in pressured speech because the other partner has cut him or her off in the past. The partner thus wants to get everything out before being cut off or having to fight. Some of these partners are also displaying their own pathology. Clients with obsessive-compulsive personality tend to obsess on details and on getting everything correct. They operate with the misguided belief that if the therapist knows all the details or content of what happened, he or she will be able to fix the problem. Some partners want to begin with stories that go back to the beginning of the relationship. The stories they tell about events may be decades old, and the partner has usually rehearsed them mentally many times or told them to others over and over. The likelihood that parts of the story have been unconsciously fabricated or confabulated is significant.

Margie and Sam had been married for 17 years. Margie initiated therapy because they were fighting so much they were on the verge of divorce. The therapist asked them what brought them to therapy and Margie stated that Sam never listened to her and did not fight fairly. She then recounted fights they had when they were first married. When the therapist tried to redirect her to the present and to talking about the patterns, she reverted to the story, saying, "I think you will understand better if I finish telling you about...." She told more of the story and the therapist again interrupted her in order to ask her about the present. It took several sessions of redirection before she got the point that her storytelling would not be allowed. Other methods include validation of the underlying feelings so that the partner feels heard (discussed in Chapter 3).

Beginning therapists often make several kinds of mistakes regarding storytelling: allowing the partner to tell the complete story with few interruptions and perhaps only asking questions that clarify the content of the story, being afraid to interrupt due to fear of client reaction, and avoiding power struggles. The problem with not interrupting is that it may cause the other partner to react in the ways discussed earlier and it focuses on content instead of patterns. Therapists also may be afraid that if they interrupt, the clients will assume that the therapist does not care about them and will consequently terminate therapy, which is indeed a possibility. The therapist may also want to avoid a power struggle with the partner over who is in control of the session. Allowing the client to take control of the session renders the therapist powerless, usually alienates the other partner, and reinforces the same pattern of storytelling in the future. In fact, the longer this pattern is allowed to continue, the more everyone becomes socialized that this is the way therapy is conducted, and the therapy becomes little more than a forum for the partner to vent thoughts and feelings. The "battle for structure" (Whitaker & Keith, 1981) is lost, and that usually leads to poor outcomes in therapy.

As was discussed earlier, the therapist must clearly establish the ground rules of therapy and enforce them. Most clients do not know what to expect in therapy or what is expected of them. Understanding the problem does not mean listening to story after story. It means getting an overview of the problem as it currently manifests (the who, what, where, when) and, if appropriate, tracing the problem back historically to the beginning of the relationship and possibly earlier. Some partners are remarried and are replaying the same problems they had in prior relationships. Some partners are replaying patterns of behavior learned in their families of origin. The therapist needs to be able to move back and forth between different temporal aspects of the problem.

Sarah and Chad, for example, had been married for 3 years. They both wanted therapy because they said they were growing further apart. They no longer experienced the intimacy they had had when first dating. Sarah picked fights to create intimacy and Chad isolated himself by working or being on the computer. A quick analysis of their families' patterns showed that neither family demonstrated much closeness. Sarah's parents fought a lot and Sarah felt distant from them. She said they mostly criticized her, which she responded to by fighting back and rebelling. Chad's parents had a parallel relationship. They rarely talked, except about the necessities, showed no affection, and were emotionally repressed. Chad commented that he felt he had raised himself because his parents were too self-absorbed. The therapy consisted of examining current patterns of behavior and connecting them to the partner's experiences in their families of origin. As therapy unfolded, Sarah and Chad could see that they were repeating what they had learned in their families. The main intervention was to have each one monitor when and how they were distancing from each other in the present. Next they were to notice how this repeated what they had learned in their families and to become more aware of the fears that had been triggered. As a result of this intervention, each discovered a pattern. Sarah feared being more intimate because she did not want to be criticized by Chad. She assumed that getting closer would lead to conflict. Chad feared being dependent on Sarah because he assumed that Sarah could only give so much of herself and that he would eventually be abandoned emotionally. The relationship was based on the unconscious expectation that neither one would threaten the other's need for distance. They had disguised this fact early on in the relationship by having a pseudo-intimate relationship. When they talked about what brought them together they stressed that they liked to do the same things and have fun. They also enjoyed sex, but it was recreational and lacked an intimate dimension.

This case demonstrates how the therapist was able to help the couple move back and forth between present and past. This allowed the partners to understand the pattern they had recreated in the current relationship without either one having to take the blame. Both partners saw the patterns from the past and did not attack each other in the present, characteristics that enhanced the therapist's ability to help them.

The following case demonstrates how a therapist can fail to deal well with the temporal aspects of a problem. Doug had an episode of sexual compulsion that probably resulted from medication interacting with an unusual history of social phobias. He had acted out with a number of women and was very remorseful. He had discontinued the medication that triggered the acting out. He came to individual therapy to work on his social phobias and marriage. The couple was also seeing another therapist for couple therapy. Carol, Doug's wife, was still committed to the marriage but was narcissistically hurt and angry over Doug's acting out. She came to his individual therapy once to say that it might take her years to forgive him and have a normal relationship again. When Doug was asked about Carol's history, it turned out that her father had had an affair that she knew about and her mother used Carol as her confidant. Her mother never forgave her father. The individual therapist urged the couple therapist to explore Carol's history, but Carol insisted on talking about only Doug's past behavior. The couple therapist was reluctant to press Carol to talk about herself, and whenever she did Carol would switch back to talking about Doug. The individual therapist coached Doug on how to get Carol to look at herself and kept urging the couple therapist to help Carol understand the strength of her feelings and how her unforgiving anger was rooted in the past. Once the couple therapist was able to gently confront Carol regarding her history, the couple's relationship began to improve significantly.

Coming to therapy may be viewed as an opportunity to change, but sometimes the existence of various underlying relational patterns is simply assumed and not scrutinized. The therapist can help clients by focusing on both the present manifestation of the problem and the way this manifestation may repeat earlier relational patterns. The appropriate use of both the present and the past is critical to clients' making therapeutic progress.

CHAPTER FIVE

Lapses in Careful Listening

Obtaining a behavioral description of the presenting problems by appropriately focusing on the temporal issues of problems is a good starting strategy for listening. But the therapist also wants to start with as complete a picture of the couple's strengths and problems as possible. Of course, the couple will only reveal some problems and some strengths after they feel more comfortable with and trusting of the therapist. As stated earlier, structuring therapy and maintaining neutrality will help to build the therapeutic relationship so that this deeper level of sharing will occur. It is crucial that the therapist maximize every opportunity to see what may be occurring in clients' situations and not miss or minimize important data. If critical information is missed, the therapist may end up working on superficial issues instead of underlying issues. In addition, therapy may stall for several reasons: the therapist is treating a symptom rather than the patterns of behavior, the clients are frustrated that the "real" issue is not being addressed, or the therapist is not sequencing therapy modalities to ensure the best outcome for the couple, among others. Some common errors therapists make include:

- Failing to recognize that couples will fail to bring up or will minimize some problems
- Failing to ask good, deliberately aimed questions
- Minimizing or discounting problems couples have
- Failing to listen with a "third ear" for couple problems
- Failing to recognize that a couple has colluded to hide a problem
- Failing to recognize that some partners are afraid to reveal certain problems

Why Couples Do Not Bring Up Problems

Partners and couples may not bring up problems for a variety of reasons. They may feel ashamed or embarrassed about the problem. Sexual problems, for example, are often mentioned only after several sessions of therapy. Problems related to incest or partner abuse may also be difficult for clients to talk about. Partners who have experienced incest may have difficulty remembering it and may think it is a false memory or be concerned that the therapist will think it is a false memory. If they do remember it, they may think that they were somehow to blame and fear that the therapist will blame them further.

When partner abuse falls in the instrumental class (see Mack, 1989), the partner is afraid to bring up the abuse because she or he thinks it will only incite more abuse or thinks it cannot be changed. The abusing partner in these cases uses violence or the threat of violence to keep the other partner in a state of dependence, fear, and intimidation. The abuser may tell the victim in advance of the first therapy session that she or he cannot bring it up, may threaten more violence, or may have socialized the victim so thoroughly that she or he knows that raising the topic will anger the abuser. The victim may not know that violence is not a normal part of relationships or that one can live without violence. It is relatively rare for couples in relationships that include instrumental violence to seek therapy. These kinds of couples may show up as a result of a court order, an arrest, or some other external motivator. More frequently, couples engage in what has been called "common couple violence" (Johnson, 1995). For them, violence is not a unique problem, and both partners engage in it to a degree. These types of couples may be more likely to gloss over the violence or not bring it up for fear of the therapist's response.

How Problems Are Revealed

A good rule of thumb to follow in assessing couple problems is for the therapist to (1) assume that clients will reveal what seems most important to them but also is reasonably safe to bring up, and (2) ask about major areas of couple functioning that the couple does not bring up on their own. It may seem so obvious as to not bear mentioning, but therapists do not always ask very good questions, and they are not always very thorough in what they do ask. Simply put, people tend not to answer questions that are not asked. Therapists must listen very carefully, but they must also ask probing questions, even in areas where there may be no indication of anything significant. It must be noted, however, that sometimes couples will not answer very directly or will actually avoid questions the therapist asks. On occasion, they will overtly say they are not going to talk about whatever the therapist has asked about.

More often, clients will generally cooperate with the therapist's questions, and in those situations the problems the partners are hesitant to address will eventually come out. At least one partner will unwittingly reveal the real problem through nonverbal interactions or through descriptions of the relationship or other problems. The problem literally leaks out as a result of descriptions of other problems and the way the couple relates. The partner may also send the therapist a coded message. This is one of the reasons why it is so important for the therapist to listen carefully to every statement and observe every action with as much diligence as possible. Without careful attention and tactful followup, the therapist may miss the crucial issue. Several types of problems may be communicated in code to the therapist. The most common are partner abuse, extramarital affairs, addictions, and severe psychopathology.

Partner Abuse

Partner abuse may be revealed nonverbally or through the description of behavior. Abused partners may communicate their fear through their body language by constantly looking at the other partner for approval of what is said, always letting the other partner take the lead, or simply looking fearful and hypervigilant. They may talk around the problem by saying they do not know how to deal with conflict, do not communicate, or feel they are always "walking on eggshells" around the partner. For example, a partner experiencing abuse might talk about not having any friends. The therapist might conjecture that this partner lacks social skills. However, the abusing partner might have driven the friends away, or the abused partner may be afraid to have others over because they will witness the abuse or intimidation. On the other hand, the therapist must avoid seeing things that are not necessarily there. Sometimes the partner with no friends has not made the effort to develop them, has poor interpersonal skills, unrealistic expectations, or a combination of these things, but blames the other partner for the problem. The therapist must use clinical judgment in this situation. Of course, countertransference issues may get in the way.

Affairs

Affairs may be difficult to bring up for several reasons. The nonaffair partner may actually know that the partner is having an affair but collude with the behavior because he or she may be deriving a benefit from the partner's affair. The affair may maintain and justify the distance the nonaffair partner needs in the relationship. It may take the pressure off the nonaffair partner for his or her lack of sexual desire or relational needs be-cause the partner can get these needs met elsewhere. The non-affair partner may not want to disrupt the continuity and super-ficial harmony in the relationship because of children, threat of dissolution of the marriage, financial or religious reasons, and so on. On the other hand, the nonaffair partner may be unaware that an affair is occurring but know something is wrong with the relationship.

There are a few ways of discerning a hidden affair: observing lack of progress, client complaints about distance in the rela-tionship, the presence of a "close friend" of one partner, jealousy, different definitions of affairs, unaccounted-for time, and act-ing as a single person. Whenever there is an active affair no real progress will be made in therapy. The clinician needs to be astute enough to know when progress should be occurring. When simple assignments are given and not done or when the sessions just do not move forward, there is some missing piece to the puzzle, and one of the possibilities is that an affair is going on. Another clue about a possible hidden affair is the nonaffair partner complaining about continuing distance in the relation-ship, lack of sexual interest, and conflict that is designed to create distance, even after therapy has been going on a while. A more obvious clue would be when the partner talks about the other partner having a close friend relationship, usually but not always of the opposite sex. Nonaffair partners may discuss sit-uations where the suspected partner and the friend do various activities together or are otherwise interacting quite frequently or personally. As a result, they suspect that the friendship is too close. The overt or subtle expression of jealousy is a good indicator of a possible hidden affair.

It is worthwhile to consider that the partners may define rela-tionship exclusivity in different ways. The therapist may have yet another definition. Some people believe that in order for a relationship to be considered an affair, sexual activity must occur, and that all relationships that do not involve sex should be considered friendships. The fact that there is no sexual involvement in their relationship with an outside person leads them to believe that they are completely innocent, and they may be unable or unwilling to consider another view of infidelity. All things being equal, and acknowledging the potential for the abuse of power that it may bring, it may be practical to define an affair as being whatever one of the partners thinks it is.

Another indicator of a possible hidden affair is unaccounted-for time, often associated with work. Glass and Staehel (2002) documented how the workplace spawns a very high percentage of affairs. The partner suspected of having an affair may be out of touch for periods of time and state that it is due to job requirements. When nonaffair partners try to locate the affair partners they cannot seem to find them and receive a blanket "I was working" response. The same inaccessibility can be true with leisure time. An obvious clue is when one partner begins acting like he or she is single again and justifies it as spending time with the "guys" or "girls." An even more obvious clue is when partners behave as if they are in love with someone new. These behaviors might include getting dressed and going out for the evening, usually getting home late, frequent "special" work or social events, and other changes often associated with a desire to impress. This behavior is not hard to spot, but it can often be "explained" away for a time.

In spite of the obvious clues, a few partners will be in denial or at least in incredulous doubt about what is transpiring, and many cheating partners will enable by maintaining increasingly implausible explanations. The therapist may also feel strongly pulled to accept the narrative the couple presents, with the cheating partner denying and the other partner not wanting to face the possibility of a most harsh reality. Unfortunately, this error happens in many cases. In one case, the husband was obviously having multiple affairs. Every weekend he went out on Friday and Saturday nights without any explanation and returned home very late in the morning or not at all. The wife was finally persuaded to hire a detective to follow him. After just one night, the detective found that the husband went to a nightclub, picked up a woman, and had sex with her in his car. When the wife was first shown the picture, she was in such denial that she could not believe it was her husband until she looked at the photo for several minutes. The therapist did not act in collusion with the wife's denial. Once her denial crumbled she was able to confront her husband. He said he was not interested in changing and she would have to accept his behavior. She eventually divorced him.

Addictions

Addictions are another problem area that may not be revealed to the therapist, or may be minimized by one or both partners. Addictions can be detected in much the same way as an affair. In fact, one useful way to look at addiction is to view it as an active affair, just with a thing or behavior instead of a person. Addictions are in many ways functionally equivalent to affairs in that many of the same dynamics are at work for avoiding bringing up the problem. The addict usually lives in denial of the addiction or simply does not believe that the resulting behavior has contributed to his or her relational problems. Sometimes partners collude in or enable the addiction because it serves some underlying psychological or practical need in them. Some couples come to treatment only after the nonaddicted partner agrees not to bring up the addiction. Often the agreement is implicit, consistent with the addiction-denying system that exists long before therapy is considered.

The therapist has to determine whether an addiction exists. The AAMFT recommends screening all clients for alcohol (Roberts & McCrady, 2003). Other addictions may be present also. The first task is to establish a relationship with the client so that the possibility of an addiction can be voiced. The therapist must be careful not to move too aggressively with the addict or with the enabling partner. Confronting them too directly and quickly and insisting on a cessation of the addiction and related behaviors will probably cause a premature termination of therapy or extreme instability in the couple's relationship.

Nonaddicted partners may give the therapist coded messages about the addiction by bringing up the problem in some indirect way. For example, they may talk about feeling lonely or about the partner's inactivity. Sometimes they will talk about feeling lonely because the partner is not present, either physically or emotionally, or because the partner is irritable and erratic. The partner may come home, sit in a chair and fall asleep or pass out early due to drinking or using drugs. The addict is "married" to the drug of choice and is not able to relate well with the partner, hence the loneliness. The complaining partner does not necessarily identify his or her competition as an addiction or addictive behavior.

A couple of case examples illustrate the difficulties inherent in communicating about addictions. The first case involved a couple coming to treatment for a variety of marital problems. At some point, the husband revealed that his wife used to be an alcoholic and compulsive gambler. She was in recovery and had been attending a 12-step program. The wife then mentioned that she was concerned about her husband's illegal behavior. She reported that he was growing marijuana in their greenhouse, but would not say he was an addict. Further exploration over the next few sessions confirmed that he used marijuana on a regular basis and was stoned whenever he was not at work. The wife found it easier to reference the illegal behavior rather than state that her husband was stoned most of the time.

In many cases, the nonaddict, let's say the wife, will say something to the effect that the husband drinks a little too much and then refuse to say more. She is afraid that the he will terminate treatment if she divulges his alcoholism. The obvious question would be how much he drinks. If the therapist asks this question, the alcoholic will feel that the therapist is trying to establish that he is an alcoholic and, predictably, therapy will not go well. A better question to ask at this point is how alcohol changes his behavior and her behavior and how it negatively affects the couple/family. The volume of alcohol consumed almost becomes irrelevant when behavioral changes are discussed and a negative impact can be established for the using partner, the other partner, the family, and possibly the addict's work.

In another case, the wife said her husband drank a little too much. Before the therapist could ask a question, the husband said he only had a beer and nursed it over the course of the evening. Listening to the husband's story, the therapist might wonder how a beer could be nursed over the course of an entire evening, especially as most people do not like to drink warm beer. As it turned out, the husband was trying to deceive the therapist with his story. The wife reported that he poured six beers into a large container and drank the contents of the container during the evening!

In short, one way to detect an addiction is to look for the consequences of addictive behavior. In addition to the consequences we already mentioned, addictions may use noticeable amounts of money. Missing money and unexplained financial hardships are good clues to addiction because the money is going to support the addiction. This is especially true if the drug is expensive or if the partner is involved in a sexual addiction or, obviously, gambling. Sex addicts can spend a tremendous amount of money on pornography and prostitution. Partners also report contracting sexually transmitted diseases. They feel embarrassed to have such a disease and the partner denies being unfaithful.

Swinging

This is another area where the therapist must listen for hidden trouble. Although swinging, or mate-swapping, was much more popular in past years, some couples still engage in it. They tend to inhabit a subculture where the behavior is normalized.

Most swinging couples keep their swinging private from non-swingers, including their therapist, but may still complain about a lack of sexual or other intimacy in their relationship. If they want to continue this lifestyle, they may not make swinging explicit for fear that the therapist will be judgmental or relate swinging to their problems. A number of swingers are also in covert conflict about the behavior. The husband is often the one to press for this lifestyle and the wife may be too passive, submissive, or afraid to disagree with his wishes. Once swinging has begun, the husband may feel threatened if his wife enjoys it too much or the wife may no longer wish to pursue the lifestyle. In any case, the therapist who fails to pick up on this may miss important elements of their relationship. Again, one or both partners may use code language, describing "friends" whom they socialize with and who may be a hidden source of jealousy or conflict. Evasiveness around their sexual practices may also be indicative of swinging, especially after a comfort level in therapy has been achieved.

Severe Psychopathology

Another problem that tends to get denied or minimized is severe psychopathology either in one or both partners. The couple may be embarrassed over the stigma attached to severe mental illness and thus deny that a severe or chronic problem exists. Severely impaired individuals often have the least insight into their problem and do not think they are ill. In one couple, the husband was schizophrenic and had been hospitalized numerous times. His wife did not want to frame their problem in terms of his schizophrenia and instead talked about their problems as if he were normal and they were just having the same type of marital problems as everyone else. In another case, a wife who was a therapist and a husband who was a professional suffering from bipolar illness but refusing to take medication came for therapy. When he was in the manic state he acted out sexually. His wife wanted to talk about the affairs but did not want to acknowledge that they were related to his mental illness. Clearly, if she accepted that one result of not taking medication was acting out, she would then have to examine why she chose a man who needed help and refused it, as well as why she continued to stay with him. It is common for partners to act as if the severely impaired partner will get better someday. This belief allows them to avoid accepting the fact that the situation will probably not change or improve.

Other Issues

The therapist must be careful not to minimize or discount problems. By listening carefully and noting nonverbal behavior, it is possible to detect problems that might otherwise be missed. Issues that may be hidden from the therapist extend beyond the ones already discussed. One couple represents a good case study for this point. The couple initiated therapy because of the wife's lack of sexual desire. This problem was the only one mentioned by the couple. Both partners were highly educated professionals. Several weeks after therapy began, something unusual happened in a session. The wife was talking in a normal tone of voice and then said something in almost a whisper in front of her husband. The therapist thought he knew what was said but was not sure. The therapist noted that the husband immediately became angry and the couple started talking to each other. The husband reminded her of their prior agreement not to talk about this issue. The therapist had to choose between letting this issue quietly pass or pursuing it. Based on what he thought he had heard, he asked the wife to repeat her statement despite knowing this was a controversial issue for the couple. She said quite clearly that she thought her husband was too close to his parents. The therapist then turned to the husband and asked about their agreement not to talk about the issue. At this point, knowing that his wife wanted to talk and realizing that it should be part of therapy, he angrily acceded to discussing the matter.

The therapist asked the wife to describe the problem. She felt that her husband was still "married" to his family. She reported that he called them approximately 20 times a day in spite of being busy as a dentist. The couple had bought a "fixer upper" house for themselves, but the husband's recently retired father was working on the house. His parents let themselves in the house every day at 7 A.M. and did not leave until after supper every night. The wife found the lack of privacy and enmeshment unbearable. Her resentment and anger over this situation had led her to develop a lack of sexual interest (Weeks & Gambescia, 2002). The therapist had been looking for the etiology of her lack of desire in the wrong places. After this new information was revealed, the therapy shifted to working on the husband's enmeshment with his parents as a problem that would need resolution if his wife were to feel sexual desire for him again.

Clients may communicate that they have a problem but be ambivalent about talking about it due to discomfort. The therapist must carefully monitor the clients to make sure he or she is getting as much information as possible and then be willing to ask further questions when more information is needed. Therapist factors can interfere with follow-through. The therapist may collude in ignoring, discounting, denying, or minimizing problems because he or she does not feel comfortable making the clients uncomfortable. An unfortunate instance in which this happens all too often is when one partner has survived incest. The incest survivor may be embarrassed and ashamed of the incest, and the partner may be angry and secretly blame the incest survivor for letting it happen and not revealing it prior to marriage. The therapist may have a countertransference reaction to the issue that causes discomfort. An example of this is shown in the following brief dialogue.

Therapist: (*to wife*) What is your theory about your lack of desire?

Wife: He wants to do things I don't like, like a lot of foreplay.

Husband: Doctor, she cringes when I do some things. It's just not normal.

Therapist: How do you think this started?

Wife: My father used to do this to me and I hated it and him.

Therapist: Did anything sexually inappropriate happen in your family?

Wife: Yes, and my husband knows about it. I was in therapy for depression and the sexual abuse several years ago.

Therapist: What happened in your therapy for the incest?

Wife: I told the therapist about it and she thought it might be related to the depression, but we didn't talk about any sexual problems.

Therapist: Do you recall the therapy for this problem and about how long you talked about it?

Wife: I just remember talking about it for two or three sessions with the therapist.

Therapist: Is that all you think you talked about it?

Wife: I think so. After those couple of sessions the therapist started talking about the depression again.

The previous therapist had minimized the problem. This led the wife to think the issue was resolved when it wasn't. We have heard stories like this one many times. It is obviously difficult for a client to talk about incest, but in these cases the therapist either is not well trained or minimizes the problem out of a countertransference reaction–or both. The client is given the impression that he or she has worked through the issue even though some of the problems stemming from the incest remain.

The therapist has a responsibility to gently guide clients to talk about the issues that concern them and help them to deal with their feelings of discomfort. The therapist may be afraid that encouraging clients to talk about uncomfortable feelings will prompt those clients to discontinue therapy. However, this probably will not happen if the therapist attends to the feeling around the discomfort before getting into the issue itself. Pressing the issue may also lead to previously submerged conflict between the couple. A therapist who does not like to deal with high levels of couple conflict may tend to avoid the issue. In general, any issue that makes the couple or partners feel uncomfortable may make the therapist feel uncomfortable. The therapist's own unresolved feelings around an issue may predispose him or her to colluding with the couple/partner in avoiding the issue or to not listening with a "third ear."

CHAPTER SIX

Inadequate Assessments and Mismatched or Mistimed Interventions

Sometimes therapists begin intervening before they have completed their assessment and have collaboratively developed a treatment plan with the couple. Metaphorically speaking, they may start construction before the architect's plans have been completed, the surveying done, and the necessary permits secured. Understandably, there will be situations where the therapist must intervene very quickly to either preserve safety or reduce a crisis-level degree of intensity that may lead to hasty and potentially unrecoverable consequences for the couple. Fortunately, most couple therapy does not proceed this way, and we urge therapists to not be too quick with their couples, which is not always easy to do. Therapists may intervene too early because they are trying to respond to the clients' sense of urgency or because they want to find a way to engender hope quickly. When couples come to treatment, they may convey a sense of urgency, sometimes quite explicitly, about their need to have the therapist "fix things" *now.* The clients' sense of urgency may in fact be related to their level of hopelessness in seeing a resolution to their problems. Clients often feel that they have tried many different solutions to no avail. In addition, they may be blaming each other for their impasses and sharing more negative communications than positive ones. No wonder couples would like to have a resolution as quickly as possible! However, the therapist needs to sort out if the problem is actually a crisis, such as a situation involving physical risk. According to Maslow (1970), it is hard to address higher-order needs such as intimacy if basic security issues are unresolved.

Some of the common mistakes that therapists make include:

- Intervening too quickly and aggressively, or intervening too slowly
- Intervening without having completed the assessment
- Intervening without a case formulation and permission/ understanding from the clients
- Failing to recognize the real problems that motivated the couple to seek treatment
- Minimizing the real problems
- Failing to refer when the problem is outside the therapist's area of competence
- Avoiding problems that trigger reactions in the therapist

Complete a Sufficient Assessment Before Intervening

There are several reasons why therapists should allow enough time to complete an assessment before intervening. First, it gives the therapist a chance to get a clearer understanding of the couple's dynamics. Couple dynamics include the influence of family of origin and relationship history, the adaptability of the couple to change, the balance between intimacy and individual growth and development, the permeability of couple boundaries to others, the nature of power and competition in the relationship, and how the couple negotiates what each partner wants. Because individuals and couple interactions can be complicated and are certainly idiosyncratic, it may take several sessions to conceptualize what is going on for the couple.

Second, as we discussed earlier, couples may be reluctant to disclose certain problems, such as partner abuse, addictions, affairs, sexual problems, and serious psychopathology, until they feel more comfortable with the therapist. Hasty interventions that are based on incomplete information are, at best, ineffective. At worst, they are detrimental to the therapy. Therapists who take the time to build clients' trust are in the best position from which to offer both support and intervention. The following dialogue shows premature treatment:

Therapist: What brings you to therapy?
Husband: My wife never wants to have sex! She is frigid, as they would say.
Therapist: (*to wife*) Is it true that you never want to have sex?
Wife: I have sex when he threatens to divorce me sometimes.
Therapist: Do you think not having sex is a problem for you?
Wife: Of course! Why do you think I got married?
Therapist: What about other problems you are having?
Husband: If we solve this problem everything will be okay.
Wife: (*long silence*)
Therapist: Okay, let's see what it will take to bring back the desire.

This example demonstrates a couple of errors. First, the therapist did not give the wife an opportunity to adequately express her complaints. The wife simply paused and the therapist set the agenda to please the husband. At that point the husband had taken control of the session. Second, the therapist did a very abrupt assessment of the only problem presented and, with inadequate information, decided on the initial course of treatment. In fact, the wife's lacked desire because her husband had a fetish that he insisted she accommodate. She felt repulsed by it but had promised her husband that she would not reveal his "deviant" behavior.

The third reason to wait before intervening is that it allows problem definitions to be refined through assessment.

Assessment includes individual factors, couple problems, and the quality of the relationship. It can be done with formal tests or informal tools. Ideally, most assessment information is also shared with the couple so that all parties can operate from a common body of known information. Fortunately, the assessment phase of treatment includes information gained via intervention in session or through homework, and this usually takes several sessions. In the longer term, it should be understood as ongoing. Patterns of interaction become clearer with time and repetition. The therapist will have a greater amount of richer information by seeing clients in various emotional states in the first several sessions. It might take several weeks to sort out what the treatment priorities are. Assessment and intervention are circular, too, in that each informs the other. It also is an evolving process, as the therapist constantly assesses new problems as they are presented and reevaluates old ones as they are being treated. Thus, the process is never-ending. What is critical is to be as fully aware of the couple's dynamics as soon as possible so as to intervene in the most judicious way.

Many couples enter therapy with a single concrete complaint or with a complaint that is vague, such as a communication problem. In fact, communication problems could be considered the "common cold" complaint of couple therapy; couples often offer this issue as their presenting problem by default, even if other issues are actually at the heart of their struggles. However, even if the couple presents with just one complaint, they are usually struggling with multiple issues. As the therapy proceeds, the couple may become more comfortable mentioning other problems, or they may become aware of other issues with the help of the therapist. The therapist may also identify issues that the couple could not identify or articulate, often at the systemic, interactional level.

When couples present with communication problems, the exact nature of the problem must be clearly described. The couple may not communicate skillfully, may have difficulty communicating during conflicts, may have differing styles of communication, or may communicate only on surface levels. In these cases, skill-building may be a sufficient intervention. Nichols (1988) suggested that skills training may be a good first step in couples therapy unless another specific problem is identified. Communication, however, is often not the real issue, and partners are often quite competent at communicating with each other. Each knows exactly what the other thinks and feels, but does not feel positively about it. In other words, they do not like what is communicated. However, in many cases the couple is not sure whether they can trust the therapist with very personal information, or they want to control the level of disclosure due to fear of increasing emotional intensity, so they say that they have a communication problem. They may evade getting to the real problem until they have established a relationship with the therapist and believe they can trust him or her.

Therapist Issues That May Interfere With Treatment

Certain therapist issues can interfere with the therapist's ability to do a good job with the couple. These issues include topics with which the therapist feels relatively uncomfortable dealing, blind spots, the minimization or avoidance of certain issues, and lack of training. We have noted that therapists may have blind spots in their training and comfort zones in which they operate. These can have quite serious implications for the clinician's work. When therapists are not knowledgeable about or comfortable with a problem, they will be less likely to ask about it; if it is revealed, they may even skirt around it or minimize it. This is a very hazardous course of action for both clients and therapist. For example, many couple therapists have received little training in partner abuse or sex therapy. If a couple reveals these as issues in their relationship, therapy can quickly stall. The therapist may be uncertain about what to do and how to do it, which severely restricts the therapeutic options available. Therapists in this situation may even feel that they are in a bind because they want to help the couple with the problems they do know how to treat, even though they do not know what to do with other issues. Therapists may be reticent about explicitly bringing up what is becoming an increasingly obvious limitation in their competence for fear of losing the client or undermining the work that may have already been done. However, with time, the couple may realize that the therapist is unable to help them and leave anyway.

Most therapists see themselves as generalists, viewing most issues as fair game within their professional scope of practice, even if their training has been sparse. Clients typically think similarly. Therapists who have some training in various problem areas may still lack actual experience in treating them and consequently may be uncomfortable dealing with them. It is also possible that the therapist may simply feel uncomfortable with the topic, regardless of training. Faced with an inability to treat clients, the therapist must take an ethical course of action by getting further supervision, entering personal therapy to deal with countertransference reactions, or referring the couple to a competent practitioner. Therapists may be blinded about making a referral because they sincerely believe that the clinical course of action they are proposing is sufficient or because they want to justify their clinical course of action by saying that the issue they are avoiding is not primary or that the order in which issues are treated is not important.

The following case demonstrates how a therapist chose to minimize a major problem because it did not fit within his schema of practice, and how therapy then failed.

Therapist: (*to wife*) You said you had a big fight last Saturday.
Wife: (*hesitatingly*) Yes...I needed to go to the store, but he wanted to take the car to go meet his friends at the lake so they could fish and party. But I had to get diapers and stuff that couldn't wait. We were really arguing and I couldn't...I just took the baby and went.

Husband: (*irritated*) So she just drives off and leaves me stuck. I told the guys I'd pick them up at 11, and now we're all screwed because she just bolted. Hello, we only have one car! It's not like we were totally out of diapers! Joey's bag had some in it, but she said they wouldn't last long enough. I wasn't going to be gone all day!

Wife: (*to husband*) Oh, bullshit! Every time you go with the guys, I never know when you're coming home! And I don't know what condition you'll be in when you finally do! You act like you're still in high school!

Therapist: So, you don't agree on how to take care of the baby's needs, and that spills into your marriage.

The therapist proceeded to examine parenting roles in each of their families of origin and never returned to the issue of the husband's activities with his friends or the overt conflict over it.

Regardless of how therapists feel about the limitations they face, there are possible repercussions for all parties that cannot be overlooked. In the case of violence, the therapist's lack of appropriate action to intervene may cause someone grave harm. In addition, treating a couple with violence as though the violence is not occurring is not likely to address the dynamics that support the violence, and the couple may not make any significant changes. Therapists' desire to be helpful where they are able to help is ultimately thwarted, despite their good intentions, by their incompetence in helping in the areas where genuine help is most needed. Referral makes obvious sense in these situations and can help the therapist avoid rather unpleasant outcomes, like lawsuits.

Of course, some therapists simply do not want to refer the client because they may think it makes them look bad or they believe they need the business. These are poor reasons for retaining a case. Additionally, clients may be daunted by referral to a specialist, seeing the referral as a possible indicator of more serious problems. The therapist can turn this situation around by stating that the problems the couple has are specialized and require the services of a therapist with specialized training. The therapist must be careful to communicate that he or she is not implying that the couple's problem is hopeless. In fact, the therapist might tell them the prognosis is very good with the right therapist. The therapist can also frame the referral in positive terms such as, "I want you to have the best help for this problem that is available. Your particular problem is fairly specialized and requires a therapist with special training. I can refer you to a specialist in this area." The couple will appreciate the therapist's commitment to helping them get the best help. Although that case might be lost for the referring clinician, there are a number of potential benefits over the long term. First, the therapist to whom the couple is referred may be similarly inclined to refer suitable couples back, and a genuinely collegial referral system will begin to develop, as well as the possibility for informal or even formal collaboration and consultation. Second, the couple will probably remember how honest and helpful the therapist was and will be more inclined to refer their friends and acquaintances to the original therapist. What may appear to the therapist as a bad business practice may in fact be just the opposite. Had the therapist continued treatment, he or she would have failed to provide the needed services and the couple would have been dissatisfied at best. Couples are not going to refer to a therapist with whom they are dissatisfied.

Suggestions for Assessment and Treatment

It is hard to avoid responding to the couple's sense of urgency when they come for therapy. A way to respond is to discuss it without prematurely intervening. Therapists can respectfully state that human beings and their interactions are complex. They can explain that although the clients have knowledge of their problems, the therapist does not and needs the clients' assistance to understand what is happening. Despite the fact that there are certain patterns of problems in couple relationships, each couple is unique. The therapist wants to be able to tailor interventions based on an assessment of what will be helpful to this particular couple, with these particular concerns, with their idiosyncratic ways of interacting, and with their strengths and resources at this time.

The matching of intervention to the couple will aid in problem resolution, something that may be clearer to the clients if the process of therapy is explained. Educating clients on the process of therapy can help them to see that there are phases to treatment—beginning, middle, and termination—each with its own objectives. If time is well used at the beginning of therapy to make assessments and to coconstruct a relational definition of the problem, clients will be better prepared to understand their problems differently. This is done through a process called reframing (discussed in detail in Chapter 10). Having a new way of understanding their situation gives clients potential new ways of interacting to solve the newly defined problem.

Perhaps a good rule of thumb to work from is that couples should leave their initial sessions optimistic that their therapist can help them. In order for this to happen, the therapist must do something to engender that hope. Simply listening and tracking with them may not be sufficient. The caveat is that the therapist should build a balanced alliance with each member of the couple before intervening. During the session, the therapist can start to create an environment that is different from home by interrupting negativity and blame. In itself, this can help to build a sense of hope that the relational situation does not always have to be the same. It can be quite difficult to balance the need to intervene in the immediacy of the moment with the need to formulate a thorough assessment and a clear treatment plan with the couple.

Further suggestions for assessment and treatment are framed below in the context of some case examples. In general, as part of the assessment process, therapists should ask about areas that many clients find difficult to discuss, such as abuse, addictions, affairs, and sex. In addition, the therapist should inquire about money, work, friends, in-laws, family of origin relationships, leisure activities, religion, parenting, housing, and any other areas that pertain to a given couple. The couple may not fully discuss the topics at that time, but raising the issues lets clients know that the therapist is interested and that these topics can be discussed. Of course, as part of the treatment planning process, therapists and clients will decide which problems to prioritize and in what order treatment will occur. In some cases, as mentioned earlier, clients may share information that leads the therapist to make a referral to another therapist.

The therapist can also facilitate the assessment process by asking questions in each of the problem areas (regarding abuse, addictions, affairs, and sex) in order to get an overview and later follow up with more detailed questions after spending some time with the couple. For example, some couples with sexual difficulties may signal early that they are experiencing these problems, even if they are embarrassed to discuss the issue. Others may present their concerns, but not in explicit terms. In fact, the couple may be waiting for the therapist to ask about their problem because it indicates to them that he or she is knowledgeable and comfortable in dealing with their issue. Once questioned, they will reveal more information to the extent that they feel comfortable with the therapist.

Asking general questions, especially about something like sex, is likely to elicit a "look good" response. Clients may want to answer in socially desirable ways, may feel defensive about revealing personal or relationship inadequacies, or may not know something is a problem unless they are specifically asked. The couple may respond to the general question by saying everything is fine. The only way to make sure this is actually the case is to follow up with specific questions such as: "Does this mean you do not have any trouble with getting an erection, ejaculating too quickly, having enough desire, having an orgasm, (etc.)?" This statement is made slowly, letting the couple respond to each potential problem, and if the answers are all no, then the therapist can say that he or she was just checking to make sure. From a statistical perspective, the answer to one or more of these questions is likely to be yes (Frank, Anderson, & Rubinstein, 1978). The therapist then pursues getting more information about these problems at the appropriate time. One additional questioning technique is to ask circular questions about whether the partners agree on the view of the problem and the impact of one partner's behavior on the other. Initially, just a general description might be enough and the therapist could then say that he or she will return to this issue when all the problems are known and the order in which they are going to be treated has been decided.

As therapists assess couples, they are also thinking about how to link problems and treatment goals. In some theoretical orientations, such as psychoanalysis and psychodynamic therapy, the therapist adopts more of an expert or authoritative stance. Other theoretical orientations, especially those with postmodern influences, stress that building a collaborative relationship with clients and coconstructing a treatment plan is highly desirable. Our approach is to identify the problems using interactional terminology to reduce blaming or side-taking (see Chapter 10), discuss the goals that clients have for each of those problems, and develop a sequenced plan of intervention. The whole process is discussed with the couple, which gives them a great deal of ownership in their treatment, as well as being interventive itself.

Accomplishing joint ownership of the therapeutic process with the couple is a critical component of launching couple therapy well. Obviously, the clients who take ownership and responsibility for their own progress are the best clients and are more likely to be satisfied with the therapy that they have participated in creating. Specifically, ownership helps clients feel empowered in the process rather than like two helpless partners who do not know how to solve their problems. We believe ownership also reduces the chances of premature termination because the couple takes part in constructing a treatment plan that prioritizes their well-being and goals. Additionally, when they are collaborators in the process from the outset, clients are less reluctant to redirect the therapist to other issues if they become more important than what is currently being worked on.

The connection between problems and goals may not be as obvious as it might appear. The therapist must be very careful not to make assumptions about the goals that follow from the problems. What therapists think is an obvious goal may not be what the client wants. Unless there is a discussion about the link between the two, the therapist and couple may find they are at odds over the direction of therapy. Once the goal is discussed and agreed upon, the next step is to decide how to get there. The therapist can briefly describe the approach to achieving the goal in order to see whether the approach is compatible with the client.

An example illustrates this point in an interesting way. A couple began treatment because they did not believe they fought fairly and they thought they fought too much. The therapist suggested a straightforward behavioral/communications approach to teaching the couple how to fight fairly. The couple liked this idea but said they wanted to understand why they fought so much. Basically, they wanted the therapist to add insight to the therapeutic mix. The therapist agreed to explore the deeper reasons for the fighting and to do some family of origin work. The couple concurred that this approach would work well for them. Couples have different ideas about how change occurs or why change occurs. Although a behavioral/communications approach might have been sufficient to remedy this couple's problem, they felt they needed more. They were both highly reflective people and had been in prior therapies that involved mostly insight. In short, the therapist's goal is to develop the treatment plan in a highly collaborative way that is congruent with what the couple wants and how they think change occurs. Even while collaborating with the couple, the therapist can exercise considerable influence as the paid consultant and educate the clients about what is likely to work best and be most efficient. The therapist simply lets the couple take the lead in defining the components of the treatment plan, the parameters of which the therapist has set out for them.

Sometimes the therapist faces an ethical dilemma when goals are being established. In one case, a couple came to treatment because the husband saw prostitutes in order to engage in sado-masochistic (S&M) behavior. The therapist might make the obvious assumption that the wife would be upset that her husband was both seeing prostitutes and engaging in what most spouses would consider a perverted behavior. However, once the wife heard about his activity, she stated that he did not need to see prostitutes because she wanted to inflict pain and be part of his S&M activities. The couple had never talked about their unusual preferences; hence, the husband assumed she would find S&M unacceptable. He had been too embarrassed to raise the issue with her. As a result of the wife's willingness to participate, the therapist was asked to help them learn how to incorporate S&M into their lovemaking.

This goal might place the therapist in an ethical dilemma. Sadism and masochism are both considered paraphilias in DSM-IV (1994), although there is some debate as to whether these diagnoses should be considered abnormal. First, the therapist may have to examine his or her own values. For example, some, perhaps even most, therapists believe that love cannot be expressed in intimate relationships using S&M. They may consider S&M indicative of an underlying pathology that needs to be addressed. Rather than endorse the behavior, the therapist might examine the husband's desire for S&M. In addition, he or she might look at the relational component of the problem. What is the wife's potential motive? Does she see his desire for S&M as nonnegotiable and therefore is participating because she fears being abandoned or rejected? Is this a way for her to take revenge in a way that is acceptable to him? Is the wife's desire for participation genuine, and will the joint activity actually build an intimate connection? Regardless of the answers to these questions, the therapist may hold such strong views on this subject as to not be able to work with the couple on their goal. This therapist would then choose the option of referring the husband for individual therapy to deal with the paraphilia.

Other therapists may hold that the client's values are the ones that must govern their choices and that what is done privately should be the couple's decision. Therapists in this case must decide whether they are competent to treat the problem. They may be able to research how this might be done, or they may have already had training they consider applicable to the situation. If they conclude that they do not have sufficient training, they can seek supervision or refer to a competent therapist.

Another case gave the therapist a different ethical dilemma. A married man came to treatment alone for help with an erectile dysfunction problem. He had been married for about 15 years and had suffered from this problem for approximately the last 5 years. He had been assessed and referred by a urologist who had determined that the erectile dysfunction was not medically based. The therapist told him that sex therapy would involve both him and his wife. The client asked about confidentiality and was assured that what he told the therapist would remain confidential as long as he was coming as an individual client. He then revealed that he was having an affair, thinking about leaving his wife, and wanted to do the therapy with his affair partner so they could have intercourse. The ethical dilemma for the therapist was whether or not to proceed with treatment with the client and his affair partner. The erectile dysfunction could probably be successfully treated, but the therapist needed to think about the impact on the marital relationship. If the problem were resolved, the client would probably leave his wife. In this instance, the therapist suggested that the client decide whether to stay with his wife or not. Only when this was re-solved would the therapist provide help with the erection prob-lem. The client said he would think about what the therapist said and never returned to therapy.

Finally, an individual client wanted help in learning how to ask for dates. Women had rejected him for years. The therapist suggested working on his fear of rejection, which was much stronger for him than for other people in his situation. The client insisted that solving his fear of rejection was not the issue. He wanted the therapist to teach him how to meet more women. The therapist suggested some of the typical ways of meeting women and he reported that he had tried all but one of those methods. The client did not see any usefulness in learning how to deal with rejection even though it was pointed out to him that if he met a woman he still had to overcome his fear of asking her out. The client's goal in this case was unrealistic. He viewed therapy as some kind of dating service. As soon as he realized what therapy could and could not do for him, he terminated treatment.

As this chapter has demonstrated, assessment and treatment must be well integrated. Assessing the problem from multi-ple dimensions must occur first, allowing the clinician to de-velop a case formulation of the couple. A variety of interven-tion mistakes—from intervening too quickly based on a lack of information to being pushed by clients for some kind of quick resolution—can lead the therapist to perform an inade-quate assessment. When this happens the therapist has a poor understanding of the couple and risks intervening prematurely or missing the real problem entirely. Linking assessment and intervention and delivering them in accord with a case formu-lation means the outcome is much more likely to be what the couple wants.

CHAPTER SEVEN

Overlooking
Process Considerations

Understanding the temporal nature of client problems, obtaining a full list of problems, and making an adequate assessment are all ways of comprehending the content of client concerns. An equally important skill to develop is the ability to listen with a "third ear" for what is not being said or to the incongruity between what is said and how it is said. This ability is based on paying attention to how clients speak and behave about issues (the process) in addition to what they say (the content). Partners respond to both the content and process of communication. In fact, partners may be so exquisitely tuned in to minor variations in tone of voice or gestures (process) that they may actually miss the content of what is being said. These clients think or have learned that actions speak louder than words. However, the vast majority of clients do not pay enough attention to process and need the therapist to help point out this aspect of their communication. Paying attention to process helps to increase clients' awareness of how they communicate or the rules they have for their relationship, which thereby gives them a wider range of options regarding future behavior. Overlooking or underemphasizing process considerations is one of the most common therapeutic mistakes. As easy as process may sound, many beginning therapists have difficulty with both the concept and its implementation. By failing to attend to process the therapist may:

- Miss the meaning of much of what is actually being communicated by the couple
- Miss, underemphasize, or misinterpret affective expression
- Fail to point out to the couple contradictions between content and process
- Fail to apprehend certain processes due to countertransference issues

This list is certainly not exhaustive, but it does identify some of the more common outcomes from not attending to the full range of communication. Clients who are working with a therapist who neglects process may feel misunderstood and will never learn how to discern and discuss process. It takes time for therapists to learn how to integrate process with content and to then teach it to couples. Knowledge about process, experience, interpersonal sensitivity and awareness (free of countertransference), and supervision are all key elements to the mastery of process.

Definition of Process and Content

The *content* of client communication in therapy refers to what the client actually says. It is the overt meaning of the words taken at face value. Understanding content is an important part of understanding the client. Content is a window through which to understand the nature of the problem and the client's behaviors, thoughts, and feelings as they are articulated or demonstrated. For clients, expressing content is usually easy. For therapists, grasping the content of the client's statements is similarly easy. People usually communicate about some issue with content that can be taken at face value. For example, a wife might state in a conjoint session that she has been thinking about divorce for several months. The content of this statement is obvious: The client is expressing concern that the marriage may end in divorce. However, the comment could be a statement of action resulting from the wife's frustration about being unable to express her feelings about the marriage. In many of the cases we treat, statements of action are often misguided attempts to express feelings and underlying problems in the relationship. The latter represent process and not content.

Understanding process is perhaps even more important than understanding content if the therapist is truly to grasp the meaning of what the clients say. *Process* refers to how statements are made. It can be thought of as all the contextual cues that are associated with the content. These may include body language, voice inflection and intonation, loudness, pressured speech and use of language or wording, and the emotion conveyed with the message. Process also refers to the larger, harder-to-see patterns or rules that govern interactions between people. These rules are not usually explicitly discussed, and most people are only occasionally consciously aware of the processes of their own relationships. One rule the couple might have imposed upon themselves is not to discuss the process in the relationship! They may intuitively know that they aren't adept at process discussions, which thus leads to conflict. Comprehending process in therapy is a much more complicated task than listening for content. Therapists must be aware of many cues simultaneously and possess a high level of interpersonal sensitivity. They must focus on and be attentive to the partners' statements and reactions while looking for patterns or sequences of behavior that occur over longer periods of time.

Communication involves both process and content. The partners usually are not aware that they are expressing more than just content. Therapists can help partners understand that they are communicating much more than just content by noticing the patterns of interaction and highlighting when a partner reacts to how things are said in addition to what is said. In session, one partner may make a statement that he or she thinks is just factual, and the other partner may respond to the process elements of the statement, even without initially being aware of it. For example, the wife contemplating divorce may convey the depth of her feelings through certain process elements such as turning away from her husband physically or using a tone of voice that is hopeless. Because nonverbal behavior conveys the emotional tone of the communication, the husband may react strongly to his wife's sense of hopelessness and act as if she were saying she wanted a divorce because the situation is hopeless. The husband's strong reaction might surprise the wife because she did not intend to convey this thought but rather was expressing the seriousness of her distress in the marriage.

How to Learn to Attend to Process

Becoming sensitive to process is something therapists (and clients) can learn through academic preparation, supervision, experience, and self-awareness. Beginning therapists often find that process, although not new in terms of their interpersonal experience, is new as an academically presented concept and is difficult to attend to adequately. As students therapists may understand the concepts of content and process theoretically but find it difficult to pay attention to both simultaneously when they enter the therapy room with clients. It is easy to feel overwhelmed by the amount of process and content data generated by a client. With a couple, obviously, the task becomes much more challenging. The therapist must pay attention to each individual, to the interaction between the partners, to his or her interactions with the couple, and to his or her own reactions to what is transpiring in session. At this point, the beginning therapist's academic preparation is complemented by supervision. The supervisor's goal is to enhance the student's ability to recognize process elements without forgetting content. As the supervisor watches the interaction, he or she may point out the process occurring between the partners as well as the process between the couple and the therapist. For example, the therapist may become distracted or fail to watch the couple for microgestures or highly transient body language. In fact, an indicator that these have happened may be in the reaction of the other partner. To facilitate this learning, therapists and their supervisors can review taped sessions and focus only on how process was attended to during the session. With feedback, the therapist learns over a period of time to become attentive and sensitive to the cues being given and to which ones may be significant.

Therapists can learn to self-monitor by constantly asking themselves some of the following questions:

- What was the content of what was just said?
- Given the way the statement was said, what were the feelings?
- What underlying meaning does the statement convey?
- Is the meaning related to prior events in the relationship or family history? Is it related to cognitive distortions?
- Is the content thematic? Does it reflect an underlying pattern or process?
- How can I move the couple from discussing content to process?

Some therapists have great difficulty understanding the idea of process and tend to allow or even encourage couples to communicate on the level of content. Therapists may have difficulty with the notion of process for a variety of reasons. They may have been reared in a family that taught them to avoid process and focus on content. Certain process elements may trigger countertransference reactions, such as fear of increasing the couple's emotional intensity if process elements are pointed out. A supervisor may be able to assist the therapist in identifying his or her problems and may recommend personal or group therapy to help the therapist gain more self-awareness and change his or her behaviors.

Making Process Explicit in Therapy

Therapists make process explicit by clarifying the meaning or underlying the intent of statements and behavior. They also hypothesize about the purpose for the timing or method of making statements or behaving in particular ways, as well as pay attention to their own actions. With the exception of those who have had therapy before or who have high levels of interpersonal sensitivity and perceptivity, clients usually have little understanding or awareness of process, and even when they *are* aware of it, they tend to react to it rather than evaluate it and respond deliberately. In a sense, clients learn about process from their therapists in much the same way that therapists learn from supervisors. With guidance and feedback from the therapist, clients learn to increase their awareness of process, as well as increase their range of choices in behavior. Once they have gained more awareness, they can choose to communicate in ways that are more congruent with their intentions.

Clients who overlook process may be especially prone to arguing, because they aren't talking about the real issue. On the other hand, if they do attempt to discuss process, they may find that it only exacerbates the problem because they are now switching between process and content and often not making their process points very well. Additionally, some couples have colluded to protect each other or their relationship by not talking about certain issues. They may even state that their communication is only "on the surface." The following dialogue demonstrates this.

Wife: Why don't you ever say you love me?
Husband: You know I love you. Look at all the things I do for you.
Wife: But I need to hear it.
Husband: I'm not a touchy-feely guy. You knew that when you married me.

Wife: I knew you were just like your family. Everyone has trouble expressing their feelings. (*a process-oriented statement*)

Husband: I don't know why you can't accept me the way I am. I'm a good husband.

This couple is struggling to communicate at a process level. The wife makes one statement about the husband's family to try to get to the deeper pattern, but her husband, missing the perhaps awkward attempt to move to a process level, goes back to a content statement. The therapist could help this couple move toward process by conversing with them in the following way:

Therapist: (*to husband*) Tell me about your family.

Husband: Everyone got along. It was a happy family.

Therapist: How did your parents deal with feelings, especially your feelings?

Husband: They didn't talk about feelings.

Therapist: Hmm...what do you think stopped them?

Husband: There were six kids in our family and my father had three jobs. He was a good provider but life was hard. My parents tried to make it a happy family but they were trying to survive.

Therapist: Did anyone ever talk about how hard life was or complain?

Husband: No, everyone had a job to do and we all knew that complaining was a waste of time.

Therapist: Do you think there was an underlying message not to complain or express any negative feelings?

Husband: (*tearful*) Yeah, life was hard, but we were told to be strong.

In this dialogue, the therapist keeps asking the husband questions designed to get him to see the underlying message in his family about feelings. Once he begins to articulate this message, he gains some awareness of how he internalized this message to be strong and keep his feelings inside.

Another issue to consider at the process level is the purpose of the client's statement or behaviors and why it is offered as it is when it is. Although the statement about divorce conveys the wife's distress, it could also be a statement of desperation or a request for attention, encouragement, or validation. Or it could be a way to provoke a response from the husband—"I don't want a divorce." In fact, the way the response is made may carry greater emotional weight than the content of the discussion about divorce. The content of deciding to divorce may be like deciding whether to have soup or a sandwich for lunch, for example, but the process underneath is probably quite different. If it isn't, that is significant. The way the couple engages in this conversation may also reflect their normative pattern of interaction. The therapist may, for example, conjecture that the couple needs to make provocative rather than calm and reasoned statements in order to make connection with each other. The therapist is developing and testing his or her hypotheses at the same time he or she is gathering information and building a relationship with the couple.

In short, the therapist must be highly aware of what the clients are saying and how they are saying them. For example, with the previous couple the therapist might reflect the content of what he or she heard by stating that the wife sounds as though she is on the verge of divorce. With greater clarification and attention to process, the therapist might say that the wife is feeling hopeless that change can occur within the marriage and that that has caused her to start thinking about divorce. The first statement implies that an action is being contemplated whereas the second stresses the emotional distress being experienced.

Generally therapists attend to the content of a statement first, clarify it if needed, and then move to process. However, there are times when process considerations are so predominant that they are considered simultaneously with content issues. The following example will clarify how this is done. During the course of sex therapy, a wife reported that she had been sexually abused but had worked through this issue in individual therapy. The client made her statement in a manner that suggested that the issue still distressed her emotionally. The therapist reflected back this emotional distress, a process intervention. He probed further with certain content questions about how long she had worked on this issue with the other therapist and what had happened during these sessions. She reported she had had three sessions, during which she had been told that the abuse had happened in the past and that she should not dwell on it. As a result of the conversation with the current therapist, the wife made a process conclusion: She had not worked on the issue and the previous therapist had discounted her abuse in the same way that her mother had discounted it when she told her about it. The emotion of her statement was so obvious that the therapist immediately addressed *how* (process) she made the statement rather than *what* (content) she said. In other words, the emotional distress was so intense that the therapist first moved to directly deal with her distress over the abuse rather than gather a lot of information about what happened.

The foregoing example also demonstrates how therapist factors may get in the way of good therapy. Therapist factors, such as the type of clients the therapist primarily serves and how the therapist deals with the emotions behind the content, can affect how content and process are handled for several reasons. Therapists who work primarily with clients with issues like violence, addictions, or criminality sometimes forget that not all clients are in denial, or lie, or cannot change. It may be hard for some therapists to imagine that a man who hits his wife only once may be so appalled at his own behavior that he feels compelled to go to therapy to make sure it never happens again. A therapist who sees one instance as the tip of the iceberg may simply refuse to believe him. The man who is treated like this by the therapist may be increasingly defensive if he sees another therapist. The point is that therapists need to be aware of their own process habits and how they interact with clients, case by case. Some therapists do not like to deal with too much emotion, particularly anger, in therapy due to countertransference reactions, because they lack the skills to manage affect, or because they assume it will cause the couple further problems. Mostly their fears are not justified, and they must learn to take risks and trust that the process will work itself out.

Following is another example of how the therapist can make explicit the process in a couple session:

Wife: I get upset when you don't do what you say you are going to do.

Husband: I always get to things eventually. It's just not on your timetable.

Therapist: (*to wife*) What is the feeling you are talking about when you say "upset"?

Wife: I've asked him to do things for years and he doesn't do them. He never offers to help in the house and doesn't notice what needs to be done. At first, I just got angry. Now I get angry and stay angry and become the "witch." I'm so angry with him that I've pulled away emotionally and that's why we never have sex.

Therapist: (*to husband*) What do you hear your wife saying and how is she feeling about the situation?

Husband: She thinks I don't pull my weight at home and she is angry.

Therapist: Yes, but how angry?

Husband: I think she is angry with me all the time. Every little thing I do makes her angry now and she doesn't want to be close to me. I feel rejected all the time.

Therapist: Now you are beginning to understand how she feels. Let's talk about what you can do to solve this problem and repair the emotional damage on both sides.

This transcript shows how the therapist made the intensity of the feelings explicit so the seriousness of the problem was clear and the feelings were fully understood. In this case, the therapist reflected back or pointed out process elements to increase the emotional intensity in a session. Once the content and process were better understood, an appropriate therapeutic agenda could be established.

Process Considerations

Weeks and Treat (2001) identified several process considerations in their book *Couples in Treatment*. These considerations are briefly reviewed here.

Voice

A partner's tone of voice conveys a great deal of information about his or her feeling state. A partner may say something relatively benign in terms of content, but the tone of voice may say much more than the words themselves. In couple therapy, the tone of voice often conveys anger, hurt, guilt, shame, aggression, submission, resentment, or a passive-aggressive attitude. Gottman (1994a) pointed out that several patterns in a marriage are highly predictive of divorce and marital unhappiness: defensiveness, contempt, criticism, and stonewalling. These patterns are also often conveyed in a partner's tone of voice. The tone of voice may be clear and the feelings and attitudes easy to read and then check out. On the other hand, they may be more subtly conveyed and leave the therapist and partner guessing what the partner intends to transmit. The therapist may also be uncertain whether and how much to probe for clarification. As the therapist becomes more familiar with the clients' normative ways of operating, the degree of guesswork involved in reading tone will decrease, although some uncertainty may always exist.

Take for example, the woman in Chapter 5 who dropped her voice to an almost inaudible level when talking about her husband's parents' involvement in the rehabilitation of the house they lived in. When she repeated the statement a little louder it was clearly said in a sarcastic way. The way the woman initiated the topic by speaking in a suddenly quiet way indicated that it was one of serious import that remained literally nearly unmentionable. Her speaking in a stage whisper conveyed meaning about its significance. In attending to process, the therapist could ask her to comment on, why she would mention her concern in a way so different than what she had just been saying.

The rate of speech can also send a number of cues about a person. Partners who speak very slowly may be clinically depressed, extraordinarily tired, or possibly under the influence of a substance. Their whole demeanor may be retarded. Alternatively, someone speaking that way may be attempting to be particularly deliberate or careful with what he or she says. Pressured speech could mean the partner is manic, hypomanic, or simply wants to make a point before being cut off. It can also be used to control the session, leaving little room for anyone else to speak. One client, Louise, came to sessions and talked incessantly and contemptuously about her husband. She would not pause and talked over her husband and therapist. Her intent was apparently to control the session. The therapist had to intervene strongly to get her to give her husband a chance to speak. As soon as the therapist gained some control, her husband had an opportunity to say that she was like this at home and that everyone she met, including her children, had at some time called her a "control freak."

Body Language

Partners may display a continuum of sensitivity to each other's body language, ranging from being mostly unaware of it to being hypersensitive to every nuance of expression to deliberately ignoring it. Once again, the therapist helps the partners become more aware of each other's body language. Ideally, the therapist wants to promote congruence between body language and other nonverbal and contextual cues and the content of what is being said. Some body language signals are more obvious than others. When partners move their chairs apart from each other, turn away from each other, do not look at each other, and show facial signs of contempt or anger the message is not difficult to decipher. Less overt signs may be more difficult to read. A flat facial expression may mask any number of feelings, giving the partner little eye contact and looking at the therapist may indicate a readiness to refute what the other partner has said, and smaller gestures such as foot swinging or finger tapping may show impatience, anxiety, or anger. Small or subtle facial expressions, such as a raised eyebrow, clenched jaw, pursed lips, yawning, or a pseudo-smile convey feelings that are no doubt significant but individual to each person. All expressions convey something; the key is for clients to be aware of what they are intending to convey by their expression and for their partner to be able to accurately read what is being conveyed.

Don and Cary were in a very distant marriage, and in counseling the therapist quickly noticed a pattern they engaged in. Whenever Cary, who was much more vocal, complained about Don, he would fold his arms and begin to stare at her. After several seconds of unbroken staring, she would look at him, and he would drop his chin slightly and look over the rim of his glasses at her with his eyebrows slightly raised. She would pause in the middle of what she was saying, and if his facial expression did not change, she would temporarily shut down, but not so quickly as to be obviously awkward. When the therapist asked about this, Don denied he was doing anything but listening, but Cary nearly jumped out of her seat and said, "It's his 'look.' I get that all the time!"

Therapist: (*to Cary*) What do you think he means with the "look"?

Cary: It means I'm supposed to shut up. I feel like a little girl in trouble with the principal.

Therapist: (*to Don*) What are you saying with that look?

Don: I'm not looking at her. I'm just listening. She can say what she wants.

Therapist: (*glancing at Cary, then speaking to Don*) I don't think she's buying that.

Cary: I'm not. He makes his eyes all big and intimidating (*to Don*) like you're doing right now!

Don: (*to therapist*) What am I doing?

Therapist: You're giving her that look. Your arms are folded across your chest and... (*Don gives the therapist the same look*) now, right now, you just dropped your chin and you're looking over your glasses at me. That's the look.

Cary: It makes me nuts!

Therapist: (*to Don*) So, what's behind the look?

Don: I'm not aware of it at all.

Therapist: Okay, but it's there all the same. What are you feeling when she complains about you and you give her that look? Or what were you feeling just a second ago when you gave me the look?

Don: I'm not sure. (*pause*) I guess I don't like it when she tries to make me feel like I don't do anything right.

The conversation at that point had begun to shift to process, and a very productive session ensued. The spouses were quite well attuned to each other's process, but they were not adept at talking about it or, perhaps, even being honest about it.

Like Don and Cary, some couples are exquisitely sensitive to each other's body language. Emotionally enmeshed couples constantly monitor each other's body language. The therapist will note that when partners make statements they glance at each other to see what kind of reaction is evoked. They are basically looking for approval or agreement from the partner and will express upset when they note something they think suggests disapproval or disagreement. The therapist can make this part of the couple's process explicit by discussing the need for approval.

The couple's body language relative to the therapist is also something to consider. The therapist may note where the couple sits. Usually the therapist's office has chairs or a couch or loveseat prearranged for the session. In one unusual case, a couple came to the first session and was asked to have a seat. The chairs were located about 5 feet in front of the therapist. Each partner walked to the chairs and simultaneously pulled them toward the therapist so they were literally sitting knee to knee to him. They also had their chairs touching each other and entwined their hands. The therapist's immediate hypothesis was that this was an enmeshed couple who only knew how to form enmeshed relationships with people. Further experience with the couple confirmed this hypothesis.

At the process level, the couple's normative body language over time indicates the nature of their relationship and their preferred ways of relating. Couples who, over the course of several sessions, including relatively nonintense ones, remain physically distant with each other or give each other minimal eye contact, for instance, are giving the therapist volumes of data on how they relate. Commenting or discussing this observation can be a powerful opportunity for change, as can commenting on the ongoing process dynamics that occur between the couple and the therapist.

Use of Language

The style in which a couple speaks is different from voice tone. Couples have an almost infinite number of ways by which to express their ideas. Certain ways of expressing ideas suggest one meaning rather than another. How a sentence is constructed may indicate very different thoughts and feelings. The use of "I" language versus "you" language is a good example. Saying "I feel sad today" is very different in meaning from saying "You make me feel sad." The therapist should note whether language is used in the form of "I" statements, "you" statements, or impersonal statements such as "it." The therapist should encourage the use of "I" language because it stresses self-responsibility and is less likely to evoke defensiveness from the partner.

The partners may also use language that is polarizing. Terms that convey an absolute, such as always, never, good, bad, right, wrong, sick, or healthy suggest a strong sense of judgment and the perception that one partner is at the polar opposite end of the characteristic from the other. In other words, if one partner says he or she is right it implies that the other is wrong. Polarizing language can also reveal the partners' extreme feelings about themselves. A partner might say, "I have never felt loved by my spouse." This statement shows that he or she views the partner as unloving. Further examination will probably show that the statement has become the current emotional reality, although there probably have been times in the past when this was not the case.

The statements a partner makes may be self-referential. The following transcript illustrates this point.

Husband: I wish you would show more interest in our finances.

Wife: I'm not as smart as you.

Husband: It has nothing to do with being smart. You just aren't interested.

Therapist: (*to wife*) What do you really mean when you say you aren't as smart as he is? Are you saying you are stupid?

Wife: Sometimes I feel really stupid and inept. When it comes to the money thing I just don't know much about money and he's really good at it.

Therapist: Where did you get the idea that you are stupid and inept?

Wife: I was never good enough for my parents. No matter what I did it was never good enough.

Therapist: Okay, let's talk about that in a few minutes. Right now I'm wondering what you feel you know and do well. It doesn't have to be perfect—just something that gives you a feeling of competence.

In this example the therapist is trying to get the wife to own some of her competence and understand where she got the idea that she was stupid and incompetent. Asking her about exceptions to her belief that she is stupid would show her that she is more competent than she tells herself, and she may begin to change her personal narrative or self-talk. The therapist also wants her to understand the roots of her faulty self-image. As suspected, they were grounded in her family of origin. The therapist could also consider and explore a variety of other possibilities, including gender roles that have become rigidly fixed, needs and expectations (especially unconscious) that the partners have of each other, power struggles, and the need to maintain a certain degree of distance.

A couple of other points about the use of language are also helpful for the therapist to understand. Language can be used to regulate the amount of distance in a relationship. Every relationship has a "set point" for closeness and distance. Many couples try to reset their closeness thermostat through the use of language. A number of statements can be used to foster greater closeness:

- I want to spend more time with you.
- I've really been missing you.
- Can we do something special tonight?
- I need to talk to you.
- I need a hug from you.
- Let's get away for the weekend.

Other statements create distance:

- You never show me any affection.
- We never do anything together.
- You are impossible.
- All you do is pick at me.
- What happened to our relationship?

Notice that the distancing statements are destructively phrased. It is appropriate to ask for distance, but in another way. For example:

- I had a terrible day and need some time alone.
- I would like to spend some time with our children/my parents alone.
- I need a little space tonight and then we can get together.
- I really want to spend some time reading tonight to unwind.

Many couples also use nonverbal behaviors to regulate distance. The stereotypical male who is not given to verbal expressions of affection but faithfully brings his wife coffee in the morning or fills her car up with gas may be showing a desire for closeness to her that she does not recognize. If he is criticized for failing to show her the closeness she desires, he may not understand how or why he is judged as failing and may be resentful that she does not appreciate him as he is. When there is a mismatch in preferred methods or currencies of expression, the couple usually has trouble. The therapist also needs to avoid imposing his or her own preferred language on the couple, especially if the couple is not troubled by their methods.

Obviously, the therapist can explain the different ways of asking for closeness and distance or separateness and togetherness. Appropriate ways of asking for each can be explained and coached in the sessions. The couple may also need to work on developing a clearer sense of how much closeness and distance they want in their relationship and why. The goal is to help them reach some consensus about how much intimacy they want and how to best achieve that goal.

Finally, the couple has a choice about whether they respond to each other reactively or purposively. A reactive response is emotionally driven and is often not deliberately chosen. It is based on a feeling of insecurity and the assumption of being attacked or abandoned by the partner. As such, it springs from too much emotional neediness. A reactive response is usually counterattacking or defensive in nature. A purposive response, on the other hand, is based on both feeling and thoughts. It is nonjudgmental and nondefensive and addresses the issue with greater equanimity. With most couples, the therapist needs to lower the emotional reactivity in the session and in the couple's relationship by monitoring the communication and asking for restatements of reactive responses. Further, the therapist can explore the underlying insecurity and assumption of attack in the reactive partner.

If one partner says to the other, "I need you to assume more responsibility in the house," the other partner may respond either reactively or purposively. Reactive responses could include:

- You're crazy. I help all the time.
- I don't know what reality you're living in.
- I guess you want me to do everything.
- I'm not a slave.
- You just want a maid.

Purposive statements might include:

- I didn't know you felt that way.
- Let's talk about what I can do.
- I'm sorry—I have been focusing too much on other things lately.
- Let's sit down and talk about how you feel.

Treating couples requires careful attention to process because of the multiple levels of communication occurring between the couple and with the therapist. The therapist must be aware of his or her own process as well as those of the couple. The therapist's tone of voice, body language, and use of language should communicate care, concern, interest, and hope. It should influence the couple in subtle ways they aren't even aware of. Poor use of process on the part of the therapist will leave the couple feeling that the therapist is not present for them or is not helpful.

CHAPTER EIGHT

The Pitfalls of Anger and Conflict

Two individuals join together to make a couple. Even if people tend to choose mates who are more similar than dissimilar to them, at some point differences will arise. Each person has a different family background, different interpersonal and personal experiences, different communication styles, different expectations about the relationship, and different levels of interpersonal skills. By the time couples come to therapy, they may have forgotten how much they valued the special and attractive characteristics and differences between them.

Fundamentally, each individual is unique. Dealing with difference and conflict is a normal part of relationships. Conflict is important because it is an inherent issue in relationships. When people feel stuck and cannot resolve conflict in mutually acceptable ways, they may seek professional help to resolve the matter. Initially in therapy, clients may want to present themselves in the best light possible, but they cannot avoid recreating their couple and conflict dynamics in session. Couples who want to "win" at all costs are engaged in a destructive behavior cycle, which probably is what brought them to therapy.

Therefore, the therapist must be competent at managing the conflict and helping the couple to find ways to change.

Some form of conflict, whether expressed overtly or covertly, is seen in virtually every couple in treatment. A therapist can make a variety of mistakes when dealing with conflict. Some of the more common mistakes are:

- Colluding with a couple who avoids dealing with conflict and anger
- Losing control of the session by letting conflict take over
- Blocking one or both partners from expressing anger and conflict out of fear, anxiety, and other countertransference reactions
- Trying to get the couple to resolve the problem too quickly
- Offering only a behavioral approach rather than addressing feelings, cognitions, family of origin, and so on
- Failing to obtain client agreement to a systematic, well-organized treatment plan to resolve conflict and anger
- Failing to manage the expression of client anger so as to minimize its destructiveness and make it useful

How Conflict Manifests

In session, concerns about conflict will manifest overtly, covertly, or usually some combination of both. Many couples will explicitly state that they cannot resolve conflict and want treatment to improve their skills. Others have problems with issues such as sex, money, parenting, or in-laws that result from lack of agreement or conflict. In the former case, the therapist knows that the clients identify conflict as a direct problem. In the latter case, the pattern of conflict or difference may need to be highlighted for the couple.

At the start of therapy, many clients try to make a good impression on the therapist and talk about their conflicts in a manner bereft of any personal investment or emotional intensity. They may even be quite adept at agreeing with each other even as they describe, often in brutal detail, how they do not agree with each other. The therapist may notice an incongruity between the descriptions of verbal, emotional, and sometimes even physical disagreement and the matter-of-fact way those descriptions are reported.

Clients may have different reasons for presenting information in this manner. They may be hoping to look "right" compared to their partner, or to appear reasonable and rational. They may simply be afraid that the therapist may decide that one or the other of them is "mentally ill," something their partner may very well welcome or even suggest overtly. Another reason may be that they are fearful of their own affect.

At home, couples may escalate conflict quickly by replacing rationality with emotion. Partners may display destructive behavior such as wanting to win at all costs, having temper tantrums, or name calling. One partner may be hyperrational and wish to score points with the therapist, whereas the other partner may control his or her emotionality for fear that the therapist will judge him or her in the same way the partner does. For this partner, it may be safer to maintain an intellectual position rather than let down his or her guard. Presenting information in a socially desirable manner, however, can be quite difficult for clients to maintain for very long, especially when the therapist pursues their reasons for seeking therapy. A couple's behavior will often change radically and rapidly when emotional issues are addressed.

Other couples do not start sessions with social niceties and calm conversation but rather with emotional exchanges. The couple may hardly even be seated before they enact their real-life dynamics in front of the therapist. They may expose their own and their partner's worst traits with great glee. The therapist may feel uncomfortable as he or she listens to these painful exchanges but will gain a great deal of information about the couple.

Deciding How Much Conflict to Allow in Session

Although spontaneous enactments of conflict can provide the therapist with valuable information, they are also risky. If therapists do not manage the intensity of conflict in session, they may lose control of the session. As a result, the couple will lose the ability to resolve the problem and participate in therapy productively. Couples may also drop out of therapy prematurely if they perceive that the level and type of conflict is the same in the therapy session as it is at home. They may become discouraged when they think the therapist is unable to reduce volatility or protect them from their angry outbursts. The therapist must find a way to allow them expression within the limits of emotional safety, which is often no small task. The therapist's second task is to help the couple learn how to manage conflict at home.

When anger and conflict begin to spiral out of control, the therapist must have a therapeutic roadmap to follow. Some therapists are not comfortable with exercising their authority and structuring the session. The therapist can set ground rules at the beginning of treatment such as no name-calling, sarcasm, or refusing to take turns. The couple can be reminded of these ground rules when they begin to violate them. Have a plan for how to proceed. The best strategies are preventive, so that the anger is kept in check. When the couple jumps from topic to topic, remember not to become engrossed in the content of what is said but rather to attend to the process by which the couple fights. Use the cognitive techniques discussed in Chapter 7 to reduce emotionality. The following excerpt shows how to transition to this technique.

Wife: Whenever he gets angry, I want to hide.

Husband: Yeah, I want to talk about it and she shuts down.

Therapist: When your husband gets angry, what are you saying to yourself about his anger?

Wife: What do you mean?

Therapist: What does the voice in your head say about what his anger means?

Wife: (*long pause*) I think it means he doesn't love me.

Therapist: That is quite a leap. So, it has dire consequences for you. He can't be angry with you and love you. (*The wife nods yes*) Where do you think you got this idea?

Wife: (*long pause*) Maybe my family. My father got angry and just left all of us. We never knew where he was.

This transcript shows how the therapist was able to uncover one cognition the wife held about anger that overdetermined its meaning for her. Additionally, the therapist was able to quickly trace the root of the cognition.

Another common error in working with couples is avoiding conflict. The therapist must be willing to deal with the problem directly. Therapists should not avoid conflict when the anger is covert and the couple is sending mixed messages about whether they want to deal with it, nor should they minimize anger or shift topics when the anger is overt and intense. These countertransference reactions on the part of the therapist are hurtful to the couple. One way therapists can become more self-aware is to note whether they block anger with the couple or with the male or female partner. Therapists may find that they attend to or block anger differently depending on the gender. This reaction may have roots in personal family of origin or other relationships. Therapists may have been reared in families that were fairly devoid of anger or they may believe that anger only has destructive consequences. If therapists are uncomfortable with dealing with highly conflicted couples, they may make therapeutic decisions that are less than optimal. For example, they may recommend separating the couple for individual therapy. This may reduce the therapist's anxiety, but it leaves the clients in a lurch. They still have to deal with each other at home, and the ultimate outcome may well be a therapist-assisted divorce. This is definitely not good therapy.

The following transcript illustrates how a therapist may block the expression of anger to the clients' detriment:

Husband: (*yelling at wife*) Stop whining! *Stop!*
Wife: We came here so you would listen to me.
Husband: (*yelling*) But you are whining again! All you do is cry and scream.
Therapist: You need to calm down so your wife can get through to you.

The therapist in this example failed to validate the husband's anger. There was no exploration of why the husband felt so angry or of his prior experiences with anger and conflict. The therapist may have believed he needed to protect the wife from the husband's intense anger, but in fact it was he who could not tolerate that level of affect in the session.

It is important to know how to explore anger without letting conflict spiral out of control during the session. The following section goes into more detail about the various ways therapists can manage clients' anger and conflict.

How to Manage Conflict

The effective management of couples' anger in session involves several steps. First, to express anger appropriately, couples must recognize that anger and conflict are normal in a relationship and not necessarily indicative of the relationship's inevitable doom. It is not a matter of *whether* there is anger and conflict but of when anger and conflict occur and how they are expressed. The normalization of anger and conflict is important for some couples because they believe that it should not be part of the relationship. There still remains a powerful romantic love mythology that strongly supports the belief that good relationships do not have conflict. Once the couple understands that conflict is a part of any close relationship, especially a couple relationship, the therapist can teach the partners how to express their anger more appropriately.

Second, each individual must recognize his or her role in the conflict. By using a neutral stance, the therapist can balance the alliance and hold each member of the couple responsible for his or her actions. Using "I" statements is a useful way of helping individuals take responsibility. One appropriate expression of anger is a statement like "I felt angry when...." This contrasts with "You made me angry," which implies blame. The expression of anger must be done well. For clients who have become adept at distancing themselves from experiencing emotion, the therapist may need to encourage them to express more of what they feel rather than less. With more intensely expressive clients, the therapist may have to help them calm down, isolate the source of the anger, and decide whether the anger is proportionate to the event.

Third, clients must question whether the meaning they assign to their partner's behavior is accurate or a helpful way to see the issue. For example, when a small infraction produces an intense response, something else is happening. Perhaps the infraction has been an ongoing problem that has been discussed multiple times without change. Perhaps the partner has ignored a problem until so much anger has built up that he or she explodes. For some partners, the fact that the problem keeps occurring means that their partner does not listen to them, respect them, or even love them. This overlay of meaning tends to intensify the feelings. The therapist might suggest that the couple adopt a commitment to assuming goodwill and intent by the partner (Weeks & Treat, 2001).

Fourth, the therapist must instill hope that the couple can learn new ways of coping. Changing behavior is difficult. The couple may have differing attitudes toward change that affect how ready each is to commit to change (Prochaska & DiClemente, 1988). The problem may be long-standing and the solutions that have been attempted have not worked. However, if the couple feels hopeful that they can make an effort to apply new skills consistently, improvements can be made.

Address Anger

Most conflict-resolution programs are behavioral and do not consider the cognitive, affective, attitudinal, and family of origin aspects of anger and conflict (see Weeks & Treat, 2001). Any problematic behavior should be considered from various viewpoints; the clinician may find that some are more relevant than others. Ask the couple a number of questions about anger, such as: What is anger? Who is allowed to be angry? How do you express your anger? How long does it last? Has anyone ever been physically hurt as a result of anger? (Further discussion about these questions is available in Weeks & Treat, 2001.) These types of questions give a much better picture of how anger is managed by the couple.

The first question regarding the nature of anger is a deceptively simple one, but it usually gives the therapist important information about the couple's attitude toward anger. Some common answers are:

- Anger is when you feel like exploding.
- Anger is when you feel annoyed.
- Anger is when you feel helpless.
- Anger just leads to more anger.
- We never resolve anything.
- Anger leads to hurt, sometimes for days.
- I am afraid of my anger or my partner's anger.
- If you don't dwell on it, it will go away.
- Anger and conflict would mean we have a bad marriage.

If the couple views anger negatively, they will see it as a destructive force and will not deal with it directly. They may reduce tension by exploding from time to time or go to great lengths to avoid anger. If the therapist tries to teach them skills or have them talk in the session, they will resist. This makes functional sense: Why deal with conflict directly if anger and conflict only have destructive, hurtful, nonproductive, and alienating consequences? They will act as if it is better to avoid the process and have a peaceful outcome than to start it and have a negative outcome.

The therapist must assess their attitude carefully, oftentimes asking them straightforward questions such as: What is your attitude toward anger and conflict? What do you think will be the outcome of getting angry and being in conflict? Do you think anger and conflict can be a constructive force in your relationship? Many couples believe that anger and conflict lead to bad outcomes, even divorce. The therapist must spend as much time as is necessary to change this negative view. Bibliotherapy can be useful; clients have a tendency to believe what they read. Books such as *The Dance of Anger* (Goldhor-Lerner, 1997), *Your Perfect Right* (Alberti & Emmons, 2001), or *Why Marriages Succeed or Fail* (Gottman, 1994a) can help change their attitudes in a positive direction. Therapists can also discuss how anger can be a constructive force in a relationship. They might describe how conflict is inevitable and explain that couples who learn to work it out are stronger, feel more united and close, experience a sense of cooperation, and can see that each other is willing to give for the sake of the relationship.

One very powerful method of challenging the couple's belief that anger is inherently negative is to look for exceptions. Solution-focused therapy maintains that there are almost always exceptions to clients' problems but that the clients tend not to see them (de Shazer, 1985). Some persistent questioning by the therapist about times when anger did not lead to a negative outcome (first in life in general, and then specifically in their relationship) can do much to show the clients that their views of anger are not entirely accurate. Identifying some situations where anger was not necessarily negative will have more impact on clients than the therapist's best teaching. By identifying exceptions, the couple will realize that they have, on at least a few occasions, experienced anger and conflict in a positive, or at least nonnegative, way. The therapist can acknowledge this fact and point out that continued avoidance will only perpetuate the negative behavior, false beliefs, and uncomfortable feelings. They must struggle together to change the pattern. Once they begin to see that the process can and does work, they will be more able to assimilate more positive beliefs.

Partners do not enter relationships with a blank slate regarding anger and conflict. They have already learned the essential lessons from their parents and other significant relationships. DeMaria, Weeks, and Hof (1999) created the "anger genogram" to give couples a better understanding of the beliefs, behaviors, and thoughts they have developed about anger from their early experiences. The early mental template on which subsequent experience is interpreted or imposed can be revealed by questions such as: Who in your family was allowed to be angry? Who was not allowed to be angry? How did your parents deal with anger/conflict? What did you learn about anger/conflict? For example, some families are conflict-avoidant. The partners will report that their parents never fought openly or, to their knowledge, rarely or never fought at all.

A case example will help to clarify the power of intergenerational beliefs about conflict. Linda, a woman who sought therapy shortly after divorcing her husband, Tim, said that to her knowledge her parents never fought and that she was told it was better to smile than be angry. Whenever she asked her parents how things were going for them, they would proclaim that everything was "fine," even when it was clear that they were having a problem or were angry with each other. Linda's predisposition to avoid conflict had fit in a complementary manner with her husband's domineering behavior. They maintained a stable relationship because Tim knew that Linda would comply with his demands and would not express her anger directly or indirectly. The arrangement worked for him, but it cost her a great deal. If she did not like something when they were together, she would hold back tears, even though she cried when describing these interactions with her husband to others. Like many women, Linda expressed her anger through quiet frustration and desperation. After many years of marriage, she exploded with anger and quickly obtained a divorce. Much of the initial work in her therapy was to help her access her legitimate feelings of anger, own them, and later let her husband know that she was angry about past events and inappropriate behaviors as she moved through the divorce process.

Although the therapist has to make sure that anger does not get out of control in the session, consistently blocking a partner from expressing anger will only intensify the anger over the long term if another means of working through it is not made available. Therapists who do not appreciate why an individual feels anger may be particularly prone to blocking its expression. Therapists must remember that clients have a lot more information about the context surrounding anger in their relationship. One of the more infuriating things for clients to be told is that their feelings are inappropriate or irrational. For example, suppose a wife becomes infuriated with her husband when he forgets to mail a letter for her. The therapist may think that the wife's anger is not proportionally related to the event triggering it and thus block the wife's expression of it. However, the intensity of the wife's anger is probably related to factors other than the immediate event. Minimizing the feeling because it does not appear justified is a potentially therapy-killing mistake. It would be wiser for the therapist to use the wife's anger as a point of departure to explore underlying feelings and the longer-term relational dynamics that have given rise to it.

Discover the Underlying Feelings and Vulnerabilities

Once the therapist has established sufficient structure in the session so that the clients can participate somewhat calmly, he or she must help the clients identify the underlying feelings associated with the conflict. This may take some time, as most couples are more comfortable expressing outrage or moral indignation than deeper vulnerabilities. One way to understand the underlying feelings is to construct an "anger iceberg" (Weeks & Treat, 2001). Explain to couples that anger is just the tip of an iceberg of feelings. Elaborate by saying that there are many feelings underlying and associated with angry feelings. The angry partner is asked to construct a list of those underlying feelings in the session and to continue assessing him- or herself at home. When the underlying feelings are not acknowledged or expressed, they get channeled through anger. The underlying feelings are usually those that are difficult to acknowledge to oneself or the partner. The client would rather disown them and use anger as a defense. In other words, as long as the client is angry, he or she can blame another person instead of acknowledging and looking at his or her own feelings.

Underlying feelings that people commonly mask with anger include fear (particularly fear of intimacy), hurt, shame, embarrassment, dependence, guilt, remorse, sadness or depression, and rejection or abandonment. Once the underlying feelings have been accessed, cataloged, and accepted, that partner can begin to express the feelings to the partner. The following transcript shows how to use the anger iceberg technique.

Husband: I get so angry when people don't respect me.
Therapist: Think of your anger as the tip of an iceberg. You can only see the tip. What are the feelings underneath it? Take your time, there are probably a lot of feelings down there.
Husband: I feel ... well, like people are ignoring me, that I don't count or I'm not worthy.
Therapist: Worthy?
Husband: I hate asking people for anything. I want to please them and I want them to like me.
Therapist: What feeling would you call that?
Husband: I don't know, maybe self-esteem.

Uncovering the underlying feelings also helps to foster understanding and a willingness to listen on the part of the other partner. The expression of anger from one partner tends to elicit anger from the other partner. When the underlying feeling is expressed, a different response is likely (Weeks & Treat, 2001). First, the acknowledgment in oneself of the feeling may dissipate the anger entirely so that it is no longer part of the interaction. Second, if anger is expressed it is usually much less intense because it is not being used as a substitute for another feeling or set of feelings.

John and Marcy illustrate these ideas. They began therapy by saying that they could never resolve anything. They were an older couple and each had been married before and had also had prior long-term relationships. Every couple of weeks Marcy would say something that offended John and he would respond by saying their relationship was a mistake. Once the argument was started, they got angry. Marcy became frustrated because John did not want to talk further to resolve the matter. He would cut her off with a blaming statement and then leave. When this occurred before they were married, he would spend the night at his house. After marriage, he would leave the house and drive around for an hour or two.

John's history revealed what might be happening. He had spent a dozen years in a relationship with one woman who was hypercritical. In addition, he noted that his mother was also hypercritical, cold, and rejecting. A close examination of his pattern of relating to both these women showed that when John felt ignored or did not receive adequate attention or affection, he felt unloved and rejected. He would never verbalize these underlying feelings in his discussions with Marcy. Instead, he was only aware of his anger, and that was the only emotion he expressed. His anger drove Marcy further away, thereby exacerbating the pattern of behavior and reinforcing his underlying fears and feelings. With assistance from the therapist, John was able to acknowledge that his anger at Marcy usually followed a period of time when he did not feel loved. Rather than react in the way he had in the past, he used these incidents to trigger himself to express his loneliness and need for attention. This defused his anger. They were then able to discuss other ways to meet his underlying needs for companionship.

Skills Training

Once the therapist has worked on the previously mentioned issues, the couple may require some skills training. According to Weeks and Treat (2001), the first step is to identify their "bad" fighting habits. Each partner is asked to identify what he or she does in an argument that is not helpful. At this point therapists may also inquire about certain habits based on their observations of client behavior in session or on reports they have heard about the couple's fights. The aim is to get each partner to commit to something he or she can do that is constructive rather than relying on old habits. The therapist helps the partners each perfect an alternative behavior and tells them that they are 100% responsible for themselves. This means that if one partner reverts to former unhelpful habits, the other partner still has no excuse to violate his or her own commitment to change. Partners can help each other keep to commitments by commenting in a nonjudgmental and nonblaming way on the bad habits they see in each other. This aspect of the treatment must be handled carefully or the partners will start a "he said, she said" argument over whether it is really something that they do. Asking them permission to do this part of the therapy is useful, and adding some humor helps them recognize that they are both human and have been operating with old beliefs and behaviors.

The therapist next teaches them a fair fighting model. Most of the models are behaviorally oriented and fairly similar. The model described here is also behaviorally oriented but a little more comprehensive. (More detailed information about the model can be obtained from *Couples in Treatment* by Weeks & Treat, 2001). The model includes two major phases, which are described to the couple before the steps are taught. Emphasize that unless phase I is complete, the couple will not be successful in phase II. Clients, especially men, have a strong tendency to skim over the first phase. During phase I, the couple shares their ideas about the problem and their feelings. They attempt to come to some agreement about the definition of the problem or, at a minimum, acknowledge each other's perceptions and feelings about the problem. For some problems, the couple only completes phase I, for example in situations that cannot be changed. In these cases, the couple must agree to disagree and learn to cope with the feelings associated with differences. A wife and mother may need to work because the family needs her income. The husband and wife may have conflicts over her working, but both know it is a financial necessity. They can certainly benefit from the steps in the first phase, but if the situation cannot be changed, phase II will not apply.

Phase II is the problem-solving part of the model. It involves discussing different solutions, choosing one, talking about problems that may arise when they implement the solution (including how each could sabotage the agreement), and congratulating each other on sticking to the process. The outcome of phase II is a behavioral change.

Couples are given graduated homework exercises. They start with conflicts that are roleplays or are topics they both agree are not emotionally laden. After demonstrating competence with these topics in the session, they begin to work on the more difficult problems at home. The couple should be forewarned that they might need to struggle to follow the rules of fair fighting at home. Sometimes couples are not capable of controlling their anger. In those cases, they are told that either partner—the one who is getting angry or the one on the receiving end of the anger—can call a time out for at least 20 minutes without question. The person who calls the time out is also responsible for setting a time to reinitiate the conversation. Otherwise, the time out just becomes a way of unilaterally terminating the conflict, which may be a part of the problem itself. If they start again and anger takes over, they are instructed to save the argument for the session. We recommend a 20-minute time out based on Gottman's (1994a, 1994b) work on anger showing that it takes at least 20 minutes for the partners' physiological arousal to return to baseline.

The following transcript demonstrates aspects of this skills training approach with a couple that was well into the process.

Therapist: You both have done a lot of hard work in getting a handle on how you have tended to deal with conflict in the past, which wasn't working very well for you. Roger, you have identified that your family experience taught you that anger was the only safe emotion to show, and you became a master at using it to protect your vulnerability and to control other people, including Diane. You were really good at intimidating her with it.

Roger: That's true. But that was what being a man was, as far as I knew.

Diane: I have to give him some credit, but he's got a ways to go still.

Therapist: No doubt. And Diane, you learned in your background to use silence and withdrawal as a means to protect yourself, and with Roger, that was perfect because he could be really hard to deal with. But then you'd get back at him by freezing him out long after he'd stopped being angry, and you punished him for his anger by not reciprocating when he'd try to get closer again. And you've taken it out on him by cheating on the budget and not being interested in sex much.

Diane: (*chuckling*) I guess I've given as good as I got. Just differently, that's all.

Therapist: So it seemed.

Roger: I don't think so. I think I was better at being a jerk than she was.

Diane: I was sneakier.

Roger: Yeah.

Therapist: Maybe you were, but that's all part of the old script. Now you're learning a new one, and it's not always easy. I'd like to ask you to talk about the budget again, because that's been a consistent area where there's been trouble, even this week. We need to come to some consensus on how to make it work better.

Roger: And then we can talk about sex?

Diane: (*laughing*) Not so fast, mister! Money first, sex maybe later.

Therapist: (*laughing*) I'm not commenting on what that just sounded like. (*All laugh*) Okay, as I recall, you had agreed to each operate on a hundred dollars a week in cash and not use plastic or write checks for anything other than bills, or unless you both agreed on a specific purchase.

Both: That's right.

Therapist: But then last week, Diane, you admitted you charged a couple of things on the debit card after using all your cash, without telling Roger.

Diane: Yeah ... I did. I knew I wasn't supposed to, but ...

Therapist: Roger, I'd like you to help Diane process through how she made a bad decision, both as accountability for her and also for what effect that had for both of you.

Roger: She knows. I was ticked.

Diane: He sure was.

Therapist: Right. So how did you handle it differently than before?

Roger: Honestly, I was this close to just going off on her again, but I remembered the time out thing, and so I just said I needed some space.

Therapist: How did you convey that?

Roger: I don't know exactly what I said, but I told her that I wasn't ready to talk about it yet. We still haven't really.

Therapist: (*to wife*) What did he do?

Diane: I could tell he was mad when he came home because he didn't look at me or say hello or anything normal. He had that "keep out of my way" attitude he gets. I assumed it was because he'd been to the ATM and saw my charges. That's part of what doesn't make sense to me. I know he goes to the bank a few times a week to make deposits and I knew he'd see what I'd done. So why did I do it? I don't know. I asked him what was wrong, and he noticeably stops and says he's not ready to discuss it with me, and then it's almost worse because he doesn't rip my head off like I expect him to. I actually felt like I wanted to criticize him for being cold toward me when he got home, you know, to get some kind of reaction.

Roger: (*to Diane*) You wanted me to punish you?

Diane: (*to Roger*) I don't know. Maybe. It's what I've come to expect from you.

Therapist: (*to Diane*) Oooh, nice zinger, Diane. You just nailed Roger for his past treatment of you, which, by the way, he did not do this time.

Diane: I did? (*looks at Roger*)

Roger: Well, not really.

Therapist: Roger, I think you're backing off all of a sudden. Did you hear what she just said? That had to sting.

Roger: Umm ... yeah, I guess it did.

Therapist: Would you tell Diane how that felt?

Roger: (*to Diane*) I hate how I've treated you with my anger so much. I'm really tired of being angry. (*pause*) I'm not saying how that felt, am I?

Therapist: Not quite. (*pause*) Try this: How did it feel for you to discover that Diane had overspent again? I bet the feelings are in the same family.

Roger: (*to Diane*) I felt... angry. It was like you hung me out to dry. We've been working so hard to get our finances together, and just when we look like we're making some progress, you torpedo it.

Therapist: That doesn't quite sound like anger.

Roger: No. It's more like... betrayal. Yeah, that's it. It sucks! (*to Diane*) It's like you don't care enough to work with me on this. It's our life, our future, and I'm on my own with it when I thought we were in it together. That ...(*becomes teary*)

Therapist: (*softly*) That sounds like abandonment.

Roger: (*nodding*) Yeah. (*Therapist looks at Diane*)

Diane: Roger, I'm sorry. I ...I don't know what else to say.

Therapist: Can you validate his feelings?

Diane: It's awful.

Therapist: And ...?

Diane: What?

Therapist: Try a little deeper. What's it like for him? Look at him and tell him what you're hearing from him.

Diane: (*to Roger*) You feel betrayed. Like I let you down. Like ... I left you?

Roger: Sort of ...yeah. (*pause*)

Therapist: (*to Diane*) What does being abandoned, being left, feel like to you?

Diane: (*tears up*) It's ...the worst thing in the world. (*Diane takes Roger's hand.*)

Therapist: You both know what that feels like. Even if it's from a simple budget. (*There is a long pause while Diane and Roger gain control of their emotions*) That's pretty powerful stuff, and hard work. I'm proud of what you both showed—a lot of vulnerability and empathy. That's a foundation for your marriage that will last. (*pause*) So, how can we make that kind of abandonment less a threat with the budget?

Diane: I have to not be stupid. I can't be so selfish.

Therapist: (*to Roger*) Do you think she was being selfish?

Roger: No, I don't. I think she's beating herself up, maybe, so I won't?

Therapist: Interesting thought.

Diane: Stop trying to rescue me. I made a commitment and I broke it. It might be easier for me to have you mad at me than for me to take responsibility for what I did, but if we're going to make changes, we both have to play our part. I have to play mine.

Therapist: Wow. I'm impressed. So, how can you help each other stick with the budget commitment? (*long pause*)

Roger: I guess... I guess it basically comes down to personal discipline. That's not one of Diane's strong points, at least with money. She's kind of like a kid that way. When she sees something she wants, she has a hard time saying no to herself, and it's cost us a lot.

Diane: Wait a minute. It's not always been just me. You've had your moments, too.

Roger: I know, but I don't think it's been split down the middle, you know.

Diane: That's not fair, Roger!

Therapist: What's happening right now?

Both: What do you mean?

Therapist: Literally in 30 seconds, you went from collaboration and empathy to insensitivity, attack, and defensiveness. That was fast! The temperature's rising quickly. What are you going to do? (*long pause*)

Roger: I need to help my wife.

Diane: And I want your help.

Therapist: Good. Good start. Keep going. Roger? (*pause*)

Roger: Well, I have a thought, but I'm hesitant to say it because I don't want to fight about it or hurt your feelings, Diane.

Diane: I'm listening.

Therapist: Remember that great line you said about playing your part in responsibility and all? Here's where it gets real.

Diane: Okay, okay! I'm really listening. (*looks at Roger*) I promise!

Roger: Man, this is going to sound like a slam. (*long pause*)

Therapist: I appreciate your sensitivity, but you have to find the middle ground between backing off and attacking her. You can switch gears like nobody.

Roger: Yeah. I do keep it interesting, huh? (*Therapist gestures toward wife*) Right. (*deep breath*) Okay, what if we take all your cards except one, and we put them away? I heard about putting credit cards in blocks of ice to make them harder to use. We could do that. You could keep one for an absolute emergency if you promise to not use it. We can even give you a little extra cash each week if it would help.

Diane: I don't know what to think about that. It makes sense, but I feel like I'm 10 and my allowance is being taken away.

Therapist: Talk more about that if you can.

Diane: I guess for me having the choice to use the cards really matters more than I thought. I don't like the limit of the cash. It makes me feel like, I don't know, like I'm not really an adult somehow. It reminds me of how strict my parents were with money. Once I had my own, I felt more independent. I liked that a lot.

Therapist: That's not unusual at all. Money translates quickly to freedom, and adulthood and freedom usually go together, right? So, if you have money limits, then I can see how you'd feel less of an adult.

Roger: But doesn't being an adult also mean being able to handle money?

Diane: You're right. I don't know why that side of it is harder for me.

Therapist: We can examine that issue more fully as we go, but for now, what do you think of Roger's idea?

Diane: I think I can live with it. (*pause*) Part of me is feeling like he's getting a better deal, though. I'm surprised I feel almost ... jealous.

Roger: Because I get to keep my cards? I don't get to use them, just like you.

Diane: I know. But I have to trust you about that.

Therapist: Good insight. You do have to trust Roger. And that means, Roger, that you have to be trustworthy, both with your money and, more importantly, with your wife's feelings of dependence that come from not having the cards. Can you be supportive when she's having trouble with it? She's taking a pretty large risk, and you need to meet her there. If she's more dependent on you because the symbol of freedom that money is is gone, you need to be dependable.

From there, the session focused on the specifics of Roger's emotional support of Diane and his being able to encourage her by helping her feel safe with less obvious freedom. Obstacles that could prove problematic were identified and how they would be handled were discussed.

Some Other Interventions

Gottman (1994b) noted that negativity could stymie an otherwise stable relationship. His research indicated that in healthy, stable relationships couples have at least five positive interactions for every negative one. He named four strategies to interrupt the cycle of negativity: calming yourself (including taking time outs), learning to speak and listen nondefensively, validating each other, and repeatedly practicing positive techniques until they become second nature.

The therapist must assess when using conflict-resolution techniques is appropriate. Occasionally, therapists may encounter couples for which conflict resolution work is not useful. These individuals tend to see problems so differently that no common ground can be found and their conflict is incessant. Their level of anger reaches rage, sometimes called "narcissistic rage." The treatment of these couples is quite different and is discussed in the next chapter.

CHAPTER NINE

Mistakes in Dealing
with Partners' Different
Perceptions

Conflict develops because two people view a problem or situation differently. It can occur in response to, for example, changes in the relationship (e.g., a partner starts working), situational stressors (chronic illness), developmental changes (transitions in the family life cycle), or perceptions of fairness in the relationship. Perceptual differences are expressed in emotions and behaviors. Couples may not agree on what the problem is, or they may differ in their descriptions, or they may see the other person's role in the problem but not their own. Couples may reduce the tension created by differences in perception by triangulating other people, including the therapist, into their conflicts. In other cases, they may live in a constant state of tension as a result of wanting to "win" at all costs. Underneath the differing perceptions are individual issues and systemic patterns. A continuum exists in the degree to which couples perceive events in the same way: Some couples agree about the kind and nature of their problems, many have some degree of disagreement, and a few agree on practically nothing. The first two groups of couples are the easiest with which to work. The third group can be among the most challenging of all couple cases, especially if the therapist lacks differentiation or has countertransferential reactions.

Several mistakes can be made in working with couples with a wide range of different perceptions of reality. These mistakes include:

- Failing to normalize different perceptions
- Failing to deal with the demoralization that some couples experience when they discover their differences
- Getting triangulated by the couple
- Not being able to see how partners project onto each other
- Not having a theoretical model to deal with narcissistically vulnerable couples

Couples may have a range of reactions to difference. Some couples, especially young ones, assume a much greater similarity of perception than actually exists. These couples may experience a sense of disappointment and loss when their expectations are not met. Others may threaten to leave the marriage. If the therapist is unable to intervene effectively or exacerbates the difference in perceptions, the partners may, at best, end up alienated from each other or, at worst, divorce each other with extreme prejudice.

Couples Who Can Agree

Couples who agree on the problem or problems and describe the problem in the same way are, of course, ideal clients. The therapist should commend their objectivity and commitment. The fact that they can agree on the nature of the problem and seek help is a sign of relationship health and their commitment to each other. These couples are generally cooperative and compliant, experience little destructive conflict, and usually have typical problems that do not include foundational threats to their relationship.

Rachael and Jim, for example, came to therapy because they wanted to become less sexually inhibited with each other. They had been married for about 15 years and reported that their only problem was that they each were reared with very negative views about sex. They realized that part of the reason they married was because neither one challenged the other to be less inhibited sexually. They were both motivated to become more educated and less inhibited, even though there was some fear associated with the unknown. Initially they showed some resistance to various homework assignments because of their fears about leaving their inhibitions behind. Once they overcame their fears, they were much more compliant and the therapy proceeded quickly and relatively smoothly.

Couples With Some Disagreements

Couples with some disagreements are the most common clients in couple therapy. These couples usually have several problems. The partners may not agree about what problems they have. In addition, when they describe something they both consider a problem, they will offer different descriptions of the problem, emphasizing aspects of it that bother each of them most and are more apparently attributable to the partner. Each partner usually sees his or her own participation in the problems mentioned by the other partner as fairly limited.

In many cases, these couples have not talked much about the problems at home. If they have, their conversations have been quite limited and tentative or have degenerated into unproductive conflict. When they respond to the therapist's questions about reasons for coming to counseling, the partners may learn that the other partner sees problems they did not know existed or realize that the list of problems is more extensive than first imagined. As a result, they feel criticized, angry, hopeless, and demoralized.

Partners typically describe the problems in different ways, even if they agree on the specific event. The therapist needs to reassure the couple that their differences in perceptions are typical by saying, for example, "You are like many of the couples we see. Each of you has a different take on the relationship. This difference in perception is normal at this stage and we will work toward sorting out these perceptions and resolving these problems." When one partner lists a number of problems that the other does not think are problems, the therapist might say, "You obviously did not know your partner felt that so many things were problems. I want to know how you feel about this. Even though you may not think these problems are real or that significant, it is important to respect your partner's feelings and perceptions. Because you're in a relationship, what is a problem for one is almost always going to turn into a problem for both. We'll need to sort out what can be done to change these perceptions so you have the relationship you want."

Another couple, Sandie and Tom, entered therapy at Sandie's insistence. They had not talked about what they were going to say before the first session. Tom said the only problem he had in the relationship was not enough sex. They could not agree on the frequency with which they currently had sex: Tom said they had sex once a month; Sandie said it was two or three times a month. She noted that at home Tom told her that they never had sex. Sandie had a list of problems. She said that Tom did not communicate with her, that she did not know how he felt about things, that he was often busy working or playing golf, that he did not give her any affection or compliments, that he was uninvolved with the children for the most part, and that he sometimes drank too much. Tom's response to her comments was that he felt blindsided by her complaints. He responded in an angry and defensive tone that if she was that unhappy she should leave the marriage.

Sandie was shocked that he was so angry and defensive and was particularly offended by his telling her to consider leaving the marriage. The therapist asked Sandie why she wanted to come to therapy, anticipating what she would probably say. She replied that she wanted to regain the passion and closeness that she once felt for Tom and make the marriage better. This response helped to calm Tom. The therapist normalized their differences in perception, as stated earlier. In addition, the therapist mentioned that women were often the emotional barometers in a relationship and usually were aware of more problems than men. At this point, instilling hope is important. The therapist may point out that none of the problems mentioned are unusual and that couples who are willing to work together can resolve issues to their mutual satisfaction. This statement gives hope and normalizes the couple's experiences. The therapist can expect a fair amount of conflict as these couples argue over whether problems are "real" or not as well as over their differing perceptions of the problems.

Couples Who Disagree on Practically Everything

This type of couple is highly reactive. Fortunately, these couples are relatively rare in treatment, but therapists may err by treating them in the same way as the first two types. They are qualitatively much different. These couples seem to disagree about almost everything and are in conflict over seemingly trivial matters constantly. They battle over all issues, regardless of importance. Their stories are very discrepant and almost seem to describe different events or experiences. One of the best indicators that a couple fits into this category is the therapist's own internal sense of confusion about the couple's stories. The therapist may also begin to wonder how the partners got into the relationship in the first place, as well as how they manage to stay!

These reactive couples are experts in trying to triangulate the therapist. Triangulation is an avoidance strategy and can have destructive consequences. For example, the couple may overtly call the therapist a referee and continually push the therapist to take one side. If the therapist does form an alliance with one partner or serves as a go-between, the couple may feel a reduction in tension but will never learn to deal with conflict. Additionally, the partner who is not being sided with may feel at a power disadvantage. These partners may also blame each other excessively for problems, thus diverting attention from resolving conflict to figuring out the cause of the problem. Finally, these couples have an extraordinary capacity to always want to "win" the battle.

Many clinicians fail to recognize the individually based issues and pathologies that dictate the systemic patterns in these couples. Many of these couples drop out after a few unproductive sessions precisely because they do not want to address the underlying individual issues. There is limited help in the literature for the therapist who wants to work with these couples. Only a few clinicians have written about the treatment of these kinds of couples with enough clarity to be helpful. Feldman (1982) was one of the first clinicians to describe this pattern. He noted that these relationships include partners with narcissistic vulnerability, meaning low levels of differentiation, and narcissistic expectation, meaning high need for being loved and adored. Narcissistically vulnerable partners generally seek ego gratification and have a very low sense of self-esteem and a fragmented sense of self. Their need for love and admiration (narcissistic expectation) is at the extreme end of the continuum and can never be fulfilled, no matter how loving, giving, and admiring the other person may be. The result is that partners are hypersensitive and believe they are being criticized nearly all the time. They become absorbed in trying to get their own needs met from the other person at all costs and lack empathy for the partner.

The core concept in Feldman's (1982) model is projective identification. Projective identification is the combination of two ego-defense mechanisms: splitting and projection. Narcissistically vulnerable people split off the parts of themselves they do not like—for example, their feelings of low self-esteem, unworthiness, and unlovability. They then project those characteristics onto the other person and negatively identify with that person. In other words all the qualities they disown in themselves are placed in the partner and then are criticized as being faults in the partner. This leads to extreme cognitive distortions. These distortions are what contributes to the therapist's feeling that the situation is unreal. The combustible combination of all the factors from narcissistic vulnerability to cognitive distortion accounts for the reactive mutual conflict in these couples. Once the perception of criticism begins, arguments quickly spiral beyond anything proportional to the event that occurred.

Feldman's (1982) article was much stronger on etiology than treatment. His approach to treatment stresses couple therapy, but he did mention that individual sessions at the beginning of therapy may be useful to help develop rapport with the clients, demonstrate understanding and caring by the therapist, and provide for the disclosure of information that might not be revealed in joint sessions. This position makes sense in light of the fact that once the partners are together they immediately begin projecting onto each other. The level of differentiation of each partner must improve before any progress in couple therapy can be made.

He described his overall approach to treatment as integrative-systemic-behavioral and psychodynamic. He did not propose any new techniques or strategies but suggested combinations of different existing treatment strategies for the factors he identified. The components of his model and their treatment are briefly reviewed here:

- *Narcissistic vulnerability.* The therapist shows concern and respect for each partner. Empathetic understanding of each partner's thoughts and feelings is demonstrated with the message that each person is worthwhile and his or her thoughts and feelings are important. Emotional awareness training is utilized to help each partner recognize the hurt feelings accompanying the conflict at the time of the conflict and how these hurtful feelings are rooted in the past.
- *Blocked empathy.* Empathy training is used to enhance each partner's understanding of the other's thoughts and feelings.

The focus is on the behavior that elicits the hurt and requests for what the partner can do in the future. It is not on the hurtful interaction itself, because that would lead to an intensification of the hurt and an escalation of the conflict.

- *Narcissistic expectations.* Cognitive awareness training is used to help the partners focus on their narcissistically unrealistic expectations and how they are related to their projections.
- *Cognitive distortions.* Cognitive awareness training is also used to facilitate each partner's understanding of the thoughts and images associated with the conflict. Partners are taught to self-monitor what they are thinking (projecting) during the conflict.
- *Narcissistic rage.* Partners are taught how to calm themselves using self-instruction training. They say things to themselves such as "calm down, you're losing control" and "what am I thinking that is making me feel so much anger and rage?"
- *Conflict.* Training in behaviorally oriented problem-solving techniques and behavioral contracting is employed to deal with the conflict. These techniques involve learning to identify the problems in specific behavioral terms and develop a behavioral contract to change the dysfunctional pattern of behavior.

In his earlier work on intimacy anxiety, Feldman (1979) noted that couples develop a collusive way of relating that protects them from having to experience some form of anxiety related to being more intimate. Using a strongly systemic focus, Middelberg (2001) extended the idea of intimacy anxiety and identified some common projective identification patterns (which she termed "dances") that dysfunctional couples use to protect themselves. Middelberg employed the same core concept of projective identification. According to her theory, partners are internally conflicted and cannot hold both the good and the bad concepts of themselves simultaneously. Therefore, they engage in splitting behaviors and projections. If one partner sees him- or herself as all good, the partner will be all bad and vice versa. The internal conflicts are then played interpersonally in the relationship conflict.

Middelberg (2001) identified five common dances that are based on projective identification:

- *The dance of conflict.* Middelberg's description of this dance is virtually identical to that of Feldman (1979). The two partners have a high degree of narcissistic vulnerability. When one partner experiences criticism or lack of empathy/attention, his or her narcissistic rage is ignited and a fight quickly escalates. The partner's underlying fear is that he or she will experience repressed negative self-images if narcissistic defenses fail.
- *The dance of distance.* Middelberg believes there are two underlying components in this dynamic: withdrawal from the other, who is seen as "all bad," and the belief that getting angry with the other partner will destroy him or her and as a result destroy both of them. To avoid intimacy anxiety, these partners use schizoid defense strategies such as withdrawal and fantasy. They fear that if they become too close they will be engulfed or enmeshed. Because there is no difference between the self and the other, they believe the destruction of one would lead to the destruction of the other.
- *The pursuer/avoider dance.* This is a common pattern in which one partner pursues with the emotion and the other distances with intellectualization. The pursuer seeks connection to meet his or her narcissistic needs. The avoider feels overwhelmed by trying to meet these needs, fears losing his or herself, and wants to deny dependency, which is considered a fatal flaw.
- *The overresponsible/underresponsible dance.* These couples are often in caretaker/patient or parent/child relationships.

The overresponsible partner disowns the need to be taken care of and the underresponsible partner disowns the need to be competent, self-sufficient, and caretaking. They strive to keep a polarized system in order to avoid the anxiety over owning aspects of themselves they have discarded.

- *The dance of triangulation.* What is unusual about triangulation in this case is that the splitting or projection takes place from two people onto a third. For example, one partner might see the triangulated person as "all good," whereas the other sees that person as "all bad" or the one who deserves to receive all the anger.

Middelberg's (2001) treatment goal is to help each partner reclaim the disowned parts of self. Therapists accomplish this goal by stopping the collusive dance, helping the partners understand what they are defending themselves against, and working to resolve the internal issues. Middelberg's approach starts treatment at the interpersonal level by identifying the pattern of behavior and then works toward resolving the intrapsychic aspects that create and maintain the behavior. Her article can be given as bibliotherapy to clients, especially if they are sophisticated lay readers of therapeutic literature.

Weeks and Treat (2001) also discussed this pattern of extreme behavior. Their theoretical model is similar to that of Feldman (1982). The key concepts in their theory of this behavior are narcissistic wounds, introjects or projective identification, repetition compulsion (the need to repeat the same pattern of early narcissistic behavior), negative and externalizing attributions, a lack of congruent communication, and lack of empathy. All these factors lead to gross differences in perception and conflict.

For example, Rob and Gwen were a highly reactive and narcissistically wounded couple. Rob was one of 10 children in a poor family. He received little attention and love. Gwen was reared in a wealthy family by cold and rejecting parents. She was raised by several different nannies. Both felt they were not worthy of being loved or understood by others, yet they both projected some degree of narcissism to the outside world and narcissistic expectation toward each other. They competed over who was most needy by making outrageous demands on each other. There was constant tension and conflict over the smallest of issues. Overtly, they said they wanted to see who could win. Covertly, they each wanted the attention of the other, but the only way they knew how to get it was through an argument. Each one would provoke the other with complaints that he or she knew would not be accepted by the other. On the one hand, this contributed to each one feeling rejected, but on the other, if they could win or get the other partner to accept their complaint they would experience victory in that their need for approval, understanding, and acceptance had been validated.

In order to treat these types of couples, the therapist can follow the seven-step treatment model developed by Weeks and Treat (2001):

1. Show constant empathy and care and model differentiation for the couple. Reversals, regressions, or setbacks are normalized and paradoxically predicted.
2. Relate the content of their arguments to early unconscious schemata that organize current emotions and thoughts of abandonment, unlovability, incompetence, and so on. This cognitive technique enables the couple to see what triggers their vulnerability.
3. Relate the unconscious negative thoughts about self to the family of origin. The roots of this pattern are deeply embedded in the family. Early family interactions led them to develop a poor self-image and differentiation. This technique reduces blame toward the partner and puts it in context.
4. Have the couples externalize and label their negative self-images and statements. Making the undifferentiated hurt and vulnerability conscious and objectifying it lets them distance from it and take control over themselves.

5. Help the couple see the negative repetitive cycles and the unconscious distortions. The therapist must actively provide feedback, connect the present feelings and thoughts to the past, and encourage congruent communication.

6. Encourage each partner to interpret the other partner's behavior in different ways. These interpretations should move from negative to neutral or positive. The couple learns to block and reject negative projections.

7. Ask each partner to take responsibility for expressing appropriate emotional needs rather than insisting on some predetermined behavior on the part of the other partner. The simple act of saying "I missed you" to a partner rather than "you must take care of me" is a significant move away from narcissistic expectation.

Carla and Bill were a couple who displayed narcissistic vulnerability. They disagreed constantly and were hurt over almost everything the other said. Each one hoped the therapist would side with him or her. The therapist needed to maintain neutrality yet show empathy and caring for each one. This involved making frequent reflective statements and statements of empathy, as well as maintaining a supportive attitude. The couple wanted to pull the therapist into their disagreements, but the therapist discussed the need to collect some early history. A genogram was done early in therapy and showed that both Bill and Carla were deeply wounded from critical parents who showed no empathy for their feelings. In fact, their feelings were constantly invalidated. It was obvious that the couple was repeating the same pattern in their marriage by interpreting events in the same way that occurred in their families of origin. The therapist helped the partners see just how wounded each had been and how they had developed an expectation of being criticized that became self-fulfilling. Once the therapist had helped them to see how they were attacking each other in anticipation of being criticized, they were able to start owning their part in feeling wounded. The therapy took months to complete with steps forward and backward along the way. Bill and Carla would slip into feeling wounded and criticized and then need to examine their projections and interpretations of statements. The therapist had to be careful not to confront too strongly but still keep reminding them of old patterns that they replayed.

As noted earlier, of all the types of relationships that a couple therapist can treat, this is the most challenging. The therapist cannot trust what is real and feels pulled by each partner to meet his or her narcissistic expectations at the expense of the other partner. Therapists lacking in differentiation will be pulled into this system as they try to satisfy each partner. This will inevitably fail, and the couple will become angry with the therapist or leave therapy. A combination of couple sessions and some individual sessions is probably the most effective strategy. The partners cannot as easily project onto the other during the individual sessions. This allows for rapport-building and confrontation without one partner losing face in front of the other. The couple sessions are designed to break the cycle stemming from narcissistic vulnerability. The therapist must be vigilant about neutrality yet support and confront the partners. These couples usually require extended treatment to achieve greater differentiation and a healthier relationship.

CHAPTER TEN

Faulty Interpretations and Reframes

As they listen to and observe the couple, therapists gain information about the content and process of what is happening in the relationship. Therapists must give feedback to the clients to check if their understanding is accurate and to incorporate further information as it is revealed. If therapists lack theoretical knowledge, are unwilling to wait long enough to establish a good relationship, or are not skillful in developing feedback, clients may reject the responses as unhelpful. The type of feedback given is not just a reflective statement for the couple but rather a reframe.

A reframe changes the emotional or cognitive meaning of the problem. It helps the couple see that they are an interlocking system of behavior rather than two separate individuals simply interacting. The two primary purposes of a reframe are to change the focus from the individuals to the system, thereby helping the partners to see their mutual contributions to the problem, and, in most cases, to change the meaning of the problem from something that is negative to something with positive connotations. Couples often resist systemic reframes because they can no longer just blame the partner for the problem.

The therapist can provide a reinterpretation of the problem in several ways, including special (bilateral) interpretations and reframes.

Therapists may make several mistakes with regard to interpretations and reframes:

- Not understanding the difference between interpretation and reframing
- Failing to have a thorough understanding of the couple's dynamics before giving an interpretation or coconstructing a reframe with the couple
- Failing to see that problems and symptoms may have useful functions for the couple
- Failing to take a systemic perspective, thereby exacerbating couple dynamics
- Confusing a systemic reframe with a linear interpretation

Interpretations

Dating back to Freud's work, the concept of interpretation is perhaps the oldest idea in psychotherapy. Interpretation has long been a mainstay of individual psychotherapy. Clients seek help from therapists to change something they have not been able to change. Therapists are assumed to have greater insight into client behavior than clients do, not only because of their broader experience with the intricacies of the human psyche, but also because their experience and analysis is based upon theory and objectivity. The purpose of interpretation is to give clients feedback about some aspect of their behavior that they do not see, usually in an explanatory fashion. Using this knowledge, clients then make different conscious choices. Interpretations are intended to produce change through insight.

Interpretations require a theoretical basis, such as analytic or dynamic therapy or the therapist's own personal theory of change. The interpretation of a behavior is filtered through this particular theoretical lens. For example, a therapist may make his or her interpretation based on clinical judgment and experience with the client, incorporating what he or she has learned about change from other clients, rather than on a particular psychological or psychotherapeutic theory. The therapist makes the interpretation from a position of authority, based on expertise, and the interpretation is imbued with a sense of truth. In a sense, the therapist is telling clients truths about themselves that they could not or would not see on their own. Suffice it to say that interpretations are useful in treatment so long as they are done well. However, there has been close and critical scrutiny of the assumption of an all-powerful and knowledgeable therapist. One of the reasons for this is that therapists may label clients as resistant if they reject the therapist's interpretation, rather than acknowledging their own inability to engender the insight necessary for change.

Prior to family therapy and its underlying paradigm of systems theory, the individual was the sole unit of treatment and the individual's internal dynamics were viewed as the basis for the problem. The early systems thinkers were both evolutionary and revolutionary in their thinking. Therapy was evolving from a focus on just the individual to the family system and larger systems in which individuals live. Unfortunately, the revolutionary part of their thinking led them to uncritically reject much of traditional individual theoretical approaches to therapy. Thus, most of the early systems thinkers eschewed individual diagnosis and treatment concepts. The concept of interpretation was, although not entirely eliminated, certainly undervalued because of the focus on the family system rather than on the individual. Most of the early family systems thinkers proclaimed that anything to do with individual therapy, such as interpretation, was misguided and obsolete.

However, even among several of the classic models of family therapy, the use of interpretation was apparent here and there. In more recent years, family therapy has rediscovered the individual, and consequently interpretation is being more commonly utilized, even within a systemic framework. Early models of relationship dynamics, such as those of Mittleman (1944), Dicks (1967), Martin (1976), and Sager (1976), included assumptions of interlocking or complementary intrapsychic patterns via which couples made their relationships work, for good or ill. Discerning and interpreting these dynamics was part of the process of treating them.

Interpretation as a Therapeutic Technique

An interpretation usually offers an explanation for behavior and is based on a level below the client's conscious awareness. Upon being made aware of this heretofore unacknowledged or unseen pattern, the individual can choose to do something different. As classically defined, the interpretation in couple therapy would be directed toward one member of the couple, with the hope of effecting awareness of something that person does or something the therapist believes is problematic for the couple relationship. In addition, because the other partner hears the interpretation, he or she may have a greater understanding and appreciation for the meaning of the person's behavior. Assuming a reservoir of goodwill exists in the relationship, the other partner has the opportunity to be supportive of change and more empathic with regard to the person's internalized and externalized struggles. This obviously has significant potential to bring about positive developments in a troubled relationship.

An example of a classic interpretation in a couple therapy context might be:

Husband: My wife is always doing things to make me angry. All I have to do is walk through the door and I can see what she has done wrong that day.
Therapist: Have you had this reaction in all your relationships?
Husband: I guess so.

Therapist: Your wife can't be that awful of a person, nor can everyone else in your past, to make you so perpetually angry. We need to explore the deeper roots of your anger.

The husband may now be aware that he is responsible for his own emotional reaction to events and that his anger is rooted in something deeper than the interactions with his wife. If the therapist makes the interpretation in front of the wife, the wife may see that the anger is not only directed toward her but also toward others and is a more pervasive pattern of behavior.

Making an interpretation in couple therapy can be useful, but there are also certain risks involved. The first risk is that the therapist unbalances therapy by interpreting one individual's behavior, especially if the interpretation can be viewed as negative or pathologizing. This can affect both partners in different ways. The one who is interpreted negatively might take on self-blame or feel that the therapist is being unfair and unbalanced. The other partner may see him- or herself as healthier and in a more powerful position and therefore disavow responsibility for his or her part in the problem or its solution. The interpretation can become another, more effective weapon for the partners to use, and the temptation to use it can be great. If the couple's underlying dynamic includes one partner's being sick and the other healthy, the mental health expert's sanction will probably add more fuel to the existing fire. This can lead the "healthier" partner to leave the relationship, decision with which the clinician and the impaired partner may reluctantly agree at best. The following interaction illustrates this point:

Husband: (*to therapist*) My wife has been seeing a psychiatrist for years for depression.

Wife: (*to therapist*) My depression has nothing to do with our marital problems.

Husband: (*to wife*) How can you say that? It has everything to do with it.

In this case the husband is trying to pathologize his wife and they are both making linear statements of causality about her depression and their relationship. In other words, they have not said anything to show that they recognize their mutual contributions to the problems.

The second risk in making interpretations is that the interpretation is completely wrong. It is essential that therapists get to know the couple before offering interpretations. Therapists should base their interpretation on enough information to have a degree of confidence in it, or be able to articulate a credible justification for it. The impact that the interpretation has on both the individual receiving it and the partner should also be carefully considered, regardless of whether the interpretation is on target or not. Clearly, if the couple relationship is not a relatively safe environment for both partners, an interpretation can leave one or both partners devastatingly vulnerable. The therapist must safeguard the couple's welfare as much as possible; when in doubt, defer or hold the interpretation.

The third risk relates to the way the interpretation is offered. The therapist should not offer the interpretation from a position of absolute authority and certainty. It is usually best to state interpretations, in a tentative way. For example, the therapist might say, "I'm wondering whether..." or "Does it make any sense to you to that...." " The partners should feel there is an implicit invitation to freely disagree with the interpretation if they think it is not correct. The following vignette illustrates some of the problems that can arise in making an interpretation.

Helen and Andrea had been dating for about a year. They got along well in all but one area, where they appeared to be in a constant power struggle. Helen described herself as stubborn and having a good sense of what was right. Andrea described herself as flexible, but strong-willed and a perfectionist. She was a particularly perfectionistic housekeeper. She had everything perfectly arranged and could not go to bed unless the kitchen was absolutely clean and tidy. She had forbidden Helen from snacking after supper because she then had to clean the entire kitchen again. Helen felt this was an unfair and absurd request. The therapist had learned that Andrea dealt with the chaos in her family of origin by becoming a perfectionist/compulsive. The therapist made an interpretation that Andrea sought to control feelings of anxiety and lack of control by being a perfectionist. Andrea accepted this interpretation, but Helen said she was not responsible for Andrea's upbringing and did not think she should have to suffer because of Andrea's childhood. The interpretation had the effect of relieving Helen from her part in the power struggle. Andrea was now the one with the problem and Helen was the suffering victim.

The onus for being open to client feedback about the accuracy and meaning of the interpretation is on the therapist. Therapists must be open to client disagreement and not view disagreement as "evidence" supporting their belief that the clients are resistant to change. They may have made an interpretation that does not fit. A good interpretation brings both partners into an examination of their processes and paves the way quite naturally for reframing.

Reframing

Reframing is probably the most widely used therapeutic strategy in couple and family therapy (Weeks & Treat, 2001). Watzlawick, Weakland, and Fisch (1974) first defined a reframe as a statement designed to change the perceptual or emotional meaning a client attributes to a behavior or event. Although Watzlawick and his colleagues were basically individual therapists and the strategy was initially used mostly with individuals, reframing quickly became adopted as a key concept in systemic therapy. There are many examples of reframing embedded in case studies in the psychotherapy literature. Interestingly, however, very little has been written about the process of reframing (see Weeks & Treat, 2001).

Reframing statements differ from interpretations in several ways, and they avoid many of the problems inherent in the latter. The specific goals of reframing are different from interpretation. Reframes move the locus of the problem from negative to positive and from the individual to the couple. Also, unlike with an interpretation, the truth or accuracy of a reframe is irrelevant. The therapist is not seeking to impart some truth based on any particular theory. Rather, a reframe is a pragmatic statement designed to loosen the client's cognitive schemata about something so change can occur. Sometimes change results from the reframe itself, but these situations are relatively rare. The reframe is usually the first strategy used in order to prepare the client for another intervention. Reframes are best known for being the frame-changing statements that facilitate paradoxical interventions (Weeks & L'Abate, 1982). Thus, it is common to see a reframing statement immediately followed by a paradoxical intervention.

Reframing statements are also different from interpretations in that they are generally based on the assumption that the symptom being described serves some useful function for the couple system. Symptoms or problems are often viewed in a negative light by therapists and especially by clients. A client who is depressed would be hard-pressed to say that the depression was a good thing or that it served some useful function. A reframe, however, might posit the depression in a different way—perhaps as a messenger bringing some unwelcome but necessary information or as a protection for the individual or the couple from something that is more threatening. For example, depression may be conveying the message that a marriage is not working. Being depressed protects the couple from having to confront or change the situation. If the couple were to confront this fact, they might be emotionally overwhelmed or even divorce.

Very little has been written about the use of reframes with couples (L'Abate & Samples, 1983; Protinsky & Quinn, 1981). As stated earlier, most examples have been embedded in case studies published in family therapy journals, particularly the *Journal of Structural and Strategic Therapy*. Reframing in couples work usually consists of two specific statements that are inextricably linked. One of the statements gives the symptom a positive meaning or connotation and the other is designed to move the couple from viewing the problem at the level of the individual to the level of the system.

General Principles of Reframing

Unfortunately, too many therapists do not understand the general principles involved in reframing: Tailor the reframe to the couple and collaborate with them in its creation. All too often therapists attempt to replicate with their clients examples they have seen in the literature, regardless of how well the reframe fits the particular couple and their situation. The therapist must understand the couple from the inside out, and the reframe should always be tailored to the couple. One size does not fit all. Many therapists think a reframe is something done to a client. However, a reframe is a collaborative process that involves understanding the couple's inner dynamics and how they perceive events. The couple will reject a reframe that departs too much from their reality. The reframe must stay within the scope of how the couple views their relationship, yet start them thinking in a different way. The change in thinking initially may be quite small and then builds as the therapist gains trust and credibility.

A metaphor may help the reader understand this process. The couple begins with a certain picture or view of their problem. Imagine that the picture is a jigsaw puzzle. When people put a jigsaw puzzle together they begin by grouping pieces that look like they go together either because of the shape or because of the artwork on the pieces. The picture the couple has is usually rigidly locked in place. Each one sees the other and the relationship in a certain way, typically dominated by the problem or problems. The goal of the therapy is to undo the picture the couple has and replace it with different, more pragmatic picture. Once the therapist has some understanding of the couple's inner dynamics, he or she can begin to ask a series of questions designed to elicit new pieces of their puzzle. The partners hear themselves talk about the problem in a new way. The process continues until the couple has enough pieces to come to a realization that there is another way of looking at the problem or until they get close enough to that picture that the therapist can make the reframe statement as a tentative hypothesis that the couple accepts. The therapist might say something like "You seem to be saying..." or "Have you considered the possibility that..." or "I'm wondering whether...." Thus, the therapist guides the conversation and incorporates the couple's feedback so that they come to their own "ah ha" experience of the reframe or are ready to shift views when the therapist suggests the reframe.

Once the therapist understands the couple's dynamics, he or she may have some particular reframe in mind. However, as the pieces of the puzzle are elicited, the reframe may need to be changed. Predicting the outcome of the process in terms of a specific reframe is difficult, although not impossible. Basically, when working with a couple the therapist must keep two goals in mind: to help the couple see how the symptom is positive and to change their attributional strategy from blaming one partner to joint responsibility for the problem.

Change the Frame

As noted earlier, one of the goals is to change the focus from negative to positive. Couples usually see only the negative aspects of the symptom. They do not see how it could be adaptive, useful, productive, or protective for them. Carlson and Marilyn were one such couple. They had been married for about 20 years. Their children were almost ready to leave home and they were beginning to see what an empty marriage they had. They both felt lonely and wondered why they were with each other because they did so little together. They had similar backgrounds. Each was reared in a family that was cold and rejecting. They had both become oppositional to their parents and could not wait to leave home. They met in high school and married a week after graduation. Both sets of parents opposed the marriage. Initially, they had what they thought of as a close relationship. They were inseparable and supported each other in not living as the parents wanted. Within a couple of years, however, they began to oppose each other and this behavior continued to grow. They were both aware that they took opposite positions for the sake of asserting themselves.

The therapist asked the couple to talk about how they met, what attracted them to each other, and their relationships with their parents. The therapist believed that they had recreated the same oppositional behavior in their marriage that they had in their families, and he wanted to lead them toward this realization. His reframe was:

"The two of you are to be congratulated for having survived in this marriage for 20 years. It is clear that your parents attempted to stifle the individuality of both of you. They wanted you to both conform to what they wanted. You were each strong enough to fight their attempts to mold you to fit their visions, and as a team you supported each other in maintaining your separateness from your parents. Unfortunately, you spent so much of your life trying to maintain your individuality that once you married you were unconsciously afraid of losing your identity to the other person. You then became oppositional to each other as a way to protect your individuality and for many years have defined yourself by being opposite from each other. I believe you are here because you are now strong enough to experience true individuality without having to be in opposition to anyone."

Each situation can be reframed in a number of ways. The content of the reframe is less important than the fact that it is positive and acceptable to the couple. The general idea is to suggest that the couple is strong and has chosen some way of relating that is now obsolete. The partners are challenged to find a better way to relate to each other. Another way to reframe the situation just described might have been:

"The two of you have been trying to find your own way of being intimate with each other for 20 years. Being intimate with another person is a concept you learn early in life. Your parents taught you that it meant giving up yourself. You had no idea that there could be anything but being completely separate from each other or losing yourself in a relationship. You have helped each other maintain selfhood by being opposite, just as you maintained your selfhood in your families by being opposite. Do you think you are strong enough now to learn to be yourself without the old fear of merging with another person or opposing them?"

Another way to conceive of a reframe is as a move from one therapy model to another. For example, there are many models of abnormal psychopathology: statistical, moral, psychiatric, and personal distress, to mention only a few. The following case example illustrates a reframe that used a change in models.

Victor called for treatment for himself. He reported that he had been struggling with the same problem for years but had been too embarrassed to seek help. He was a salesman and traveled within a certain territory. When traveling he would visit men's rooms that were known to be places where gay men had sex. With their permission, he simply watched but never participated actively. The therapist thoroughly assessed whether he might be gay and ruled that diagnosis out. Victor was a fundamentalist Christian and, not surprisingly, felt enormous guilt over his behavior. He believed he could not tell his minister but did feel that, to alleviate some of his guilt, he must tell his wife what he had been doing. She, too, was a fundamentalist and they were regular attendees at church. Victor wanted the therapist's help in telling his wife. He was framing his problem as a moral weakness and it seemed clear to him that his wife would do the same. He predicted that his wife would, at best, feel ambivalent about his disclosure. On the one hand, she might feel that he was committing a sin and possibly even leave him. On the other hand, she might feel that it was her Christian duty to forgive him and help him resist temptation. The therapist advised Victor that revealing this information could destroy the marriage and he acknowledged that possibility. He still felt compelled to tell her.

The therapist wanted to change Victor's way of viewing the problem, hoping that his wife would accept this new frame. He said to Victor:

"It is not clear why you are compelled to engage in this behavior that you find so repulsive. A lot of work will be needed to understand it. This behavior also goes against all your moral thinking and you punish yourself with guilt for doing what you do. What you need to know is that you are suffering from a psychiatric disorder known as voyeurism. Voyeurism is a condition that involves watching other people, usually a heterosexual couple or individual, having sex. It is a compulsion. The only thing that makes your voyeurism unusual is that you like to watch men and you are not gay. The good news is that we can treat it. If we can get your wife to help you, the treatment will probably work better. I'll talk to her when she comes in with you."

Victor still viewed the problem morally, but he now accepted another frame of reference for his compulsion. He was relieved to know that other people had the same problem and that it was something that could be treated.

Victor's wife, Sue, came to the next session. Victor was anxious and wanted to tell her right away. The therapist told Sue that Victor had come to him for help because he wanted to overcome a problem he had. The therapist also said that Victor was an honest man and wanted to tell her the truth. He had been so ashamed of his problem that he had not been able to tell her. Victor then told Sue about what he had been doing. Sue looked shocked and said that what he was doing was a sin. The therapist then said:

"Sue, this must be quite a shock for you. What Victor is doing is a sin and he has been praying for help with this problem. He came to see me because he thought I might be the answer to his prayers. Your husband has a psychiatric condition that involves a certain type of compulsion known as voyeurism. People with this condition cannot help themselves stop what they are doing without psychiatric help. He is facing a real challenge and he needs your support. I know that you are a good Christian wife and will do the right thing."

Sue thought about what the therapist said for a minute and then commented that it was still a sin but she would help him. Victor felt better that he had told Sue and they began to work on his compulsive behavior. The therapy continued initially mostly with Victor. Occasional couple sessions were held and it was apparent that the marriage was one characterized by great emotional distance. The real shock came a few months later when Sue said she needed to tell Victor something. She said that she had been having an emotional affair for some time with a man who was blind and attended their church. She also felt that she was sinning and wanted to stop. Perhaps this affair was also one of the reasons that she was willing to help Victor. The therapy eventually shifted to help her individually and then to work more with the couple. After a few of years of therapy, the case came to a successful conclusion.

Change the Focus From the Individual to the Couple

The second goal of a reframe is to change the locus of the problem from the individual to the couple. This involves changing the partners' attributional strategy from one that is linear to one that is circular. A linear attributional strategy consists of one partner's placing blame or responsibility for the problem on the other partner. A circular strategy allows each partner to conceptualize his or her part in the problem. Shifting the attributional strategy can be done in two ways. This point has not been made in the literature (see Weeks & Treat, 2001), although it is apparent from some case examples. The first option is to make bilateral interpretations or frames, usually of a positive nature, that tie together the couple's behavior. The other option is to make a single systemic reframe that captures the couple's primary dynamic. The two following examples illustrate the use of each technique in dealing with a lack of intimacy.

Bilateral interpretation or reframe. The terminology of this intervention is a bit confusing. A classic interpretation is focused on one person and his or her dynamics. What we call a "bilateral interpretation or reframe" incorporates the idea of an individual interpretation but also ties one partner's behavior to that of the other. Thus, the aim is to show how they have formed an interlocking system of behavior. For example: "Ian, you were reared in a family where you were told that you were not smart and were worthless. You learned to hide how you felt about yourself. We call this 'fear of exposure'. What you learned in your family has also affected your marriage. You keep your distance from your wife because you are afraid she will learn that you see yourself as someone who does not deserve love and who is incompetent."

"Miriam, you were reared in a family that was emotionally abusive. You learned that if you were seen you might become the target of anger or become a scapegoat. You felt afraid and small when you were subjected to irrational anger. Both of you should continue to keep your distance in your marriage for now, because you know that being close means that you are a potential target of anger or exposure. You should only change when you each feel strong enough to deal with these problems individually and as a couple."

Systemic reframe. The systemic reframe focuses on one core dynamic in the couple and puts both partners on the same level. An example of this type of reframe for Ian and Miriam could be: "The two of you came to this relationship with underlying fears of intimacy. These fears are not readily apparent because they are unconscious and you are repeating what you learned in your families. You unconsciously chose each other knowing that you would protect each other from having to be too close. This relationship has helped you avoid your underlying fears, but now you both want to overcome those fears and have a closer relationship."

As noted earlier, the couple's dynamic must be understood if the reframe is to be on target. The reframe must fit the clients' view but also diverge enough to set in motion a new way of thinking about the problem. Therapists trained in individual therapy may make interpretations, but we advise that it be done cautiously. The proper use of reframing is much more productive to change because it is generally positive and more readily systemic.

CHAPTER ELEVEN

Failing to Foster Commitment

Commitment is the foundational glue that holds couple relationships together. Along with intimacy and passion, it is one component of the triangular theory of love developed by Sternberg (1986, 1997) based on research in social psychology and personality. At some point in the couple's relationship, they made a decision to commit to each other. As part of this commitment, especially if they marry, they made promises that also have societal sanction. Commitment may also be manifested through sexual fidelity (Sternberg, 1997). Social psychologist Harold Kelley (1983) noted that commitment is sustained by the rewards-cost balance (greater rewards than costs), irretrievable investments (intangible things that make a relationship special or unique), understanding (the sense of "we-ness" in the relationship), and attractiveness of alternatives (for example, divorce or affair).

Couples may come to therapy with differing definitions and levels of commitment. The ideal situation for therapy is a couple with equal positive levels of commitment. Some couples may have no commitment and are thinking of divorce. Others may have ambivalent commitments and may be in an affair.

They may have unequal levels of commitment where one partner wants to continue the relationship and the other does not.
In addition, couple commitment may vary over the life of the
relationship and may even be affected by the actions by the
partners.

Because commitment is a foundation upon which couples
build relationships, handling it well in therapy is important.
Waite and Gallagher (2000) noted in *The Case for Marriage* that
commitment underlies many of the benefits of marriage. Commitment must be viewed both as a separate component of a
couple's relationship and as inextricably foundational to everything else about it. The therapist who wants to help a couple improve their relationship must be mindful of this fact. Struggling
couples frequently have found their commitments weakening
as their relationships leave them disappointed and hurt, which
in turn makes their commitments all the more vulnerable. This
cycle can escalate, and many couples that seek therapy and are
not thinking of divorce are nevertheless aware at some level of
the potential threat to the relationship if things do not improve.

Therapists can err in dealing with couples and their commitment by:

- Failing to understand the importance of commitment to the
  outcome of therapy
- Failing to value commitment by the couple
- Failing to recognize differences in views about commitment,
  either between the partners or between the therapist and
  the couple
- Failing to raise the issue of commitment appropriately
- Failing to understand their own impact on couple commitment

Psychotherapeutic Assumptions Regarding Commitment

It might seem odd to ask why commitment matters. After all,
couple and family therapists are interested in fostering good,

committed relationships. However, the field is hardly unified in its understanding of how a good relationship is defined and to whom the good applies. Examining a number of often overlooked assumptions in our field, many of which are more controversial than what those outside the field would expect, is helpful if therapists are to successfully manage commitment issues.

Within Western culture there has been an increasing emphasis on individualism. This was a byproduct of an increasingly mobile population with an unprecedented level of material prosperity. In short, people believed that they needed each other and community less for essential survival functions. It became increasingly possible, and then somewhat normal, for individuals to think about themselves in autonomous and highly self-focused, self-sufficient ways. By the 20th century, interpersonal connectedness was lessening even in the family and, principally, in marriage. Being committed by necessity for the community's good evolved into commitment by choice. Thus, individuals evaluated their family and especially their marital relationships according to a new set of progressive criteria, including feelings of love, compatibility, and intimacy. This was consistent with the rise of the companionate model of marriage. The shift from a community to an individual focus resulted in increasing social and personal alienation and the concomitant difficulties that came with such a normative view. Therapists have had a long history in our culture of helping their clients manage to get along with less social support, or what has been termed "community" (Richardson, Fowers, & Guignon, 1999). Therapy was, and continues to be, largely about helping clients solve problems by increasing, in some manner, their self-efficacy. This is true even in more systemically oriented therapy, such as couple and family therapy.

Therapists, who are themselves heavily influenced by the larger cultural context, tend to prioritize individual well-being, regardless of the individuals' relational contexts. Our diagnostic system itself is individually focused, assuming that individuals have disorders, even if their disorders are intricately intertwined with their relationships. Individual therapy focuses treatment at the individual level and may even attempt to protect or safeguard individuals and their well-being from other relationships. In other words, a bad relationship may well be seen as worse than no relationship. For example, Doherty (1995) has argued that therapists have been too focused on liberating people from the toxic constraints typically found in marriage, family, community, and religion. Indeed, there has been a growing literature addressing what some suggest is essentially psychotherapeutically assisted relational suicide, because therapists fairly casually dismiss commitment as a powerful and beneficial element critical in intimate relationships in favor of a more individualistically oriented, rights-based, "what's in it for me" cost-benefit equation.

In our highly individualistic culture, therapists occupy a position as creators of culture. That is, how we influence clients powerfully affects what they do in their lives, and their actions that follow from our influence thus form the context within which our culture is framed and perpetuated. If a systemic focus is to be taken in therapy, the implications for the manner in which commitment is handled may change. Therapists must examine how they value commitment as a relational and, ultimately, social good. They must examine much of their training, their personal value systems and experiences, and their cultural immersion to combat the tendency to undervalue commitment or to see commitment as a sign of pathology, especially when it occurs in a relationship that is not clearly rewarding or satisfying or likely to become so relatively quickly. In other words, too often therapists simply apply a lens toward couples that does not prioritize their commitment to each other or acknowledge the importance of honoring their commitments. In fact, couples often have a higher regard for their commitment than the therapist does.

Susan and Jason came to therapy to change their conflicts. They reported to the therapist that they had become increasingly nasty in their conflicts and were doing things that surprised them, and they believed that they needed to halt these developments to keep them from getting out of control. The therapist did not share their position, as shown in the following transcript. Predictably, the clients discontinued with the therapist and found another who valued what they valued.

Jason: We've both been...really destructive. We never fought dirty before, and the fact that we've done that in the last year or so has scared us. (*pause*) I can't believe it. Some of the things I've said, and even thought, I'm ashamed of.

Susan: I never thought we would have a verbal abuse problem. Jason's more controlled with his emotions than I am, and it's always been me with the mouth, but even he's been crossing the line with what he's said. He's really hurt me, and I know I've hurt him. We want to stop....This is a direction we have to stop.

Therapist: So, if I'm hearing you right, you've seen a consistent deterioration in how you've handled conflict in the last few years, and you're both afraid of where it may lead. Like divorce?

Both: Yes.

Therapist: My experience with couples in these situations is that often their relationships are changing in critical ways over time, because that's just what happens, and the fear people feel is really an indicator of some larger underlying fear of change. It's normal, but it's not healthy. I wonder why either of you may fear the end result of this change in your relationship.

Assessing Commitment

Commitment can be a difficult issue to tackle. The concept has different meaning for different cultures, yet couples may develop idiosyncratic ways of defining it. For example, the concept can be so variable that it can apply to "open" marriages. In addition, there are times when the therapist and the client couple have vastly different views of commitment. As noted earliest, it is common for couples to have a firm commitment to their relationship, but be working with a therapist who views the relationship as questionable or worse. Occasionally the couple's commitment is minimal but the therapists sees it as something to be fixed, regardless of the reason why commitment is minimal. In any case, commitment is critical to what happens both in the relationship and in therapy, and the therapist must work with or on the commitment well.

One of the first tasks that the couple therapist accomplishes is assessing the degree and nature of commitment between the partners. Couples in therapy may take various stances with respect to commitment: They may assume it, be ambivalent toward it, or overtly have problems with it. Commitment between the partners is often a given, and the therapist may not ask about it or even notice that he or she is not thinking about it. The couple presents for treatment intent on improving a problem or set of problems that they experience, but the question of whether the relationship will continue is not on the table and, in fact, may not have even entered the mind of either partner. Therapy proceeds, problems and issues are addressed, changes are made or not, and the couple's relationship continues. The commitment is not brought up in treatment or thought about by any participant. Rather, it is assumed, and correctly so.

However, for many couples, underlying their presenting concerns are deeper questions, or perhaps fallback positions, about the viability of their relationship. In other words, if things do not improve, there may be an implicit threat of ending the relationship. It can be hard to determine without explicit investigation how clearly developed that threat is for couples who do not overtly state it in their concerns. The therapist can assess for commitment by asking the partners what their definition of commitment is and how committed they are to the relationship.

Alternatively, the couple can be asked what brought them to their current thinking about commitment. The couple may respond that their level of commitment reflects problems with intimacy or passion, in which case these issues would become the goal of therapy. The therapist may need to probe repeatedly to understand what is happening. Other couples may be much more overt and state quite emphatically in the opening stages of therapy that this is the last chance for their relationship. Whether such a sentiment is actually accurate is another story. In the moment, the message is that the relationship is in jeopardy and help is urgently needed. Longer term, the partners may still be together, regardless of the success of therapy, sometimes with a better relationship and sometimes with no changes.

For some therapists, such declarations of the potential end to a relationship add a degree of pressure and urgency to the therapy, which can be counterproductive. The therapist suddenly may feel the weight of the couple's hopes, expectations, and desperation about their relationship. The therapist must remember that the couple has the ultimate responsibility for their relationship. This is not to suggest that the therapist does not have a critical role in what happens, but rather that the therapist must be clear about what his or her responsibility is. In any event, the couple's commitment to each other is something the therapist will probably influence, deliberately or inadvertently, so it is wise to consider how one approaches it.

As mentioned, the question of commitment often does not come up in couple therapy. Sometimes it should but does not; sometimes it should not but does. Either of these situations is an error to be avoided. The first issue, then, is determining whether commitment should be explicitly discussed. The next issue is what to do with commitment when it is explicitly discussed.

When to Discuss Commitment

Commitment should be discussed when couples overtly raise the issue, when they have little positive to say and are concerned that therapy might not help, when they make ambiguous statements and veiled threats, when there is not much vitality to the relationship, and in cases of infidelity, violence, or addiction. Sometimes it is remarkably easy to know when to discuss issues pertaining to commitment. When a couple overtly raises it themselves, the issue is obviously a subject for therapy. But there are many situations where it is not so clear. The first that comes to mind is when a couple has very little positive to say about their relationship and they express doubt that it can improve at all, even with effort in therapy. Clues that one or both partners are thinking of an exit are good indicators that the therapist should initiate a discussion of commitment. The therapist must use good clinical judgment and not enter discussions lightly, however, as some situations can become traps for the therapist.

An example of this can be seen with Toni and Dave. They came to therapy together and both were quite articulate in outlining problems in the relationship. Not surprisingly, they were both able to see clearly that the other person was the source of the struggle, and there was the fairly typical initial session with the couple bickering over this and that fact. They did not discuss positive areas of their relationship or things they appreciated about their partner. Each made some ambiguous comments about what they might need to do if things did not get better, but the therapist noticed that neither partner commented on the underlying threat of relationship dissolution. This couple was sending mixed messages. They did not overtly threaten divorce, but made vague references to something happening if their situation did not improve.

The therapist asked them to talk explicitly about what each of them had in mind if things did not improve in their relationship. Commitment was now overtly a topic for discussion, and the stakes were seriously raised. Dave stated that he had decided that the relationship was probably beyond salvaging. He had begun to look at ads for apartments in the local newspaper and thought that he would move out by the first of the next month, a week and a half away. Toni was dumbfounded. She was at a loss for words when she heard Dave state such concrete thoughts about leaving. She had not considered terminating their relationship.

The therapist had the task of helping them work through the immediate crisis. First, he had to assess the seriousness of Dave's announcement; in other words, was he saying this simply for effect or because he could tell his wife in the relative safety of the therapist's office where she would have some help from someone beside him? In this case, the therapist judged that Dave was quite serious, and he turned his attention to Toni to manage the fallout from Dave's statement. Once that was done, he set about examining the degree to which Dave's intentions were firm. Later, depending on the answers, he could develop several plans of action collaboratively with them depending on what course of action they wanted to take. Developing collaborative goals before asking the question about commitment would have been premature for this couple. Had the therapist proceeded to set up goals for couple therapy, it is unlikely that therapy would have progressed.

In this case, Dave was honest about his level of commitment and his plan of action. There is always a risk, of course, that either or both partners will avoid the question and make hollow pronouncements of their intentions to stay together. It is not unusual for couples to do this early in treatment. Therapists astute enough to hear ambiguity or veiled threats about divorce may receive denials when they confront clients about those comments. Time will tell, however, whether or not such denials are genuine or manufactured because of a fear of honesty about the potential end of a relationship. If one or both partners continue to be ambivalent about the relationship, it is simply a matter of time before the question must come up one way or another in therapy. At that point, their past and current explicit statements about the relationship can be used to gauge subsequent motivation. In addition, other indicators of lack of commitment include couples' finding other things to do besides attend their therapy sessions, or when one partner discontinues, leaving the therapist and remaining partner wondering what exactly all of them are doing.

Another case vignette illustrates a situation in which commitment needed to be raised explicitly. Jolene and Fred came to therapy seeking help with "communication difficulties." It quickly became clear, however, that they actually were quite accomplished at communicating with each other—both expertly avoided conflict and the other person's underlying bids for attention. They were not overtly in much conflict but rather fairly passive and comfortable staying on the surface. They found it difficult to engage in meaningful conversation in therapy. Fred found it easier to work or watch television than to interact with Jolene. Jolene did not seem to mind very much, reserving her complaints more for what Fred did not do around the house. After a few sessions, it was fairly evident that the two of them did not see their marriage as having much vitality, and the therapist was left wondering what each really wanted.

The therapist had assumed that the couple was interested in staying in the marriage and had proceeded accordingly. After a few sessions with little therapeutic progress he raised the question of their commitment explicitly. The couple's response was quite telling; ordinarily, Jolene and Fred responded fairly quickly if unenthusiastically to questions and did not interrupt each other, but did not really pay much attention to most of what their partner said. When commitment was raised, they actually hesitated and attended to each other. Jolene stated that she had thought about divorce from time to time for many years, and still at times thought it would be the best solution, especially now that their children were no longer at home. While explaining herself, it was evident that she was gauging Fred's reaction and that he was listening closely to what she said. Although his reaction was not strong in any direction, it was clear that he was very interested in what course of action she thought she wanted to take. When it was his turn to respond, he made a more vulnerable and genuine disclosure than he had before, saying that he knew she had thought about it in the past and had wondered why she had not already left. He volunteered that he was glad she had stayed but that he also understood her views, because he largely shared them. He stated he also had thought about leaving. They then proceeded to have a deeper conversation about their relationship and its future, mostly without the therapist's intervention. They eventually decided that they wanted to make their marriage work and continued with that goal in mind.

The point here is not about what course of action they chose. Rather, the therapist's willingness to explicitly raise the commitment issue allowed the couple to discuss the nature of their relationship, something they had been unable to do. Had the therapist continued to work on communication skills and never gotten to questions of their commitment, the couple may have ended treatment. Some therapists might argue that with more effective communication skills, the couple would have inevitably broached commitment as an area of exploration, however frightening, but such an assumption may be wrong. It is entirely possible for skills training to never produce any significant increase in risk-taking or personal disclosure in vulnerable areas. In fact, the therapist who presides over such skills training and does not notice the fact that there is little increase in the depth of communication is not getting the larger job done well, in our view.

Another issue that raises questions of commitment is infidelity. Infidelity causes a reexamination of the assumption of relationship exclusivity and breaks the trust between the partners in a committed relationship. The most damaging aspect of infidelity is that the boundary around the relationship has been breached. The partner who has been betrayed almost inevitably questions the level of commitment in the relationship. He or she may threaten divorce, and the previously reluctant partner may take these threats seriously enough to enter counseling. Although therapists typically will not do couples therapy while an affair is actively occurring, therapists should not make the error of avoiding discussions about commitment when such issues arise. Commitment and the trust that accompanies it are important to the healing process after infidelity.

If one or both partners have had an affair, commitment issues may be raised by the couple, but not in a judicious manner. The therapist working with a couple that has experienced infidelity must bring up commitment issues in a serious and deliberate way. It is common for these partners to express emotions intensely. They may deliver ultimatums, but they may not mean what they say. In many cases the betrayed partner who says that the relationship is over is actually just trying to express the amount of hurt and anger he or she feels. This is an important distinction to draw for the couple. Because the commitment is tenuous and conditional, the therapist will have to return to the discussion of commitment with some regularity. In addition, the betrayed partner may suddenly have a new degree of influence over the other partner. The therapist must address the implications of the power issues for the relationship on an ongoing basis, as there may be other risks for unilateral action, for example reciprocal infidelity or divorce, that may have as much or more impact on the relationship as the original infidelity.

The therapist must be able to invite the couple to discuss their commitment to each other. There are a number of dimensions involved in this. First, the partner who had the affair must be able to articulate what his or her commitment is to the betrayed partner. It is entirely possible that there may be some ambivalence here. Cliff and Penny, for instance, came to therapy after Cliff's affair was discovered. In the first few interviews,

Cliff's palpable ambivalence was a major topic for discussion. He stated that the woman with whom he had become involved was a true soulmate for him and that he deeply desired to pursue that relationship, yet he was aware that for many reasons such a course was wrong. Second, the betrayed partner's commitment to the betraying partner must be examined. Penny had a very difficult time hearing Cliff state that he wanted to be with the other woman but knew that making his marriage relationship work was "the right thing to do". His ambivalence resonated with hers. Her ambivalence was based in both the breaking of the marital vow and the overt statement that she was clearly not his first choice any longer. However, after a number of sessions and many weeks of navigating the uncomfortable uncertainty, they agreed that their commitment to each other, to God, and to their children and families, as well as the investment of history of their marriage, were of greater importance than either of their more immediate desires.

Once commitment has been established, specific behavioral indicators must be put into place to keep that commitment measurable and both partners accountable to it. This is not always easy to do, given the potentially volatile nature of couples who have experienced affairs. The couple may make progress for many weeks or even months and then blow up when a new revelation of some detail of the story is made, a suspicious phone call or email shows up, an anniversary date passes, or a chance viewing of a television show on affairs brings up a fresh batch of anger, jealousy, hurt, and betrayal. The therapist must validate the feelings of both partners while maintaining the momentum toward healing by highlighting the commitment they have made. Using an externalizing approach can be helpful here, as both partners can be encouraged not to let their mutual "enemy" defeat them. Developing acceptable behavioral indicators is no easy task for many couples, and the therapist will often be in the role of mediator, but not as a neutral one. This is a delicate balance to maintain. If the therapist fails to acknowledge the debt from the betrayal, he or she may be inadvertently viewed as taking the side of the betrayer, but too much acknowledgement will alienate the betraying partner. Negotiation is crucial during this time, all the while reinforcing the importance of the couple's commitment both to therapy and the relationship.

Commitment is also central to working with couples where there is violence or an addiction. The therapist should assess violent couples first. Commitment discussions are not advised if there is a threat to one partner if he or she leaves, or if the therapist senses that commitment is coerced. It is generally unwise to address the issue without an a priori safety plan. If violence persists or intimidation merely changes forms, the necessary components involved in a decision to remain in a relationship, or at least give it a chance to change, are undermined. This possibility needs explicit discussion in therapy, with the therapist most often acting in the role of guide, pushing for adherence to what has been agreed.

Dealing with violent couples is in some ways easier than dealing with addicted couples, because there tend to be more obvious indicators of both commitment to change and accountability for the change. Therapists will find that addictions are similar to infidelity in that there is quite frequently a secret or a series of secrets that work against trust and boundary maintenance. Accountability is harder to maintain because the addictive behavior can frequently be hidden and the enabling dynamic in the relationship may continue to be exploited, as it may have been prior to therapy. In addition, if clients express two or more issues such as violence and addiction, they will find that creating committed and satisfying relationships is more challenging. However, although couples in these relationships may state that they do not like their relationship, they still may not separate from each other because the excitement caused by their issues allows them to avoid deeper, probably long-standing pain from which they are desperate to escape.

What to Do With Commitment When It Is Raised

As therapists evaluate or diagnose a given relationship, they tend to utilize criteria associated with the companionate, romantic love model of relationships that dominates our public philosophy (Fowers, 1998). This model of love suggests that partners in a good relationship are soulmates who enjoy emotional closeness, sexual and romantic passion, and self-expression and disclosure, with personal fulfillment as an expected result. It should be no surprise that as the expectations rise for what a relationship should be, the opportunities for it to fall short also abound. Therapists unwittingly contribute to this problem and then compound it by encouraging clients to make their commitment to their relationships based upon criteria that may well be exceptionally difficult to achieve.

It is certainly worth critically examining how therapists contribute to the culture's development through the ways we influence our clients. The public benefits of marriage and committed stable relationships have become more widely understood and appreciated; therapists should evaluate how they either perpetuate or hinder the development of such relationships. As mentioned earlier, therapists have tended to emphasize the individual aspects, particularly the emotional rewards and costs, of maintaining commitment in relationships, and thus they have typically prioritized individual choice, personal happiness, and freedom over commitment, obligation, and responsibility.

A relatively inexperienced, young, single, female Caucasian therapist saw Angelica and Rafael, a Hispanic couple married for 5 years. Their problems were not unusual, manifesting in conflicts about roles and communication styles. In addition, they participated in a pursuer/avoider dynamic. Angelica was the more expressive partner, and she pursued Rafael, usually ineffectively. He withdrew in the face of what he viewed as her pressure. He characterized her as a nag, and she characterized him as being childish and insensitive to her. They were stuck in their relationship. They had not mentioned the possibility of divorce in therapy, yet after several sessions where little change had been accomplished, the therapist finally asked why they were still together. This is not a bad question in itself, but the way in which she asked the question was problematic. Her subtext was "I see you two as clearly incompatible, with few rewards and little mutuality, and I don't understand why you stay with each other, yet I can't say that explicitly." The couple, however, caught her underlying message and responded with affirmations of their love and commitment to each other. They also reminded the therapist that divorce was not really an option, as their families of origin and their religion (Roman Catholicism) explicitly forbade it. When they asked the therapist her opinion of the prospects of their relationship, she spoke from her worldview. She said that she was quite concerned about the level of apparent discord in their marriage. She stated that she felt pessimistic that they would be successful at overcoming their differences without imposing major restrictions on their individuality, which she did not think was fair or would be successful in the long term. In particular, she had concerns that Rafael did not value his wife as much as his wife needed him to and that if he could not become more responsive to her, she deserved a chance at something better to be happy. Although the therapist delivered these comments in a nonconfrontational way, she missed the cultural and relational context for this couple.

The therapist failed to appreciate that her view of commitment and the couple's view of commitment were radically different. Worse, she communicated, however subtly, to them that their commitment to each other needed to change and that their relationship was somehow "wrong." In her view, staying in the marriage indicated individual or relational pathology and she implicitly suggested that they do what made sense to her–divorce. She never fully considered what effect a divorce might have on either partner. The therapist paid no attention to the couple's ethnic context, which, although the partners were fairly well acculturated, still included an extensive and involved extended family network on both sides. Nor did she consider what divorce might mean for the couple, their family, and their network of friends. In addition, the therapist dismissed the importance of their religious beliefs in favor of her own worldview. Although she was not as overt as she could have been, she nonetheless subtly attempted to "proselytize" them into her own view of their relational world, under the guise of happiness and "mental" or "relational health." The clients discontinued therapy after this session, presumably because they did not think that the therapist could help them do the admittedly hard work of keeping their commitment.

The foregoing case demonstrates that undervaluing commitment that is held strongly by clients does not work well. Rather than responding to the couple's question about the prospect of their relationship, the therapist should have had the couple talk about their own definition of commitment. This would have allowed the cultural context, as well as the level of commitment by each partner, to become more clear. In addition, discussion may have revealed information about the balance between commitment, intimacy, and passion the clients wanted, whether they could express each component, whether they had realistic perceptions of what was involved, and whether they had the capacity and the behavior to support these elements (see Weeks & Treat, 2001, for further discussion). Therapist influence does carry weight with couples considering their relationship's future, including the possibility of ending the relationship. In these situations, therapists must consider whether they may err by undervaluing commitment generically.

It may be obvious, but it is worth mentioning that therapists often need to educate couples about the normal changes that can be expected in relationships over time. Without this background, couples often take a much more proximal view of their relationship and tend to see it more negatively than is warranted. Feelings can fluctuate rapidly or slowly and widely, and all relationships can expect to have seasons during which feelings of love, attraction, romance, intimacy, or common interests may be largely absent. Many couples come into treatment during these seasons, and for many it no longer seems to be a season; metaphorically, it has become an ice age. Such a relationship may be quite disappointing, and partners can become very distressed about it. Couples need to be able to examine their expectations and their habits for meeting these expectations within the context of a commitment they made to each other that accounts for developmental change. Normalizing the couple's experiences without necessarily giving the partners the impression that they are stuck where they are helps them appreciate that there may be nothing fundamentally wrong in their relationship and gives them hope that they can make it better. It is an error to assume that there must be a fatal flaw or inevitable ending if couples are not as close or happy as they want to be or think they should be.

Because of the political weight given to not marginalizing different kinds of couple relationships, therapists have ended up running the risk of viewing all kinds of intimate relationships as inherently the same. Specifically, cohabitation and marriage, the dominant relationship choices in society today, are increasingly defaulted into the same category. There is ample evidence to show that such a collapsing of distinctiveness is erroneous (Waite & Gallagher, 2000). Marriage is a qualitatively different kind of relationship than cohabitation, even though some married couples may have less commitment than some cohabiting couples.

Therapists approaching marital therapy must assume that married couples' commitment level at the time they married was probably much higher than that of cohabiting couples. The married couple at some point chose to commit, presumably and usually explicitly, to permanent marriage to their spouse. When the couple is ambivalent about staying together or splitting, the therapist's response, or lack thereof, is likely to be significant in their decision. Although therapists are ethically prohibited from using their position to tell their clients whether to marry, divorce, have children, or the like, it is naïve to assume that the therapists' biases, whatever they may be, will be completely detached from what happens. Therapists should attend to and understand their own biases regarding relationship commitment, as they may affect discussions about commitment with the couple. The therapist should respectfully invite the partners to consider the significance of their decision on every level possible. This process should involve engaging the couple in a discussion about their reasons for commiting to each other and how they continue to reaffirm their commitment through their belief system and actions. The stakes are usually much higher for married couples, although it is probably worth noting that most cohabiting couples who seek therapy have an established commitment far greater than couples who do not seek treatment.

The following case example demonstrates how partners may look at commitment differently. Dee and Rod came to therapy in serious trouble in their marriage. They had been married for nearly 15 years; this was his first marriage and her second. Dee's first marriage had been right out of high school and had lasted for about 5 years. She had three children with her first husband. She described that marriage as a nightmare, ending with her husband's suicide in front of her and the children. She had managed to take care of the family alone for a time, and when she met Rod, he seemed to be a particularly good choice. He was very good with the children, seemed stable professionally, and was, as she put it, a "very level headed, good hearted" man. They had married after about a year's courtship and a few years later had a child together. There was no report of any violence, infidelity, or substance use.

Their major concern was that Dee had very little feeling of love or interest in Rod, and she was contemplating leaving him. He very strongly indicated that he wanted the marriage to continue and made it clear that he would do whatever it took to "win her heart" again. But he also said he felt helpless because he seemed irrelevant to her. She agreed that he was a good man but stated that she had little hope that she would really be able to love him and did not want to live out the rest of her adult life in a loveless marriage.

After addressing some of the latent effects of the first marriage that were playing themselves out in the current situation in some individual work, the therapist returned to the original presenting issue. Dee's position was still the same, although she admitted that she felt more hopeful about her life overall now that she had worked through issues from her first marriage. At that point, the therapist took a different tactic, noting that Dee had married Rod mostly becauses of his ability to care for her and the children in a way vastly different from the first husband. She agreed that that was true. The therapist pointed out that the criteria Dee had used to evaluate Rod had never been significantly tied to her feelings of love, though she did say that she had found him attractive and had been interested in him during their courtship and early marriage. The therapist confronted Dee about the significance of her commitment and what it meant to dismiss it not only to her but also to everyone else affected by it without making every reasonable effort to honor it. The therapist asked her a decidedly morally based question: "Is it fair to Rod, to the children, or even yourself to decide the fate of the marriage if the criteria used to evaluate it have significantly changed from what they were originally, which he satisfied well, without giving him the chance to meet the new criteria?" Dee was surprised but responded that she did indeed owe everyone that consideration. Couple therapy then proceeded forward, and after several months of hard work, the marriage became quite more in line with what both Dee and Rod had hoped it would become.

This case, as well as that of Toni and Dave discussed earlier, are about mismatched levels of commitment. One partner is intent on preserving or remedying the relationship whereas the other is more interested in moving out of the relationship, or certainly is less committed to keeping it alive. As mentioned with Dave and Toni, if a partner learns for the first time in session of the other partner's intent to leave, the therapist's first task is to take care of the crisis for the one who wants to work it out. Once that is done, what to do with the couple becomes the key issue.

There are several assumptions that are often made at this point, and they may need to be explicitly discussed with the couple to check their validity. First, find out whether the "leaving" partner has made an irreversible decision. The fact that person is even in therapy may indicate some flexibility. Frequently the partner's decision to leave is more word than action. Second, do not assume that what has been said is the truth. Either or both of the partners may not fully believe the other's stated intentions and instead believe that they are negotiating or in a power struggle with each other. This might be another example of the couple's past and current interactional dynamics. Over time and with careful observation and sometimes pointed questions, the therapist can illuminate what is actually happening when there are threats to leave, as well as the partners' desire to change or save the marriage. Third, do not make assumptions about what "should" happen. This again is where the risk of undervaluing commitment looms. It is also possible, but less common, that the therapist is taking a default "save the relationship" position; this must also be avoided.

Weeks and Treat (2001) discussed in detail how to work effectively with couples where there is ambivalence in one partner, and Brothers (1997) wrote extensively on the topic in *When One Partner Is Willing and the Other Is Not.* Here, we will briefly suggest some things that the therapist may work on with the couple. First, clarifying what commitment means to each of the partners is paramount. They must know what they are committing to. Some clients may only be willing to commit to looking at their commitment. In other words, they may only be willing to commit to treatment for a time to make a decision about the relationship. Treatment at this point is less an interactional intervention and more an overt cost-benefit analysis. Curiously, many couples begin to move closer to each other, even during these sessions, as their focus becomes more collaborative, if also emotionally intense. They may find that they begin to get along better when they simply consider their possibilities rather than attempt to resolve their problems. Of course, this may occur because they are not dealing directly with intractable issues. In fact, the nature of their interaction as they explore what they want to do may tell the therapist a great deal about their actual relational status. In any event, unless both partners agree on an acceptable starting point, therapy will go nowhere.

Partners must also account for why they are willing or unwilling to make the commitments they are considering. This again is where the clients' expectations can be examined explicitly and countered, challenged, or validated as need be. The therapist should stress honesty and an appreciation of the past that the couple has built together, as well as the broad consequences of whatever decision they make. This latter concern too often does not get adequate consideration.

Second, for many couples with mismatched commitment levels, it can be helpful to adopt a more future-oriented approach. The partners can be asked to examine what benefits they would like to see in the future that would make commitment attractive. Asking them specifically how they would accomplish these benefits may help them to actually begin accomplishing them, and this reinforces the commitment. It is important, however, for the therapist to balance out the constraints the couple may have about leaving the relationship against the attractions they have to staying; an overemphasis on either does not adequately prepare the clients to make the best decision.

CHAPTER TWELVE

Overlooking or Inadvertently Imposing Spirituality

Historically the psychotherapy field has tended to avoid religious or spiritual issues. It has not, however, been completely absent in the literature. For example, Viktor Frankl (1955) was a well-known pioneering therapist who discussed the role of the meaning of life or "spiritual" issues. In general, though, with a few notable exceptions, religion and spirituality have been seen as indicative of neurosis and thus a problem to be treated. Fortunately, this has begun to change markedly in recent years. Increasingly therapists are trying to incorporate sensitivity to spiritual issues into counseling.

Understandably, there are still many barriers to including religion or spirituality in counseling. These include a very pragmatic belief in the separation of church and state in the United States. Additionally, there are diverging opinions about therapist power and proselytizing, wide disagreement regarding the nature of truth, a dominant belief in the profession that counseling is a science, and an intrinsic conflict between an orientation to spiritual healing using the internal resources of the person versus the external resources of treatment (Walsh, 1999). Moreover, few clinicians have any notable training regarding spirituality or religion; indeed, as Kahle and Robbins (2004) observed, spirituality and religion are glaringly absent from most multicultural counseling courses, appear cursorily at most in ethics courses, and appear nowhere else in the typical professional's training experience. In fact, many professionals sense that spirituality and religion are not to be included in training or counseling (Kahle & Robbins, 2004).

The ethical responsibility that all the mental health disciplines have to consider diversity (ACA, 1995, AAMFT, 2001, APA, 2002), however, includes sensitivity to clients' religious or spiritual issues. This implies that the therapist must be aware of clients' religious or spiritual realities and work well with them, or at least not harm them. This is a rather remarkable adjustment if one considers the field's history, because it essentially acknowledges that, far from being solely a scientific and empirical exercise, the counseling profession should view people holistically and must be able to address existential issues in their lives. Therefore, counseling can be seen as a spiritual practice if the therapist regards it as spiritual, if the client regards it as spiritual, or if some or all of what happens in the room is seen by either or both as spiritual (West, 2000).

There are several basic errors the therapist can make with regard to spirituality and religion in general practice; with couples, there are some more specific errors. Common general failures pertaining to spirituality and religion by therapists include:

- Lack of a conceptual framework for spirituality or religion
- Failing to include spirituality or religion in counseling when it is clearly appropriate
- Forcing spirituality and religion into counseling when clients do not want to include these issues
- Failing to address ethical issues related to including spirituality in counseling
- Failing to know one's own spirituality and its impact on the counseling relationship

- Failing to appreciate the significance or importance of spirituality to clients, especially when it is different from the therapist's (in other words, influencing clients away from their faith and toward that of the therapist)
- Failing to make use of clients' spiritual or religious resources in their treatment when appropriate

Errors that pertain specifically to work with couples include:

- When treating couples with different or incompatible spiritualities, creating an alliance or coalition with one of the partners based on the belief that he or she is "correct"
- Discouraging couples from organizing their relationships around their spiritual beliefs and practices
- Failing to see or failing to help clients see the implications of their spiritual beliefs on their relationship, and vice versa

Definitions of Religion and Spirituality

A review of the literature reveals no single, agreed-upon definition of spirituality. Defining spirituality implies that it can be understood much like other ideas and concepts, a suggestion that some would find controversial. However, if we are to discuss spirituality we must define it, even if that definition is lacking in some ways. Further, it has become commonplace to distinguish between religion and spirituality. Walsh (1999), for example, makes the common distinction that religion is organized, institutionalized, has beliefs about God or a Higher Power, and involves a like-minded community that provides standards grounded in core beliefs supported by rituals and ceremonies. In contrast, spirituality is "an overarching construct [that] refers more generally to transcendent beliefs and practices [and] can be experienced either within or outside formal religious structures" (p. 8). Others have noted that spirituality is complex and multidimensional (Elkins, Hedstorm, Hughes, Leaf, & Saunders,1988; Miller, 1999). Doherty (1999) suggested that the definitions typically used in the literature may be too broad and individualistic and have too little connection to the moral realm. It is worth noting that distinguishing spirituality from religion is a rather modern, American conceptualization generated out of our heavily individualistic culture. As Doherty stated, spirituality as it is often defined today has an implicit bias away from a commitment to and involvement in a larger community not only of belief and historic significance, but also of moral action, accountability, and ritual practice.

For the purposes of this chapter, we will define spirituality as a connection to or belief in the Transcendent (God, Higher Power, Divine, etc.), which may encompass thought, emotion, and behavior and offers a tangible sense of purpose and meaning to life. The relationship with the Transcendent leads to a "profoundly relational and moral way of being... [and] relations of respect, mutuality, accountability, compassion, and love with all humanity and with all creation" (Carlson, Erickson, & Seewald-Marquardt, 2002, p. 218).

Reasons to Include Spirituality in Counseling

Why include spirituality issues in counseling? First, Gallup poll information shows, over a 60-year period, fairly consistent percentages of Americans who find religion important in their lives. For example, according to Gallup (1996) 90% of all adults say religion is important in their lives and nearly 75% of respondents report that their family relationships have been strengthened by religion in the home. More than 80% say that religion was important in their family of origin when they were growing up. More than 90% identify with a particular religion, predominantly Christian (85%). The increasing percentage of non-Christians demonstrates that there is increasing diversity in religious practice: 3.6% in 1900 to nearly 15% in 1995.

Second, counseling should include religion and spirituality because clients desire it. Kahle and Robbins (2004) indicated that there are considerable data that clients want their therapists to include spirituality and religion in their treatment, although they may not explicitly request it. Some clients prefer therapists who are overtly religious or spiritual, even if the clinician is not of the same faith as they are, and clients want to be able to discuss issues pertaining to faith in counseling.

Therapists, particularly psychologists, tend to be less religious than their clientele and may evidence some bias against religion; as a whole, marriage and family therapists may be more religious than social workers, psychologists, and psychiatrists (Bergin & Jensen, 1990). Still, mental health professionals of all stripes tend to be less religious than clients. Furthermore, the vast majority has had little or no training in matters pertaining to spirituality and often have even received negative implicit or explicit messages about spirituality in their professional preparation and practice (Kahle & Robbins, 2004). Clearly, there is a gap to be closed.

Third, there is evidence from meta-analyses conducted by a number of researchers showing a positive correlation between spirituality, religion, and mental health. McCullough and Larson (1999), for instance, found that persons who both participated in a religious group and valued their faith had an up to 60% reduced risk for depressive disorders compared to those with no religious link. The National Institute for Health Care Research constituted three panels in 1996 and 1997 to look at the relationship of spirituality to physical health, mental health, and alcohol and drug problems. "When spiritual and religious involvement has been measured (even poorly), it has with surprising consistency been found to be positively related to health and inversely related to disorders" (Miller, 1999, p. 11). The reasons for this protective relationship are poorly understood. Sperry (2001) summarized over 200 published studies and stated that higher levels of spirituality are related to lower risk for disease, fewer medical and psychiatric problems, and higher levels of psychosocial functioning. Specifically, subjects with higher levels of spiritual and religious commitment tend to report higher levels of well-being and life satisfaction, have greater marital satisfaction, less divorce, lower rates of premarital sex, teenage pregnancy, and juvenile delinquency, less anxiety, less depression and substance abuse and dependence, fewer suicidal impulses, and less likelihood of committing suicide. Additionally, those using prayer, meditation, reading sacred writings, and seeking spiritual counsel tend to adjust better to crises.

Family process researchers have found that transcendent spiritual beliefs and practices are key ingredients in healthy family functioning (Beavers & Hampson, 1990; Stinnett & DeFrain, 1985). Family life cycle issues—for example, marriage and having children—often bring religious issues to the fore. In interfaith couples, the rituals associated with marriage itself can be a challenge for both the individuals and the extended families. Once children are born, parents who thought they viewed religion as unimportant may be surprised to find that one or both deeply care about how the children are raised with regard to matters of faith. This can be especially difficult for Jewish people who are concerned about their future due to high rates of intermarriage (Walsh, 1999). Religious involvement follows a life cycle pattern: young adults, particularly in college, often distance themselves from their religious upbringing (Elkind, 1971) and 16% of 18- to 29-year-olds say that they have no religious preference (Gallup, 1996). In midlife to later life, people grapple with questions about meaning and face their own and others' mortality (Erikson, Erikson, & Kivnick, 1986; Walsh, 1998). Attendance at worship services increases with age: 30% of 18- to 29-year-olds, 40% of 30- to 49-year-olds, and 46% of people age 50 and older have attended in the past seven days (Carroll, 2004).

In addition, suffering may be understood ultimately as a spiritual issue and may be viewed and responded to differently in various religious traditions. Family belief systems are powerful influences in making meaning of adversity and suffering; they can facilitate or constrain change (Dallos, 1991; Wright, et al., 1996 quoted in Walsh, 1999, p. 37). Sperry (2001) noted that a couple's spiritual orientation and religiosity influence various aspects of their lives, such as gender roles, sexuality and intimacy, and ideas about how to raise children, and can serve as either a resource or barrier to treatment.

Ethical Issues

Ethical considerations applicable to the inclusion of spirituality in counseling come from codes of ethics requirements and from principles. One foundational problem with applying ethical codes or principles, however, is that the sources of authority for those codes and principles are rarely explicit and not traditionally religious. Typically, professionals do not examine in any depth the sources of their ethical codes, but rather accept (or reject) them and generally act accordingly.

Robichaud (2003) listed ethical requirements including client welfare, informed consent, dual relationships, imposition of values, and training and competence. For example, Corey, Corey, and Callanan (2003) suggested that working within a client's belief system is a way to protect and enhance client welfare. Addressing spiritual or religious issues as they arise is another way to honor the client's best interest in this domain (Frame, 2003). Frame suggested that the client be informed at the beginning of therapy if the therapist is willing to work with religious or spiritual concerns. For some clients, a therapists' having a neutral stance with respect to religion or spirituality may inhibit joining and development of trust (Boyd-Franklin & Lockwood, 1999) and could potentially cause harm. Of course, as any multicultural counseling course will emphasize, making assumptions about clients' stances toward spirituality and religion based on their ethnicity or external appearance is unwise.

Same-faith therapist-client relationships can also be a concern, especially if the therapist and the clients have a relationship with each other outside counseling. If they belong to the same religious community, especially in a smaller locality, confidentiality can be jeopardized. In addition, the client may not understand or appreciate the professional constraint the therapist must respect if they happen upon each other in the faith community. The idea that the therapist, with whom the client shares a spiritual community *and* a deeply personal relationship, would willfully ignore the client in that setting may be quite harmful. Obviously, the concern here is that the client may be confused by the dual relationship or the therapist's judgment may be vulnerable to impairment. The most serious concern is when a pastor or spiritual leader is doing the counseling. The client may feel they must say what the church teaches even though part of the problem may stem from the church's teachings.

In some cases, religious leaders act as both minister and counselor simultaneously. This can lead to role confusion. Miller (2003) suggested various potential solutions including providing free counseling in a religious setting and limiting counseling to religious or spiritual problems, consulting with colleagues, and being clear at the beginning of counseling regarding communications and interactions within the community. Such solutions may be easier to suggest than implement.

Frame (2003) noted that counseling is not value-free. Therapists working with clients on religious or spiritual issues may be vulnerable to violating the ethical standard not to impose values. Examples of imposition of values include making judgments about client lifestyle choices or using a religious or spiritually based intervention without the consent of the client. Suggested courses of action include understanding one's own religious or spiritual values and how they can affect the counseling relationship, letting the client bring up religious or spiritual issues first, discussing the treatment plan and one's level of expertise with the client, and making referrals if needed (Frame, 2003; Miller, 2003). This does not mean that the therapist cannot clarify client beliefs and help the client to identify which beliefs may be helpful or not. Of course, transference or countertransference can confound clear understanding of imposition of values.

Codes of ethics (ACA, 1995; AAMFT, 2001) mandate that therapists do not practice outside of their training and competence. Because there has been a dearth of training in spirituality and religion, therapists who work with these issues must take steps to increase competence through training to gain self-awareness, obtain knowledge of the client's religious or spiritual culture (see Richards & Bergin, 2000) or the various ways to map spiritual development (West, 2000), and learn skills and methods that can be incorporated into practice for dealing with this area. Various books deal with these issues, and there are many offerings at professional conventions, conferences, and workshops. West suggested several other actions: joining with others to study this area or obtaining competent supervision, which is sometimes difficult to find.

Therapists should also consider the setting in which they work as they approach this topic. Frame (2003) suggested that professionals work within the law and within agency policies and procedures. For therapists working in publicly funded, secular settings, discussion of religion and spirituality may be looked at with some suspicion. Unfortunately, this may especially pertain to Christianity. For example, a client presented for treatment at a publicly funded, state-operated clinic. Shortly into treatment, the client began to discuss religious issues that were a source of difficulty. In the course of the conversation, she revealed that she was Christian. She asked the therapist what religion she was, and the therapist replied that she was also Christian. (Some would question the wisdom of the therapist's revealing that piece of data, which again points to how uncomfortable therapists may be with the subject of religion and spirituality.) The client asked the therapist if they could pray together at the end of their sessions because the client thought it would be helpful to her. The therapist agreed, with some enthusiasm. When the administrator of the clinic heard about the case during staffing, his response was swift and unmistakable. The therapist was forbidden to pray with the client because the clinic was not "faith based" and would brook no appearance of religious favoritism. Less than a month later, a second case was discussed in staffing, wherein a client asked the therapist if he would be willing to perform a Native American religious ritual with the client in session. The therapist, who was excited to be part of it, agreed. The administrator's response to this was again swift and unmistakable. The therapist was praised for his openness to the diversity of religious experience and expression, and the clinic was praised for its willingness to be inclusive and work with clients. Unfortunately, the irony, not to mention the discrimination, was lost upon nearly the entire staff. When the clinic defined the intervention as overtly religious it was forbidden, but when defined as accepting diversity it was approved.

For therapists working within more explicit religious or private settings, the difficulty is less often the discussion itself and more often the untoward results of the discussion. Among these concerns is usurping or displacing the authority of a spiritual or religious leader or making derogatory or critical remarks about the practices and beliefs of religious leaders (Frame, 2003). Discussing religious dogma, doctrine, and practice or ritual is also very tricky.

An alternate way to look at ethically handling spiritual issues is within a framework of principles. Odell (2003) suggested that there are four interrelated principles that should undergird spiritual and religious work in therapy: agency, fidelity, responsibility, and safety. Agency means that clients are free to choose what they believe and how to act, because they are free moral agents. Therapists who cannot acknowledge this principle may be covertly or overtly imposing their values and should either obtain the clients' explicit informed consent to include spiritual issues or refer. Fidelity is the consistent living out of one's beliefs. In order to support fidelity, therapists must not assume that they and the client share a common worldview, but rather must ask the client to educate them on the client's belief system. Therapists, using client language, can ask respectfully about any inconsistencies, which may prompt the client to either change his or her behaviors or beliefs, increasing fidelity. The client operates in a context of relationships and thus has responsibilities to his or her family, faith community, and larger society, which must be taken into account. This is particularly true with regard to the subject of commitment. Therapists must carefully consider the implications of challenging clients to remove themselves from family and communities that may support them. Safety must be preserved physically, emotionally, psychologically, and relationally.

Assessment and Treatment Considerations

Some may believe that assessing or measuring spirituality is an oxymoron or even hubris. However, as Gorsuch and Miller (1999) stated, assessment can be important for prognosis, context, outcome, and intervention. Knowing about a client's religious involvement can provide some information on risk and protective factors, much like family history, social support, and stress do, because religious involvement is often inversely related to physical, mental, and substance abuse disorders. Of course, this must be done in sufficient detail and in relation to other data. Because spirituality is ultimately what forms and frames a client's reality, understanding it will help put the presenting problem in context. In addition, assessment helps to answer questions about potential personal and community resources clients may have, important values that might affect deeply held ethical positions, the impact of the presenting problem on involvement in their community (some may stop participating in it), and misunderstandings about faith positions, which clergy may be able to clarify. Spiritual functioning is dynamic and changes over time. In addition, although spirituality is generally protective, some beliefs increase risk; for example, a concept of God as wrathful and punitive increases the risk of substance abuse (Gorsuch, 1994). Thus, treatment can affect spiritual functioning, especially if coping strategies are made more functional. Spiritual variables can also be important for intervention. Assuming that spirituality is relevant to treatment and that the client has consented, incorporating or building on the client's spirituality may enhance treatment, for example by using meditation, acceptance and forgiveness, hope, or prayer, all of which are discussed by Miller (1999).

Assessing for Spiritual Health

One approach to assessment is to consider whether a client's spirituality is healthy or unhealthy, either individually or relationally. Of course, such a statement implies that there is a set of universally accepted metavalues by which the otherwise foundational values provided by spirituality or religion can be evaluated, which there are not. In other words, spirituality is evaluated in psychological terms, which is not something all clients, nor all therapists, accept. If one has to choose between being faithful to one's spirituality and being evaluated as psychologically healthy (according to a different set of criteria), there will certainly not be unanimity, and it may well be that some people would choose the former over the latter. This is a reality often overlooked in the literature on spirituality. Therapists must ensure that they have adequate training and consult when necessary to make these assessments.

Individual assessment. There is a literature related to conceptions of healthy individual spirituality or spiritual development. Allport and Ross (1967), for example, made a distinction between immature/extrinsic and mature/intrinsic religion. The therapeutic implication of this is the understanding that people having an immature religion use it for their own ends, whereas those with mature religion try to embrace or internalize their beliefs and follow them fully. Vaughn (1991), from a transpersonal and modern Western perspective, stated that healthy spirituality supports personal freedom, autonomy, and self-esteem as well as social responsibility. He also noted that healthy spirituality does not deny humanity or depend on suppression or denial of emotions. Spiritual addictions may be present if spirituality is based on wishful thinking or abdication of personal responsibility, or if a high is sought through religious or spiritual rituals or practices.

Richards and Bergin (1997) summarized several other empirically tested theories of religious and spiritual well-being, development, and maturity, such as Fowler's six-stage model of faith development, Paloutzian and Ellison's two-dimensional model of spiritual well-being, Malony's eight-dimensional model of Christian maturity, and Clinebell's informal and empirically untested tests for mentally healthy religion. The clinician wanting more information can consult Sperry (2001), who summarized and critiqued various stage models of development that might affect the spiritual dimension and discussed spiritual journey. Lukoff (1998) noted that it may not be easy to discern healthy spiritual experiences because there is a continuum from pure mystical experience to pure psychosis. It is not just the content of the experience but also the ability of the person to establish intersubjective reality with others and manage everyday life that is important.

Relational assessment. Assessment can also be done relationally. Couple systems can be characterized by three metaconstructs: boundaries or inclusion, power or control, and intimacy (Fish & Fish, 1986). Similarly, these constructs can be useful in assessing and formulating treatment issues with couples and families (Sperry, 2001). Are members forming coalitions with God in an effort to gain extra power, control, or authority? Is religious conflict used to present underlying family conflict? Does conflict arise out of fundamentally different religious commitments (Pattison, 1982)? The therapist can ask questions to determine the degree to which religion or spirituality influences feelings, thoughts, and behaviors in the couple system. The eventual goal is to discriminate between healthy and dysfunctional spirituality in the couple system. How does spirituality or religion contribute to marital affect (from defensiveness to openness), thinking (from certainty to tentativeness), and behavior (from revenge to forgiveness) (Giblin, 1993)? Patterns of intimacy/distance between couples are assumed to be similar to those perceived in relation to God. Changes in the closeness or distance perceived in the marital relationship may affect the perception of the relationship with God and vice versa (Sperry, 2001).

What to Assess

Many different authors have posited various ways of asking questions about religion and spirituality (Cole & Pargament, 1999; Crohn, 1996; Gorsuch & Miller, 1999; Richards & Bergin, 1997; Walsh, 1999; Wright, 1999; Yahne & Miller, 1999). In essence, the questions revolve around the importance of religion or spirituality to the person, how religious or spiritual beliefs are put into practice, and the impact of family of origin on beliefs, practices, and the couple relationship (especially if there is an interfaith marriage). Questions about religious orientation are also included in DeMaria, Weeks, and Hof (1999). In addition, Matthews (1998) suggested that therapists conclude assessment by asking clients whether they would like them to address their religious or spiritual beliefs and practices with them.

Some useful assessment models have been developed in the pastoral counseling field. Fitchett (1993) proposed a functional, multidimensional, holistic framework for gathering information in a conversational manner. The dimensions included medical, psychological, psychosocial, family-systems, ethnic and cultural, societal, and spiritual. The spiritual dimension is further defined by looking at beliefs and meaning, vocation and consequences, experience and emotion, courage and growth, ritual and practice, community, and authority and guidance. Denton (1998) had an alternate approach based loosely on the concept of independent axes used by DSM-IV. His axes are ethical guilt, covenantal betrayal, and existential defilement. Feelings of being punished and guilty are assessed on the first axis. Failures in relationships of trust either with others or God is assessed on the second axis. The third axis is used to note someone wrestling with life-and-death spiritual themes.

Contraindications

Richards and Bergin (1997) offered a list of contraindications to the use of spirituality in psychotherapy. Their list has both absolute and relative contraindications. Absolute contraindications for spiritual strategies include clients who do not want such an approach, clients who are delusional or psychotic, cases where these strategies are not relevant to the presenting problems, and when parental consent has not been obtained for clients who are minors. In considering client welfare as well as the potential for the imposition of values, therapists should consider the relative contraindications for certain clients: young children and adolescents, severely psychologically disturbed clients, antireligious or nonreligious persons, those who are spiritually immature or who consider God as distant and condemning, and those who have a deferring or passive religious problem-solving style.

How to Address Issues That May Be Raised

Helmeke and Bischof (2002) listed the kinds of issues that might be raised by clients and therapists. Clients may raise spiritual issues such as general discontent with life, questions of meaning, dealing with loss or trauma, or struggles between actions and values. Conflicts due to different religious backgrounds, abuse by clergy, or positive statements of practices that lead to coping are also examples of religious issues that clients may raise. Therapists may initiate discussions of spiritual issues while assessing for resources or strengths, conducting life reviews, helping with addiction recovery, or when using rituals; religious discussions might evolve from completing religious genograms, exploring cutoffs with God or a faith community, or while doing premarital counseling. Richards and Bergin (1997) noted that there is more risk for ethical violations when interventions are therapist-initiated, denominationally specific, religiously explicit, and in-session. In addition, interventions are likely to be more risky and less effective if the therapeutic alliance is weak and when therapists and clients have low religious value similarity.

For therapists who feel timid about using spiritual or religious interventions, Helmeke and Bischof (2002) outlined treatment considerations based on whether the client or therapist raises the issue. If clients raise spiritual issues, therapists can acknowledge them, question their impact, explore the experience or language used, and assess if the client's spirituality can be part of a solution. They can also research the issue, collaborate with a minister (with consent of the client), help the client work out power conflicts, and pay attention to their own countertransference. Therapists who raise spiritual issues with clients should use a tentative, cautious approach when questioning ways that beliefs may constrain or empower clients. Paying attention to the impact of losses and addiction and to the feedback from client can assist in the journey of discovery. For therapists who want to raise religious issues, Helmeke and Bischof stressed not making assumptions about any religious beliefs.

Other Treatment Considerations

Assuming there are no contraindications and the therapeutic alliance has been built, interventions should respect client autonomy and freedom, be sensitive to religious and spiritual beliefs, and be flexible and responsive to client values and needs. Treatment must be tailored to the unique combination of needs, beliefs, and circumstances of each couple. At the same time, interventions must take into account the spiritual or religious community within which the couple live their lives. Having a couple watch a pornographic video together as a homework assignment directed at loosening sexual inhibitions, for example, would be ill-advised for clients who belong to a faith community that frowns on such activities. The couple would be forced to choose between therapeutic change as suggested by the therapist and the moral boundaries and spiritual understanding of marriage as offered by their beliefs and the community that supports them.

Language. Matching client language can be used to help tailor interventions. Doherty (1999) conceptualized three overlapping domains: spiritual, clinical, and moral. Language differs in the three domains: for example, God's will, calling, faith, and grace in the spiritual domain; personality, family dysfunction, and self-esteem in the clinical domain; right/wrong, obligation, and fairness in the moral domain. Language is also different in the overlapping areas: serenity, centeredness, and hope in the clinical-spiritual domain; commitment, responsibility, and honesty in the clinical-moral domain; and commandments, golden rule, and evil in the spiritual-moral domain. Doherty (1999) saw healing, values, growth, guilt, forgiveness, meaning, and community as being part of the language of all three domains. Thus, if individuals use rote language from one domain, language from an overlap area might help the client; in areas of conflict, language from the overlap areas can be used to find areas of agreement. Giblin (1993) suggested that ambivalent spaces in the relationship can be reframed as holy spaces. Griffith (1999) advised therapists to explore the language around spiritual/religious issues with curiosity. Therapists may become entrapped in thinking that they know what the couple is saying due to assumptions about religious denomination, language, or images about God, or because of their own countertransferential need to have the client know the God they know.

Values. Values are another target of therapeutic intervention. Therapists may focus on this area when there are incongruities between values and behavior, self-punishing ideals, confusion between values, or unhealthy client values (Richards, Rector, & Tjeltveit, 1999). Kimball and Knudson-Martin (2002) urged therapists to be cautious of agreeing with a position that carries moral consequences, such as gender inequality, without allowing clients to consider the implications of their decisions. In addition, looking for common denominators in values can obscure cultural or spiritual contrasts that need to be acknowledged in couples who have a mixture of cultures, ethnicities, or faith (Crohn, 1996).

Spiritual practices. One challenge for therapists working with couples is that much of the literature on spirituality and counseling has focused on practices that individuals undertake including prayer, meditation, spiritual relaxation and imagery, and religious bibliotherapy. Richards and Bergin (1997) described these practices, the therapeutic benefits associated with them, and research evidence to support their use or outcomes. They noted the usefulness of these practices but reminded therapists that there is a risk of role boundary confusion if these practices are done in-session. They also stated that therapists must make sure that they are working within the client's belief systems to avoid imposing their own beliefs or practices. Referrals to religious leaders may be made if the client wants to understand practices better. Forgiveness, worship and ritual, and fellowship and service are practices done within relationships. Encouraging forgiveness is one of the most frequently used spiritual interventions by psychotherapists (Richards & Bergin, 1997) and is used to forgive others, the self, and God. Encouraging clients to participate in worship, ritual, fellowship, and service can connect them to important other relationships.

Relational considerations. Becvar (1997) used a systemic orientation that focuses less on technique and more on the orientation to and relationship with clients, including acknowledging connectedness, suspending judgment, and creating new realities. She noted the power of acknowledging connectedness in systems (each person, including the therapist, is affected by the other) on many levels, including the soul. The primary focus should be the kind of relationship we have and want. Growth and healing can come as one person helps the other. Her message reinforces the importance of carefully handling commitments in relationships. Clients come to therapy stuck in repetitive patterns of behavior and need new information or stories to create a new context. Stories can be shaped differently if clients can, at least temporarily, suspend judgment. This can be done by a focus on the here and now and by assuming good intentions by the various parties. This allows clients to reflect and create a new reality. As mentioned, reframing is an important part of creating new realities. Therapists can help clients see crisis as an opportunity to develop new qualities, meaning, or purpose. Certain questions can be helpful in this regard, for example. "In what way does this situation, or in what way *could* this situation, add meaning to your life?" "How might you use this situation to benefit yourself or others in your world?" "Are there themes or patterns that link this situation to others in your life?" Rituals can also be created to support clients' ability to trust that change is happening—for example, writing down prior hurts on cards and burning them as an acknowledgment that the past cannot be changed but that a changed response to these events reflected in new stories can recreate the past.

Change and growth may not be similar for members of a couple. For example, representations of God or a Higher Power may be distant, intimate, nonexistent; religious or spiritual practices may be different; and the individual be either intrinsically or extrinsically oriented to religious matters. We have already noted that what the differences actually are may be less important than how the couple negotiates those differences. The spiritual dimension may affect how these negotiations and decisions are made, so asking clients whether and how this dimension affects them may give important clues about resources and barriers. In addition, given a systemic orientation, attention must be paid to the impact of individual or couple decisions on others.

Errors With Couples

As mentioned, one common error that therapists can make when working with couples who have incompatible spiritualities or religions is to attempt to convince one or the other, or both, that their beliefs are wrong. Doing so typically involves a coalition with one partner against the other. In particular, because religion and spirituality tend to be important to people, their responses to being attacked in this domain tend to be quite strong. The following case shows how this error was avoided.

A couple presented for counseling with several major areas of conflict, the most obvious one being polar differences in their spiritual beliefs. The marriage was the second for both of them, and they had dated for quite some time. The wife was deeply religious and involved in a church, and her husband was a devout atheist who had agreed during their courtship to "investigate" her beliefs. This was a condition under which she would continue to see him. They had progressed far enough in their relationship to agree to marry, and came to therapy about a year later. Since the wedding, the husband had concluded that his wife's beliefs were "stupid and irrational" and he had discontinued "investigating." In addition, he overtly disapproved of her or the children displaying any religious symbols, praying before meals, or conducting other rituals established in her home. Understandably, the wife was angry, both at herself for "compromising" and at him for what she believed was his deception. He was angry that his wife seemed to love God more than she loved him, and that she kept trying to "push her religion" on him.

Although the content of therapy early on was focused on the specifics of behaviors related to religion and attempts to negotiate acceptable compromises, the issue in question really was one of priority. Ultimately, the compromises were untenable for both of them. The wife wanted her husband at the least to let her be demonstrably religious in the home and with the children, and the husband wanted the wife to totally abandon all religious behaviors. It became necessary to examine the nature of their commitments to each other vis-à-vis their commitments to their worldviews. They both agreed that they had not been very wise in their courtship! The therapist was religious, but could not and did not attempt to argue with the husband, nor did he side with the wife. Rather, he steadfastly insisted that they evaluate their commitments and their choices and then consider the ramifications of any course of action they would take with regard to themselves, their marriage, the children, and their larger social communities. Ultimately, the husband sought a divorce; because of her faith, the wife did not believe herself free to do so. However, upon his leaving, she believed herself to be released from the marriage as well.

In the foregoing situation, the differences between the clients' worldviews are obvious. In many cases, the differences are much more subtle and errors are easier to make. Consider the following case in which a couple, Sean and Tara, discussed roles in their marriage in the context of their religion. The therapist did not share either partner's belief system.

Tara: I'm so frustrated sometimes with how little Sean helps me with the kids. I know he's incredibly busy at work, but when he gets home I'd really appreciate his picking up with them. Homework, or something! I hate having to tell him what to do.

Sean: We've had this discussion about a thousand times. I'm dead tired when I get home, and it takes me a while to change gears into "family man." But that's too long for her. And I already have a boss, so I don't want another one at home.

Tara: It's not fair. (*pause*) I want to be the submissive wife that the Bible talks about, but I don't think that means Sean gives the orders and I take them.

Sean: It means you need to respect my authority. You shouldn't tell me what to do. For my part, yeah, I need to hold up my end.

Therapist: Pardon me, but what you just said strikes me as kind of sexist. Just what does holding up your end mean, and why would you want a marriage built around things like authority and submission? That doesn't sound very healthy to me.

Tara: Look, I just need some help with the kids more often, and I don't want to nag.

Therapist: Don't run from the issue or try to protect your husband. It seems we're getting into foundational problems with power in your marriage, and I'm concerned that the way you've organized your relationship is ... well, flawed.

The therapist's reaction to the clients' religious language and beliefs was negative and led him to miss the issue with which they needed help. Rather than accept how they defined their relationship around religiously informed issues like authority and submission and then working within their frame of reference, he took issue with what he perceived to be inherently flawed power inequities and addressed their source—religion—overtly. Because he assumed that Tara was the stereotypical exploited female married to the privileged male, he readily dismissed the clients' worldview. If he were to continue treatment without exploring more specifically how they understood and implemented their religious beliefs, he would most likely fail with them.

Therapists can also err by failing to utilize the clients' belief system to organize their relationship in helpful ways, or by discouraging couples from using their religious or spiritual resources to combat problems they identify. The following case illustrates how this error can occur.

Howard and Renee came to treatment with a presenting issue of conflict over Howard's use of Internet pornography and Renee's response to it. They both shared the same religious beliefs, and Renee's difficulty with her husband's behavior was explicitly predicated on her belief that his actions were essentially adulterous according to their religion's doctrine and scriptures. Howard agreed with her, but said that his use of it was partially related to her unwillingness to have sexual relations with him to the extent that he desired. Underneath the content, there was a power and blame struggle at the process level of their relationship that was manifesting in Renee's use of spiritual "one-upsmanship" with Howard. The therapist, who did not share their religious perspective, was leery of religion and avoided the religious language altogether. He instead chose to deal directly with the question of power. He emphasized that use of pornography is normal and not necessarily the major issue. He pushed the couple toward considering changing their behavior by negotiating for what they wanted through quid pro quo agreements, and they were responsive. From the therapist's point of view, it was problematic that both Renee and Howard kept returning to the meaning of the pornography as a form of infidelity, with Renee usually the initiator of the conversation. The therapist did not know how to address this, but wisely did not discount their concerns about it.

The therapy would probably have been more effective had the therapist made use of the religious language the clients used. Had the therapist researched some of the religious texts the couple mentioned, he could have pointed out that Renee's refusal to have sex with her husband was also problematic in their scriptures, something that would have countered the consistent power dynamic in a way that would have been easier for her to accept. She may have then been better positioned to be faithful to what she believed (i.e., to be a person of virtue according to her religion), which may have softened her and ultimately contributed to both forgiveness between them and a greater willingness to honor each other's sexual boundaries, needs, and preferences. This vulnerability would have made the power struggle much less significant and removed much of the blaming cycle.

Therapists can make mistakes with couples by failing to see or failing to help them see the reciprocal implications of their beliefs and practices for their relationships. Most religions are fairly pro-marriage, and the degree to which people live out or fail to live out their faiths has serious consequences, for good or ill, for their relationships. The converse is also true. The following case example shows how a couple's first therapist failed to see the use of religious beliefs in reframing their situation to support the continuance of marriage, whereas the second did not.

Ted and Ellen presented for counseling, saying they were afraid they were on the verge of a divorce that they both fervently wanted to avoid. They had previously seen a therapist for several sessions over a few months and had addressed a number of issues that all seemed to be connected to a serious underlying incompatibility. The partners were notably different from each other with regard to everything from hobbies and interests to personality type. The one foundational thing that they shared, however, was their spiritual beliefs, and they said they believed God had brought them together. Their former therapist had attempted to help them find ways to overcome the difficulties they were experiencing, but after little progress had been made, they were all feeling understandably frustrated.

In one session with the first clinician, Ellen reported that she had said she sometimes felt like God had made a mistake in bringing them together. The therapist, who did not share their religious beliefs, interpreted that statement as a sign of doubt about her religion and suggested that perhaps her thought was not unreasonable. Maybe, she said, God had erred, or perhaps they had misread God's plan for them. Further, the therapist said, she found it hard to believe that God would want them to be so miserable together, and even if divorce was a sin according to their beliefs, God would surely forgive them if they divorced. Because the couple did not accept the reframe, they stopped attending, although they did not tell the therapist why. Presumably, the therapist may have concluded that the clients were somehow pathologically committed to each other and had an overly literal or fundamental rigidity in their religious beliefs. It would not be hard to imagine that she pathologized their choice to stay together.

When the couple began working with the second therapist, who accepted their religiously generated commitment even though she did not share their beliefs, they found that she was able to help them by tapping into their belief system rather than challenging it. She asked them how God could be using their marital struggles as a way of strengthening each of their characters and showing an example of marital commitment in a culture in which such a commitment is rare. She wondered collaboratively with the couple about what God's intention was for bringing two very different people together in a marriage that from the start would be difficult. Joining with them in this way offered a powerful reframe that freed the couple to attempt to be different with each other out of love for God and spouse. It also strengthened their confidence in God's decision to put them together. The second therapist emphasized that accomplishing the changes that would be necessary would be both a cause and a result of their living in accordance with their faith. Their counseling was successful.

It is worth noting that the first therapist attempted to help the clients see the implications of choosing to stay together for religious reasons, but she went off track by suggesting that their religious reasons were questionable. In her mind, their religion was an unnecessary constraint, and she was implicitly proselytizing. The second therapist accepted their beliefs while highlighting the fact that their marriage would be difficult, even with their convictions about staying together. She was able to work within and through their religion.

When spirituality and psychology are integrated, therapists see humans as physical, mental, emotional, and spiritual beings. The therapy process, then, can access the spiritual for healing and resilience, challenge constraining beliefs or destructive actions, and support clients as they move from despair and brokenness to hope and healing.

References

Alberti, R., & Emmons, M. (2001). *Your perfect right* (8th ed.). Atascadero, CA: Impact.

Allport, G. W., & Ross, J. M. (1967). Personal religious orientation and prejudice. *Journal of Personality and Social Psychology, 5*, 432–443.

American Association of Marriage and Family Therapy. (2001). *AAMFT code of ethics.* Washington, D.C.: Author.

American Counseling Association. (1995). *Code of ethics and standards of practice.* Alexandria, VA: Author.

American Psychiatric Association. (1994). *Diagnostic and statistical manual of mental disorders* (4th ed.). Washington, D.C.: Author.

American Psychological Association. (2002). *Ethical principles of psychologists and code of conduct.* Washington, D.C.: Author.

Beach, S. R. H. (2003). Affective disorders. *Journal of Marital and Family Therapy, 29*(2), 247–262.

Beavers, W. R., & Hampson, R. B. (1990). *Successful families: Assessment and intervention.* New York: Norton.

Becvar, D. S. (1997). *Soul healing: A spiritual orientation in counseling and therapy.* New York: Basic.

Bergin, A. E., & Jensen, S. P. (1990). Religiosity of psychotherapists: A national survey. *Psychotherapy, 27,* 2–7.

Boyd-Franklin, N., & Lockwood, T. W. (1999). Spirituality and religion: Implications for psychotherapy with African American clients and families. In F. Walsh (Ed.), *Spiritual resources in family therapy* (pp. 90–103). New York: Guilford.

Brothers, B. (1997). *When one partner is willing and the other is not.* New York: Haworth.

Carlson, T. D., Erickson, M. J., & Seewald-Marquardt, A. (2002). The spiritualities of therapists' lives: Using therapists' spiritual beliefs as a resource for relational ethics. *Journal of Family Psychotherapy, 13*(3/4), 215–236.

Carroll, J. (2004, March 2). American public opinion about religion. *The Gallup Organization Focus on Religion.* Retrieved September 5, 2004, from http://www.gallup.com/poll/focus/sr040302.asp?ci=10813.

Charney, I., & Parnass, S. (1995). The impact of extramarital relationships on the continuation of marriages. *Journal of Sex and Marital Therapy, 21*(2), 110–115.

Cole, B. S., & Pargament, K. I. (1999). Spiritual surrender: A paradoxical path to control. In W. R. Miller (Ed.), *Integrating spirituality into treatment: Resources for practitioners* (pp. 179–198). Washington, D.C.: American Psychological Association.

Corey, G., Corey, M., & Callanan, P. (Eds.). (2003). *Issues and ethics in the helping profession* (6th ed.). Pacific Grove, CA: Brooks/Cole.

Crohn, J. (1996). Interracial, interethnic & interfaith relationships. In H. Kessler (Ed.). *Treating couples.* San Francisco: Jossey-Bass.

Dallos, R. (1991). Family belief systems, therapy, and change. Philadelphia: Open University Press.

DeMaria, R., Weeks, G., & Hof, L. (1999). *Focused genograms: Intergenerational assessment of individuals, couples, and families.* Philadelphia: Brunner/Mazel.

Denton, D. D. (1998). *Religious diagnosis in a secular society: A staff for the journey.* Lanham, MD: University Press of America.

de Shazer, S. (1985). *Keys to solution in brief therapy.* New York: Norton.

Dicks, H. V. (1967). *Marital tensions.* New York: Basic.

Doherty, W. (1995). *Soul searching: Why psychotherapy must promote moral responsibility.* New York: Basic.

Doherty, W. J. (1999). Morality and spirituality in therapy. In F. Walsh (Ed.), *Spiritual resources in family therapy* (pp. 179–192). New York: Guilford.

Elkind, D. (1971). The development of religious understanding in children and adolescents. In M. P. Strommen (Ed.), *Research of religious development* (pp. 655–685). New York: Hawthorn.

Elkins, D. N., Hedstorm, L. J., Hughes, L. L., Leaf, J. A., & Saunders, C. (1988). Towards a humanistic-phenomenological spirituality. *Journal of Humanistic Psychology, 28*(4), 5–18.

Erickson, E. H., Erikson, J. M., & Kivnick, H. Q. (1986). *Vital involvement in old age.* New York: Norton.

Feldman, L. B. (1979). Marital conflict and marital intimacy: An integrative psychodynamic-behavioral-systemic model. *Family Process, 18*(1), 69–78.

Feldman, L. B. (1982). Dysfunctional marital conflict: An integrative interpersonal-intrapsychic model. *Journal of Marital and Family Therapy, 8*(4), 417–428.

Fish, R., & Fish, L. (1986). Quid pro quo revisited: The basics of marital therapy. *American Journal of Orthopsychiatry, 56*(3), 371–384.

Fitchett, G. (1993). *Assessing spiritual needs: A guide for caregivers.* Minneapolis, MN: Augsburg.

Fowers, B. (1998). Psychology and the good marriage: Social theory as practice. *American Behavioral Scientist, 41,* 516–541.

Frame, M. W. (2003). *Integrating religion and spirituality into counseling: A comprehensive approach.* Pacific Grove, CA: Brooks/Cole.

Frank, E., Anderson, C., & Rubinstein, D. (1978). Frequency of sexual dysfunction in "normal" couples. *The New England Journal of Medicine, 299,* 111–115.

Frankl, V. (1955). *The doctor and the soul: From psychotherapy to logotherapy.* New York: Knopf.

Gallup, G., Jr. (1996). *Religion in America: 1996 report.* Princeton, NJ: Princeton Research Center.

Giblin, P. (1993). Marital conflict and marital spirituality. In R. Wicks & R. Parsons (Eds.), *Clinical handbook of pastoral counseling: Volume II.* New York: Paulist Press.

Glass, S. & Staehel, J. C. (2002). *Not "just friends": Protect your relationship from infidelity and heal the trauma of betrayal.* New York: Free Press.

Goldhor-Lerner, H. (1997). *The dance of anger.* New York: Quill.

Gorsuch, R. L. (1994). Religious aspects of substance abuse and recovery. *Journal of Social Issues, 51,* 65–83.

Gorsuch, R. L., & Miller, W. R. (1999). Assessing spirituality. In W. R. Miller (Ed.), *Integrating spirituality into treatment: Resources for practitioners* (pp. 47–64). Washington, D.C.: American Psychological Association.

Gottman, J. (1994a). *What predicts divorce? The relationship between marital process and marital outcomes.* Hillsdale, NJ: Erlbaum.

Gottman, J. (1994b). *Why marriages succeed or fail.* New York: Simon & Schuster.

Griffith, M. E. (1999). Opening therapy to conversations with a personal God. In F. Walsh (Ed.), *Spiritual resources in family therapy* (pp. 209–222). New York: Guilford.

Helmeke, K. B., & Bischof, G. H. (2002). Recognizing and raising spiritual and religious issues in therapy: Guidelines for the timid. In T. D. Carlson & M. J. Erickson (Eds.), *Spirituality and family therapy* (pp. 195–214). New York: Haworth.

Howard, B., & Weeks, G. R. (1995). A happy marriage: Pairing couples therapy and treatment of depression. In G. R. Weeks & L. Hof (Eds.), *Integrative solutions: Treating common problems in couples therapy* (pp. 95–123). New York: Brunner/Mazel.

Johnson, M. P. (1995). Intimate terrorism and common couple violence: Two forms of violence against women. *The Journal of Marriage and the Family, 57,* 283–294.

Johnson, S. M. (1996). *Creating connection: The practice of emotionally focused marital therapy.* New York: Brunner/Mazel.

Johnson, S. M. (2003). The revolution in couple therapy: A practitioner-scientist perspective. *Journal of Marital and Family Therapy, 29*(3), 365–384.

Kahle, P. A., & Robbins, J. M. (2004). *The power of spirituality in therapy: Integrating spiritual and religious beliefs in mental health practice.* New York: Haworth.

Karpel, M. (1980). Family secrets: I. Conceptual and ethical issues in the relational context II. Ethical and practical consideration in therapeutic management. *Family Process, 19*, 295–306.

Kelley, H. (1983). Love and commitment. In H. Kelley, E. Bersheid, A. Christensen, T. Huston, G. Levinger, E. McClintock, L. Peplau, & D. Peterson (Eds.), *Close relationships* (pp. 20–67). New York: Freeman.

Kimball, L. S., & Knudson-Martin, C. (2002). A cultural trinity: Spirituality, religion, and gender in clinical practice. In T. D. Carlson & M. J. Erickson (Eds.), *Spirituality and family therapy* (pp. 145–166). New York: Haworth.

L'Abate, L., & Samples, G. T. (1983). Intimacy letters–invariable prescription for closeness-avoidant couples. *Family Therapy, 10*(1), 37–45.

Lukoff, D. (1998). From spiritual emergency to spiritual problem: The transpersonal roots of the new DSM-IV category. *Journal of Humanistic Psychology, 38*(2), 21–50.

Mack, R. (1989). Spouse abuse: A dyadic approach. In G. R. Weeks (Ed.), *Treating couples: The intersystem model of the Marriage Council of Philadelphia* (pp. 191–214). Philadelphia: Brunner/Mazel.

Martin, P. A. (1976). *A marital therapy manual.* New York: Brunner/ Mazel.

Maslow, A. (1970). Motivation and personality (Rev. ed.). New York: Harper & Row.

Matthews, D. (1998). *The faith factor: Proof of the healing power of prayer.* New York: Viking.

McCullough, M. E., & Larson, D. B. (1999). Religion and depression: A review of the literature. *Twin Research, 2*, 126–136.

Middelberg, C. V. (2001). Projective identification in common couple dances. *Journal of Marital & Family Therapy, 27*(3), 341–352.

Miller, G. (2003). *Incorporating spirituality into counseling and psychotherapy.* New Jersey: Wiley.

Miller, W. R. (1999). *Integrating spirituality into treatment: Resources for practitioners.* Washington, D.C.: American Psychological Association.

Mittleman, B. (1944). Complementary neurotic reactions in intimate relationships. *The Psychoanalytic Quarterly, 13*, 479–491.

Nichols, W. C. (1988). *Marital therapy: An integrative approach.* New York: Guilford.

Odell, M. (2003). Intersecting worldviews: Including vs. imposing spirituality in therapy. *Family Therapy Magazine, 2*(5), 26–30.

Odell, M., & Campbell, C. E. (1998). *The practical practice of marriage and family therapy.* New York: Haworth.

Odell, M., Dielman, M. B., & Butler, T. J. (in press). An exploratory study of clients' experiences of therapeutic alliance and outcome in solution-focused marital therapy. *Journal of Couple and Relationship Therapy.*

Pattison, E. (1982). Management of religious issues in family therapy. *International Journal of Family Therapy, 4,* 140–163.

Prochaska, J., & DiClemente, C. (1988). *A transtheoretical approach to therapy.* Chicago: Dorsey.

Protinsky, H., & Quinn, W. (1981). Paradoxical marital therapy with symptom triangulation. *Family Therapy, 8*(2), 135–140.

Richards, P. S., & Bergin, A. E. (1997). *A spiritual strategy for counseling and psychotherapy.* Washington, D.C.: American Psychological Association.

Richards, P. S., & Bergin, A. E. (2000). *Handbook of psychotherapy and religious diversity.* Washington, D.C.: American Psychological Association.

Richards, P. S., Rector, J. M., & Tjeltveit, A. C. (1999). Values, spirituality, and psychotherapy. In W. R. Miller (Ed.), *Integrating spirituality into treatment: Resources for practitioners* (pp. 133–160). Washington, D.C.: American Psychological Association.

Richardson, F., Fowers, B., & Guignon, C. (1999). *Re-envisioning psychotherapy: Moral dimensions of theory and practice.* San Francisco: Jossey-Bass.

Roberts, L. J., & McCrady, B. S. (2003). *Alcohol problems in intimate relationships: Identification and intervention, a guide for marriage and family therapists* (NIH Publication No. 03-5284). Washington, D.C.: U.S. Government Printing Office.

Robichaud, E. (2003). *Is spirituality effective as a component in the counseling process?* Unpublished manuscript, University of Nevada, Las Vegas.

Sager, C. (1976). *Marriage contracts and couples therapy: Hidden forces in intimate relationships.* New York: Brunner/Mazel.

Sexton, T. L., Weeks, G. R., & Robbins, M. S. (2003). *Handbook of family therapy: The science and practice of working with families and couples.* Philadelphia: Brunner-Routledge.

Sperry, L. (2001). Spirituality in clinical practice: Incorporating the spiritual dimension in psychotherapy and counseling. Philadelphia: Brunner-Routlege.

Sprenkle, D. H. (Ed.). (2002). *Effectiveness research in marriage and family therapy.* Alexandria, VA: American Association for Marriage and Family Therapy.

Starbuck, G. (2002). *Families in context.* Belmont, CA: Wadsworth/Thomson Learning.

Sternberg, R. (1986). A triangular theory of love. *Psychological Review, 93*(2), 119–135.

Sternberg, R. (1997). Construct validation of a triangular love scale. *European Journal of Social Psychology, 27,* 313–335.

Stinnett, N., & DeFrain, J. (1985). *Secrets of strong families.* Boston: Little, Brown.

Swinton, J. (2001). *Spirituality and mental health care: Rediscovering a "forgotten" dimension.* London: Jessica Kingsley.

Vaughn, F. (1991). Spiritual issues in psychotherapy. *Journal of Transpersonal Psychology, 23*(2), 121–137.

Waite, L., & Gallagher, M. (2000). *The case for marriage.* New York: Broadway.

Walsh, F. (1998). Families in later life: Challenges and opportunities. In B. Carter & M. McGoldrick (Eds.), *The expanded family life cycle* (3rd ed., pp. 307–326). Needham Heights, MA: Allyn & Bacon.

Walsh, F. (Ed.). (1999). *Spiritual resources in family therapy.* New York: Guilford.

Watzlawick, P., Weakland, J., & Fisch, R. (1974). *Change: Principles of problem formation and problem resolution.* New York: Norton.

Weeks, G. R. (1994). The intersystem model: An integrative approach to treatment. In G. R. Weeks & L. Hof (Eds.), *The marital relationship therapy casebook: Theory and application of the intersystem model* (pp. 3–34). New York: Brunner/Mazel.

Weeks, G. R., & Gambescia, N. (2000). *Erectile dysfunction: Integrating couple therapy, sex therapy, and medical treatment.* New York: Norton.

Weeks, G., & Gambescia, N. (2002). *Hypoactive sexual desire: Integrating sex and couple therapy.* New York: Norton.

Weeks, G. R., & Hof, L. (1994). *The marital relationship therapy casebook: Theory and application of the intersystem model.* New York: Brunner/Mazel.

Weeks, G. R., & Hof, L. (1995). *Integrative solutions: Treating common problems in couples therapy.* New York: Brunner/Mazel.

Weeks, G. R., & L'Abate, L. (1982). *Paradoxical psychotherapy: Theory and practice with individuals, couples, and families.* New York: Brunner/Mazel.

Weeks, G. R., & Treat, S. (1992). *Couples in treatment: Techniques and approaches for effective practice.* New York: Brunner/Mazel.

Weeks, G. R., & Treat, S. (2001). *Couples in treatment: Techniques and approaches for effective practice* (2nd ed.). Philadelphia: Brunner-Routledge.

West, W. (2000). *Psychotherapy & spirituality: Crossing the line between therapy and religion.* London: Sage Publications.

Whitaker, C. A. & Keith, D. V. (1981). Symbolic-experiential family therapy. In A. S. Gurman & D. P. Kniskern (Eds.), *Handbook of family therapy* (pp. 187–225). New York: Brunner/Mazel.

Wright, L., Watson, W. L. & Bell, J. M. (1996). *Beliefs: The heart of healing in families and illness.* New York: Basic Books.

Wright, L. M. (1999). Spirituality, suffering, and beliefs: The soul of healing with families. In F. Walsh (Ed.), *Spiritual resources in family therapy* (pp. 61–75). New York : Guilford.

Yahne, C. E., & Miller, W. R. (1999). Evoking hope. In W. R. Miller (Ed.), *Integrating spirituality into treatment: Resources for practitioners* (pp. 217–233). Washington, D.C.: American Psychological Association.

Index

GERALD R. WEEKS, Ph.D., ABPP, ABS, is a professor at the University of Nevada, Las Vegas. He has published sixteen professional books in the fields of psychotherapy, couples, sex, and family therapy.

SUSANNE METHVEN has an MS in Counseling from the University of Nevada, Las Vegas and is pursuing a Masters of Divinity at the Episcopal Theological Seminary of the Southwest in Austin, Texas.

MARK ODELL, Ph.D., is owner and director of GlacierHaven, a counseling and consulting practice in northwest Montana designed for leaders and leadership development. He spent ten years in academia as a trainer of therapists and has published in a variety of areas.